Series Editor:
Paul Wehman, Ph.D.

The Brookes
Transition to
Adulthood Series

ESSENTIALS OF
Transition
Planning

The Brookes
Transition to
Adulthood Series

ESSENTIALS OF
Transition
Planning

by

Paul Wehman, Ph.D.
Virginia Commonwealth University
Richmond

with invited contributors

·P A U L·H·
BROOKES
PUBLISHING CO.®

Baltimore • London • Sydney

Paul H. Brookes Publishing Co.
Post Office Box 10624
Baltimore, Maryland 21285-0624
USA

www.brookespublishing.com

Typeset by Auburn Associates, Inc., Baltimore, Maryland.
Manufactured in the United States of America by
Versa Press, Inc., East Peoria, Illinois.

Some individuals described in this book are composites or real people whose situations are masked and are based on the authors' experiences. In these instances, names and identifying details have been changed to protect confidentiality.

Library of Congress Cataloging-in-Publication Data

Wehman, Paul
    Essentials of transition planning / by Paul Wehman.
        p.   cm. – (The Brookes transition to adulthood series)
    Includes bibliographical references and index.
    ISBN-13: 978-1-59857-098-4 (pbk.)
    ISBN-10: 1-59857-098-6 (pbk.)
1. Students with disabilities–Education (Secondary)–United States.   2. Students with disabilities–Vocational guidance–United States.   3. School-to-work transition–United States.   I. Title.
LC4031.W423 2011
371.9′473–dc22   2010032134

British Library Cataloguing in Publication data are available from the British Library.

2020   2019   2018   2017

10   9   8   7   6   5   4

Contents

Series Preface vii
Editorial Advisory Board viii
About the Authors ix
Preface xiii
Acknowledgments xv

1 Transition: An Overview and Background 1

The Importance of Transition
The Individuals with Disabilities Education Act
The Need for Transition Planning
About the Transition Planning Team
Vocational Assessment
The Planning Process
Planning Components

2 Individual and Community Transition Planning.........................23

Individualized Transition Planning
Community Participation and Collaboration
Transition Supports
Self-Determination
School and Community Inclusion

3 Developing the Transition Curriculum
   DiAnne B. Davidsen and Karren D. Streagle 41

How to Determine a Student's Career Goals
High-Stakes Testing and Diploma Decisions
Access to the General Education Curriculum
Community-Based Instruction
Postsecondary Education
Achieving Social Competence
Putting It All Together
Ten Precious Minutes

4   Planning for the Future: One Student at a Time
     Pamela Sherron Targett and Paul Wehman 75

     What to Address in the Transition
        Individualized Education Program
     When to Begin Planning
     Some Strategies for Planning
     Key Players on the Transition Team
     Ways to Involve Families
     Ways to Involve the Student

5   Writing the Transition Individualized Education Program
     Wendy Parent and Paul Wehman 95

     Where to Begin
     What to Do if More Information Is Needed
     How to Decide on Goals
     How to Get Started
     What to Include in the Transition Individualized Education Program
     Examples of Successful Postschool Outcomes
     How to Obtain Support from Community Agencies and Resources

6   Implementing the Transition Individualized Education Program............111

     The Interagency Planning Team
     Interagency Collaboration
     Cooperative Relationships

7   Employment: Community-Based Choices
     Pamela Sherron Targett and Paul Wehman 127

     Vocational Education, Career, and Training Models
     Vocational Support Service Models
     Practices Supporting Higher Education
     Next Steps

8   Strategies for Funding and Resources Needed for Transition
     Individualized Education Programs
     W. Grant Revell, Jr. and Paul Wehman 145

     Community Training and Employment Support Programs
     Transition Resources in the Adult Service System

     References..161
     Index..171

Series Preface

The Brookes Transition to Adulthood Series was developed for the purpose of meeting the critical educational needs of students with disabilities who will be moving from school to adulthood. It is no longer acceptable to simply equip a student with a set of isolated life skills that may or may not be relevant to his or her adult life. Nor is it sufficient to treat the student as if he or she will remain unchanged throughout life. As we allow for growth and change in real-life environments, so must we allow for growth and change in the individuals who will operate within the environments. Today, transition must concern itself with the whole life pattern of each student as it relates to his or her future. However, integrating the two constructs of self and the real adult world for one student at a time is not always straightforward. It requires skills and knowledge. It requires a well-thought-out, well-orchestrated team effort. It takes individualization, ingenuity, perseverance, and more.

The results of these first-rate efforts can be seen when they culminate in a student with a disability who exits school prepared to move to his or her life beyond the classroom. Unfortunately, though, this does not always happen. This is because transition has become a splintered concept, too weighted down by process and removed from building on the student's aspirations and desires for "a good life." However, it does not have to be this way.

This book series is designed to help the teachers, transition specialists, rehabilitation counselors, community service providers, administrators, policy makers, other professionals, and families who are looking for useful information on a daily basis by translating the evidence-based transition research into practice. Each volume addresses specific objectives that are related to the all-important and overarching goal of helping students meet the demands of school and society and gain a greater understanding of themselves so that they are equipped for success in the adult world.

Editorial Advisory Board

About the Authors

Paul Wehman, Ph.D., is Professor of Physical Medicine and Rehabilitation, with joint appointments in the Departments of Rehabilitation Counseling and Special Education and Disability Policy at Virginia Commonwealth University (VCU). He serves as Chairman of the Division of Rehabilitation Research in the Department of Physical Medicine and Rehabilitation at the Medical College of Virginia. Dr. Wehman has his doctorate in behavioral disabilities from University of Wisconsin–Madison. He helped to develop supported employment at VCU in the early 1980s and has published more than 200 articles and authored or edited 40 books primarily on transition, severe disabilities, and employment for people with disabilities. He received the Kennedy Foundation Award in Mental Retardation in 1990 and the Distinguished Service Award from the President's Committee on Employment for Persons with Disabilities in 1992. He received the Lifetime Achievement Award from the Association for Persons in Supported Employment (APSE) in 2006 and the VCU School of Medicine Research Recognition Award in 2007. Dr. Wehman was also recognized as one of the 50 most influential special educators of the millennium by the *Remedial and Special Education* journal in December 2000. He is Editor-in-Chief of the *Journal of Vocational Rehabilitation.*

DiAnne B. Davidsen, M.Ed., received her master of education degree in special education from The College of William and Mary, Williamsburg, Virginia, and is currently in her final year of doctoral studies in urban services leadership/ special education at Virginia Commonwealth University (VCU). Since 1970, Ms. Davidsen has taught students in prekindergarten through high school in public school settings from all disability categories and in all service delivery models. She has been Transition Specialist for a school district in Virginia and one of the founders of the Peninsula Transition Forum as well as Director of Special Education for a school district in Arizona establishing Teacher/Parent/ Student Transition Information Nights to prepare families of children and youth with disabilities for transition issues at all levels. Ms. Davidsen is currently an assistant professor at VCU in the Department of Special Education and Disability Policy in the School of Education. Beyond transition and curriculum development, instruction in characteristics and methods classes, and supervision of student teachers, her areas of interest are in preparing students for success at the postsecondary education level and in working with individuals from diverse populations. She has published on postsecondary education transition and has presented at local, state, national, and international conferences on transition, use of assistive technology, collaboration, and inclusion.

Wendy Parent, Ph.D., is Research Associate Professor and Assistant Director, Kansas University Center on Developmental Disabilities, a Center for Excellence in Developmental Disabilities at The University of Kansas. She has more than 25 years of experience in the areas of supported and customized employment and transition from school to work for individuals with severe disabilities.

Dr. Parent has published numerous book chapters and peer-reviewed journal articles related to transition and supported/customized employment and has coauthored several books on supported employment. In her efforts to build systems capacity and enhance employment and self-employment outcomes, she provides training and technical assistance to teachers, transition coordinators, families, rehabilitation counselors, job coaches, and individuals with disabilities. She is currently the president of the Kansas Rehabilitation Association and Kansas Association for Persons on Supported Employment (APSE): The Network on Employment and serves on the national Boards of the APSE Foundation and the National Rehabilitation Association. She serves on the editorial board of two journals: *Focus on Autism and Other Developmental Disabilities* and the *Journal of Rehabilitation.* Her areas of interest and research are supported/customized employment and transition from school to work for individuals with severe disabilities, with an emphasis on creative funding and support strategies, individual and family involvement, job-coach training and leadership, interagency collaboration and service delivery issues, and systems change.

W. Grant Revell, Jr., M.S., M.Ed., serves as a research associate at the Virginia Commonwealth University (VCU) Rehabilitation Research and Training Center (RRTC) on Workplace Supports and Job Retention. He has extensive experience in the areas of policy analysis and funding related to state level and national implementation of employment supports for individuals with significant disabilities. He has served as a project director for a variety of national technical assistance and research projects, including the National Supported Employment Technical Assistance Center and the Supported Employment Consortium (SEC). The SEC was a 4-year national study funded by the Rehabilitation Services Administration of the U.S. Department of Education to research best practices in supported employment services to people with significant disabilities and to disseminate information on these best practices through technical assistance and training. He recently served as a State Training Liaison for the Region III Community Rehabilitation Providers Regional Continuing Education Program (CRP RCEP) and is currently conducting a variety of research studies in the area of self-employment. Prior to coming to the VCU RRTC, he worked as a program specialist in supported employment and as a vocational rehabilitation counselor at the Virginia Department of Rehabilitation Services.

Karren D. Streagle, M.Ed., received her master of education degree in early childhood special education from Virginia Commonwealth University (VCU), in Richmond, Virginia. She has an additional endorsement in severe and profound disabilities. She is currently in her final year of doctoral studies in special education and disability policy at VCU. Since 1995, Ms. Streagle has taught students in preschool and elementary school as an inclusion teacher for students with noncategorical disabilities and as a self-contained teacher for students with multiple and severe intellectual disabilities in an urban and rural school district in central Virginia. She has also served as a school-level special education department chair. Ms. Streagle is currently Coordinator of Testing for Goochland County Public Schools, in charge of Standards of Learning testing (Virginia's assessment and accountability assessment program), alternate and alternative assessments, and GED testing. She has served on several state-level standard-setting and range-finding committees for the Virginia Alternate Assessment Program. She is an adjunct faculty member at VCU in the Department of Special Education and Disability Policy and the Certifying Online Virginia Educators grant program. Her areas of interest include alternate and alternative assessments and best practices in academic instruction for students with significant intellectual disabilities.

Pamela Sherron Targett, M.Ed., has worked in the area of disability and employment since 1986. For 22 years she oversaw the day-to-day operations of a fee-for-service supported employment program that assisted individuals with significant disabilities with going to work. During this time she also worked with schools to develop community-based vocational education programs. Her special interests include transition to work for youth with disabilities and individuals with significant support needs, such as brain injury and autism.

Preface

Well over 8 million students annually receive special education services, but as these individuals reach the ages of 18–21, there is not usually a well-crafted plan in place to gain access to the community, independent living, a real job, and other aspects of entering adulthood such as financial literacy, travel, and social relationships. The reasons for the lack of carefully designed planning to help students with disabilities make this bridge to adulthood are twofold. Most school districts really do not know how or have the time to gather all of the necessary participants together and engage in the planning. Second, in the cases in which this critical planning does occur, the resources to implement the plan are lacking.

There is good news, however. After 2 decades we know how to help solve this problem. We know how to build the bridge to help students leave school and enter into communities successfully, thanks to available research and examples showing how these plans can and are working. What this book does is to pull together in a logical sequence the steps involved in making transitions a reality, from their beginnings in schools into the community and workplace.

Chapter 1 provides a brief overview of law and policy related to transition planning, followed by a discussion of why transition planning is required.

Transition planning must be considered at two different levels: individual and community. Although these two levels must intersect for the end result to be effective, each requires different thought processes and planning in order to be effectively implemented. Chapter 2 examines each. Areas that can affect the quality of the transition individualized education program (IEP) are also reviewed, including supports, self-determination, and inclusion.

Chapter 3 provides information on how to develop a transition curriculum. Ways to promote student involvement and identify critical academic and functional skills needed for the future are also included. In addition, access to the general curriculum and community-based options are examined.

Chapter 4 shifts emphasis from the foundations of transition that were addressed in the first three chapters to programmatic implementation. This chapter focuses on the elements of a transition IEP, including assessment practices that guide program development as well as ongoing monitoring of student progress toward reaching goals. The roles of professionals who serve on the team are explored along with ways to promote family involvement and engage those students with more significant support needs.

Transition is an outcome-oriented process that is individually driven by the student's vision of an adult life. The postschool goals drive the transition planning process and the annual IEP provides the mechanism to take action and outlines the specific steps to get there. Chapter 5 offers a practical, step-by-step process. It begins by examining where to start and concludes with writing the transition IEP. Information on how to obtain support from community agencies and resources is also provided.

Once a plan is developed, it must be implemented. Chapter 6 focuses on who needs to do what to make a transition plan a reality. The importance of involving adult service professionals and taking the steps necessary to make sure the student and family drive the process is emphasized.

Chapter 7 takes a look at student vocational training options in business and postsecondary education settings. Next, vocational support service delivery models are reviewed. This is followed by information on ways to support students who choose to pursue higher education.

Youth with disabilities, once they reach age 22 or complete their secondary level program, no longer have legal rights to the variety of services covered by the Individuals with Disabilities Education Improvement Act (IDEA) of 2004 (PL 108-446). Chapter 8 takes a look at transition service coordination from both an individual and systemic perspective. It examines case management and service coordination. Some of the barriers that may be faced, along with some recommendations on how to effectively work with a highly bureaucratic and fragmented service delivery system, are examined.

In closing, this is a comprehensive yet practical book on transition planning that will be of interest to a wide range of audiences. From school personnel such as special education teachers, transition specialists, and administrators to adult service providers such as one-stop career center staff, vocational rehabilitation counselors, and case managers, this book is for anyone involved with transition services, which may also include family members, advocates, and policy makers. In essence, this book will be useful to anyone who is interested in improving and enhancing the transition to adulthood for youth with disabilities.

REFERENCE

Individuals with Disabilities Education Improvement Act (IDEA) of 2004, PL 108-446, 20 U.S.C. §§ 1400 *et seq.*

Acknowledgments

It has been a pleasure to write this first book for *The Brookes Transition to Adulthood Series*. This is an idea initially launched through frequent conversations between myself and the innovative Rebecca Lazo, Senior Acquisitions Editor at Paul H. Brookes Publishing Co. It should go without saying that her leadership in getting the Editorial Advisory Board together, her research and frequent calls to others in the field, and her persistent (but always pleasant) communication with me have been the signature aspects of how the series got started.

In doing this initial book I have asked for a lot of help from experts in the field who have read drafts and helped make this as evidence-based as possible. I would like to acknowledge my contributors and coauthors, DiAnne B. Davidsen, Wendy Parent, W. Grant Revell, Jr., Karren D. Streagle, and Pamela Sherron Targett, for their participation in this project. I have much gratitude for their willingness to help and more than that, their insights as to what is the most important information to include.

I give deep thanks to Jeanne Dalton, my program specialist support colleague, for all of the work she did on permissions, finding references and organizing them, and her patience in moving the project along rapidly. Jeanne does great work and, as I know Paul H. Brookes Publishing Co. would attest, plays a major role in these projects.

The person whom I absolutely want to thank and single out for her tireless work on this project is Pam Targett. During the winter months of 2010, when I had to be away for family health reasons, she stepped up and really kept this project on track, meeting extremely tight timelines. She has stayed on top of all of the deadlines through difficult snowstorms and other barriers and also has added important perspectives on content as well, with her more than 20 years of disability experience. I am most indebted to her for these efforts and wish to fully recognize and thank her.

Finally, I have to acknowledge the thousands of parents who are waiting for help for their teenagers with disabilities and who are looking for the best blueprint for helping their children move into the world of work; academia; and the community of shopping malls, transportation systems, banks, fitness centers, and other places where people can experience whole lives. This book is a start in the right direction. This book especially, and this series, is for these parents and for professionals who want to help parents and youth with disabilities. We hope with all of our combined energies that it works for them and is highly useful.

To the thousands of parents
who are looking for the best ways to
understand and plan for the transition of
their son or daughter into a normal, whole life
that includes real work for real pay,
friends, community involvement, and
the opportunity to be happy

1

Transition

An Overview and Background

Mary is 19 years old and has a moderate intellectual disability. She is currently in the 11th grade, and she is about to enroll in the state vocational rehabilitation supported transition program.

A number of vocational situational assessments were set up for Mary at the start of 10th grade. The first took place at a large retail store. As a result of the assessment, both Mary and her vocational teacher, Sandra, learned more about Mary's work preferences. Although Mary was able to learn a number of skills with one-to-one instruction, Sandra thought Mary would need some additional support to meet the established performance standards.

Next, Sandra set up an assessment at a fast-food restaurant. While there, Sandra instructed Mary on how to perform a variety of different job tasks, including cleaning the customer dining area. Once again, Mary learned a number of job skills. Mary seemed to enjoy the work in the main restaurant, where she was in the customer's eye. For example, she smiled a lot, greeted customers, and said good-bye to them. She also kept pace performing certain tasks. Although the restaurant was extremely busy at times, Mary did not seem to get overwhelmed or frustrated. Near the end of the fourth day of this situational vocational assessment, the shift supervisor told Sandra that management was seeking to fill a front-of-the-house customer service position with hours from around 2 p.m. to 5 p.m. He encouraged Sandra to have Mary apply for the job and said he would put in a good word for Mary.

Sandra discussed the job opportunity with Mary's mother and explained why she felt it might be a good job match, and stated that the school would provide transportation on school days. Mary's parents talked that evening and agreed that they wanted their daughter to pursue the opportunity. When asked about working there, Mary would repeat the name of the restaurant with a smile and say, "friends to me." This information, paired with other observations Sandra had made during the situational assessment, seemed to indicate Mary's desire to work at the restaurant.

A few days later Sandra spoke to the hiring manager about Mary's abilities and supports that would be provided, such as on-site coaching to learn the job. The next day, Mary met the manager and was offered the job. A job coach accompanied her to work and provided on-the-job skills training and support services.

After about 6 weeks, the job coach was able to fade his presence from the job site. Today, Mary works 15 to 25 hours a week. On the weekends she works longer shifts, and her parents provide transportation. The job coach provides long-term follow-up services, visiting the restaurant at least twice a month to see how Mary is doing. Additional training and on-the-job support is provided as needed to help Mary continue to do a great job.

What really surprised everyone was how Mary's independence and confidence grew each day she worked at the restaurant. Mary's parents were not expecting the intangibles that she got from being employed. For example, she made two new friends and learned to ride the bus. Mary opened a bank account and is learning how to use an automatic teller machine to deposit and retrieve funds. Mary has also bonded with her managers, coworkers, and regular customers. Several customers say they come in several times a week just to see Mary.

Mary's is a success story. The planning and process that went into these outcomes should not be minimized. These activities could never be replicated in just a classroom situation. There is little doubt that without the federal law setting the stage for these services, trained personnel, advocates, and Mary herself having a clear road map from school to the community and work, she could have easily ended up like thousands of young people with disabilities in this country—at home with no friends, no job, and no excitement about having a whole life.

THE IMPORTANCE OF TRANSITION

According to Turnbull and Turnbull (2009), it is important for young people with disabilities to have what they term *whole lives*. Although the interpretation of what constitutes a whole life is open to discussion, having a whole life is reflected in students having self-determination, choice, and direction in terms of where to live, where to work, how to meet people and maintain social networks of friends, and how to feel movement and progress in their lives. All young people with disabilities are entitled to an opportunity to develop a whole life.

This book shows how to help young people with disabilities live meaningful and full lives through transition planning. It discusses why transition planning is important, what the legal and legislative mandates around transition outcomes are, and who should be involved in the transition planning process. It touches on individual and transition planning; specific how-tos for writing and implementing transition individualized education programs (IEPs); post–high school options, such as work or postsecondary education; quality indicators for success; and funding. Numerous resources are offered as well. The information in this book is consistent with the National Transition Goals outlined by Hasazi and colleagues (2005):

1. To promote students' self-determination and self-advocacy
2. To ensure that students have access to the general standards-based curriculum
3. To increase the graduation rate of students with disabilities
4. To ensure access to and full participation in postsecondary education and employment
5. To increase parent participation and involvement
6. To improve collaboration and links between systems to support student achievement of meaningful school and postschool outcomes
7. To ensure the availability of a qualified workforce
8. To ensure that students have full, active participation in all aspects of community life, including social, recreation, and leisure opportunities

THE INDIVIDUALS WITH DISABILITIES EDUCATION ACT

The Individuals with Disabilities Education Act (IDEA) of 1990 (PL 101-476) ensures that all children with disabilities have a free appropriate public education (FAPE) that emphasizes special education and related services designed to meet their unique needs and prepare them for further education, employment, and independent living (34 C.F.R. 300.1 [a] and 20 U.S.C. 1400 [d] [1] [A]). Changes to IDEA in 1997 (PL 105-17) and 2004 (PL 108-446) strengthened the transition process for students with disabilities (Johnson, 2005). The 1997 amendments were the first to include the definition of transition services and an age requirement for the initiation of services (Wehman, 2002). Shaw noted, "Recent federal legislation, particularly IDEA 2004, has sought to foster productive transition to help students fulfill postsecondary goals" (2006, p. 108). IDEA 2004 mandates that IEP teams ensure students meet graduation requirements that relate to their postsecondary goals (Kochar-Bryant, Shaw, & Izzo, 2007). The statute has also made the transition process a driving force in planning student outcomes.

Related services are now paired with required transition services, suggesting that policy makers want transition IEP teams to consider the supports that students may need to benefit from available transition services. Related services are all of the services needed for a child with a disability to benefit from his or her specialized instruction. They are not the actual instruction, but can be thought of as noneducational services necessary to make the educational services accessible and effective. Related services include, but are not limited to, the following:

- Transportation
- Physical and occupational therapy
- Orientation and mobility services
- Counseling
- Psychological services
- Social work services
- Recreation, including therapeutic recreation
- Rehabilitation services
- Rehabilitation counseling

This is consistent with the underlying legislative philosophy of providing students with access to the general curriculum and inclusive settings. Secondary students in special education have traditionally received few related services. For example, few students receive IEP services after the age of 16, the age at which the statute requires a transition plan to be in place. The addition of related services for transition in 1997 forced special education and related service providers to examine whether supports should be provided that enable a student to have access to a more integrated work, education, or independent living environment; to demonstrate higher skills and abilities; or to accomplish objectives leading toward his or her transition goals.

Some of the many revisions to IDEA in 2004 include references to the transition-age student, a definition of transition services, age requirements, mention of IEP content (including postsecondary goals), and the new Summary of Performance (SOP).

Transition Services

Andrew Halpern, a true giant in the field of transition, published a comprehensive and frequently cited definition of secondary transition for students with disabilities that provided theoretical and practical background for the language that would later appear in the Individuals with Disabilities Education Act (IDEA) Amendments of 1997 (PL 105-17) and 2004 (PL 108-446). Halpern defined *transition* as

> A change in status from behaving primarily as a student to assuming emergent adult roles in the community. These roles include employment, participating in post-secondary education, maintaining a home, becoming appropriately involved in the community, and experiencing satisfactory personal and social relationships. The process of enhancing transition involves the participation and coordination of school programs, adult service agencies, and natural supports within the community. The foundations of transition should be laid during the elementary and middle school years, guided by the broad concept of career development. Transition planning should begin no later than age 14, and students should be encouraged, to the full extent of their capabilities, to assume a maximum amount of responsibility for such planning. (1994, p. 116)

The term *transition services* means a coordinated set of activities for a child with a disability that 1) is designed to be within a results-oriented process that is focused on improving the academic and functional achievement of the child with a disability to facilitate the child's movement from school to postschool activities, including postsecondary education, vocational education, integrated employment (including supported employment), continuing and adult education, adult services, independent living, and community participation; 2) is based on the individual child's needs, taking into account the child's strengths, preferences, and interests; and 3) includes instruction, related services, community experiences, the development of employment and other postschool adult living objectives, and, if appropriate, acquisition of daily living skills and functional vocational evaluation. (See 20 U.S.C. 1401(34) and 34 CFR §300.43(a).)

Individualized Education Program Content and Postsecondary Goals

According to IDEA 2004, the IEP for any student ages 16 years or older must include a statement of

- "Appropriate measurable postsecondary goals based upon age-appropriate transition assessments related to training, education, employment, and, where appropriate, independent living skills
- The transition services (including courses of study) needed to help the student reach those goals." (34 C.F.R. 300.320 [b] and [c] 20 U.S.C. 1414 [d] [1] [A] [i] [VIII])

Certo et al. (2008) noted that the transition IEP is essentially an implicit national policy that young people with disabilities be employed and integrated into the community:

> The IDEA Amendments of 1997 eliminated the separation between the individualized transition plan and the IEP. Implicit in this requirement is the national policy stated in the law that publicly supported education for students with disabilities should culminate in postschool employment and independent living. That is, graduates should be working in direct-hire, individualized jobs; should be able to

access stores and services in their communities; and should be attending postsecondary institutions as needed and as appropriate to their career goals. (2008, p. 86)

Transition assessment is an ongoing, coordinated process that begins in middle school and helps students with disabilities identify and plan for postschool goals and adult roles (Sitlington, Neubert, Begun, Lombard, & Leconte, 2007). Each student's measurable postsecondary goals are based on data gleaned from transition and vocational evaluation assessments.

Summary of Performance

One of the requirements of IDEA 2004 is the preparation of an SOP for each student. Each school district is required to provide a summary of the student's academic and functional performance as well as recommendations on how to assist him or her in meeting postsecondary goals (300.305[e][3]). The SOP is designed to help educators and service providers quickly review all of the pertinent information about a student. It should summarize the student's current strengths and weaknesses in key areas and should describe the accommodations, modifications, and assistive technology that the student actually uses, rather than what may be needed.

This information can enhance a student's knowledge and self-advocacy. For example, if a student is moving on to postsecondary education, the SOP can provide an insight into what may be needed to help that student succeed. It also provides postsecondary institutions with more immediate information about what an incoming student may need. The information may also be shared with employment service providers who may be assisting students in obtaining or continuing work in the community. But no matter how it is used, the SOP is an important aspect of transition planning because it focuses on "the bottom line" of where the student, family, and team want to go.

Increased Accountability

IDEA 2004 requires states to develop annual state performance plans based on 20 indicators, 2 of which relate specifically to transition. Indicator 13 requires data on the percentage of students "aged 16 and above with an IEP with goals and transition services that will reasonably enable the student to meet the post secondary goals" (20 U.S.C. 1416[a][3][B]). This information should indicate how the team is addressing a student's course of study, employment experiences, and independent living needs to achieve postschool goals and who the adult services representatives are who are involved in the plan (National Secondary Transition Technical Assistance Center, n.d.).

Indicator 14 requires data on the "percentage of students who at one time had an IEP but who are no longer in secondary school and were employed, enrolled in some type of postsecondary school, or both within 1 year of leaving school"(20 U.S.C. 1416[a][3][B]).

NSTTAC has developed checklists to help states collect data for Indicator 13. Schools may want to use them as a guide for developing a compliance checklist to use with each student. Checklists can be found at http://www.nsttac.org/indicator13/indicator13_checklist.aspx

THE NEED FOR TRANSITION PLANNING

It is important for students to have a viable transition plan that reflects their and their family's needs, wishes, and desires. Such a transition IEP moves the students into adulthood, enabling them to gain access to accommodations and supports, social competence, postsecondary education, and employment. Through this process, they develop maturity, self-determination, and self-advocacy. Finding ways to promote growth by learning self-determination skills should help ensure individualized, high-quality outcomes for every student.

Growth and Maturity

It is usually assumed that as students enter their teenage years, they begin to mature. Consider those students who are floundering: They appear to have no passion for any interests in or out of school, no friends e-mailing or calling, no confidence, no work experience. Setting goals and then achieving them reinforces success for these students. The transition plan must identify specific interventions and supports and specify the resources necessary to achieve certain outcomes.

Self-Determination and Self-Advocacy Skills

Self-determination skills are necessary for transition planning to succeed. McGuire and McDonnell (2008) studied the relationship between recreation and levels of self-determination in teenagers with disabilities and found that those students with better recreation skills scored higher on a self-determination scale. Students with disabilities need to learn the skills to advocate on their own behalf. To be effective self-advocates, students have to learn both how to advocate and what to advocate for. Students have ample opportunities to learn and practice self-advocacy skills within the context of the education planning process. Too often, students' perspectives have been lost because they have not had the opportunities or the skills to express them within IEP, transition, or general education planning meetings. A first step toward enabling students to express their wants and needs during these meetings is to educate students about their rights and responsibilities under IDEA; their civil rights under the Americans with Disabilities Act (ADA) of 1990 (PL 101-336); or, more generally, rights available to all citizens.

In addition, teaching effective decision-making and problem-solving skills enhances positive transition outcomes for students and young adults. Khemka (2000) found that teaching young women with intellectual disabilities to make more effective decisions improved their capacity to identify potentially abusive social interactions. Datillo and Hoge (1999) found that teaching decision making to adolescents with cognitive disabilities in the context of a leisure education program improved students' leisure knowledge and skills. Limitations in social problem-solving skills have been linked to difficulties in employment, community, and independent living situations for people with developmental disabilities (Gumpel, Tappe, & Araki, 2000). Storey (2002) reviewed the empirical literature pertaining to improving social interactions for workers with disabilities and determined that problem-solving skills contributed to more positive workplace social interactions. O'Reilly, Lancioni, and O'Kane (2000) found that incorporating instruction in problem solving into social skills instruction improved employment outcomes for supported workers with traumatic brain injuries.

Quality Outcomes

Transition planning should also ensure quality outcomes. Each transition IEP must plan for certain topic areas (see Chapter 4 for the specific domains), including finances, self-determination, independent living, transportation, postsecondary education, and work. Unfortunately, many transition IEPs do not reflect what students actually need to move into adulthood. Powers et al. (2005) analyzed the transition components of 399 IEPs. In many cases, transition goal areas either were not addressed or were inadequately detailed. Effective practices, such as career planning and self-determination enhancement, were not incorporated within most plans, and frequently the students were solely responsible for carrying out action steps to achieve their goals. What is evident from the research is not only that the content of transition IEPs is of limited quality but also that strategies, teaching, and access to accommodations are all too often not available.

Access to Accommodations and Supports

The ability to use accommodations and supports helps bridge youth and adulthood. According to the National Longitudinal Transition Study–2 (Cameto, Newman, & Wagner, 2006), only 6% of accommodations and supports are mentioned in transition planning, an incredibly low percentage. This is most disillusioning when one considers how critical accommodations and supports are to many students as they seek work. This lack of needed accommodations and supports may provide an insight into the dismal employment rates of people with disabilities. According to a Harris Survey (National Organization on Disability, 2004),

- Only 35% of people with disabilities report being employed full or part time, compared with 78% of those who do not have disabilities.
- Compared with people without disabilities, 3 times as many people with disabilities live in poverty, with annual household incomes of less than $15,000 (26% vs. 9%, respectively).

The field of special education has much to offer to improve employment outcomes for people with disabilities. But special educators, especially transition personnel, need to recognize that a student's disability is seldom to blame for poor results.

According to Agran, Cain, and Cavin (2002), although rehabilitation counselors play a pivotal role in providing adult services for many students, special education teachers reported that such counselors were never or rarely invited to IEP transition meetings. The counselors frequently reported that neither parents nor school districts contacted them as resources.

Many young people with disabilities do not know how to gain access to accommodations and may not

In a study of the procedural compliance of 282 transition plans in one state, Tillman and Ford (2001) found that only 30% of the plans demonstrated linkages to community agencies, despite the finding that 73% of the plans indicated that students needed assistance with employment and other postschool living needs (Etscheidt, 2006).

have the opportunities or resources to take advantage of valuable assistive technology or supports (Hughes & Carter, 2001).

Social Competence

Another reason for planning transition is to promote greater social competence and social networking. For people with disabilities, social competence is critical for job tenure, friendships, and general self-esteem.

Getting along with people, developing interpersonal skills, and establishing social competence in the community are among the most important features of a successful life. Unfortunately, many young people with disabilities are ultimately unable to achieve this level of competence. Being able to use effective social skills and knowing how to behave in a variety of challenging social situations can make the difference in achieving successful outcomes in the workplace as well as at home and in the community.

Eisenman (2007) detailed the social networks of five workers with intellectual disabilities and concluded that social networking was effective in getting and holding a job. This conclusion concurs with recommended practice and can be readily planned for by professionals, families, and young adults. For example, creating a vocational profile can be an early step in planning for employment. The profile should list family members, neighbors, friends, employers, and social groups to which the person belongs. Furthermore, it should include a list of businesses near the person's home and those that are readily accessible through means of transportation available to the person. Such a list represents an initial network of career opportunities to be systematically explored.

Joining social groups and leisure activities can increase students' social skills and confidence as well as extend their social networks. (See Table 1.1 for examples of social relationships.)

Individuals in a social network can provide direct and indirect leads for employment. Social networking using the Internet can also be a powerful mechanism for rapidly expanding the number of people a student feels connected with (Targett, 2006).

The strongest predictor of policy compliance with recommended practice in local education agencies was the existence of a school-based interagency transition team of parents, guardians, educators, and adult service professionals. Transition training of these participants was a weaker predictor of recommended practice (McMahan & Baer, 2001).

College and Career Advancement

Career advancement is heavily dependent on having the skills and capacity to learn how to demonstrate different talents in a variety of settings. College can help with this. Some students will want to pursue higher education, and this is yet another reason why appropriate transition planning must occur (Camarena & Sarigiani, 2009). Consider, for example, an adolescent with Asperger syndrome who wants to go to college. Without a transition IEP that details how to research colleges friendly to people with autism spectrum disorders, what the recommendations and expectations are for a Section 504 Plan (Miller & Newbill, 1998), and what the necessary documentation is for accommodation and proof of disability, this student will have a very difficult time fulfilling this dream. Trainor observed,

Table 1.1. Social relationships that can develop between students with and without disabilities

Social relationship	Example
Peer tutor	Leigh role-plays social introductions with Margo, providing feedback and praise for Margo's performance.
Eating companion	Jennifer and Rick eat lunch with Linda in the cafeteria and talk about their favorite music groups.
Art, home economics, individual arts, music, or physical education companion	In art class, students were instructed to paint a sunset. Tom sat next to Dan and offered suggestions and guidance about the best colors to use and how to complete the task.
General class companion	A fifth-grade class is doing a "Know Our Town" lesson in social studies. Ben helps Karen plan a trip through their neighborhood.
During-school companion	After lunch and before the bell for class rang, Molly and Phyllis went to the student lounge for a soda.
Friend	David, a member of a varsity basketball team, invited Ralph, a student with severe disabilities, to his house to watch a game on T.V.
Extracurricular companion	Sarah and Winona prepare their articles for the school newspaper together and then work on the layout in the journalism lab.
After-school project companion	On Saturday afternoon, Mike, who is not disabled, and Bill go to the shopping mall.
Travel companion	David walks with Ralph when he wheels from last-period class to the gym, where Ralph helps the basketball team as a student manager.
Neighbor	Parents of nondisabled students in the neighborhood regularly exchange greetings with Mary when they are at school, around the neighborhood, at local stores, at the mall, and at the grocery store.

Brown. L., et al. (1989). The home school: Why students with severe intellectual disabilities must attend the schools of their brothers, sisters, friends, and neighbors. *Journal of The Association of Persons with Severe Handicaps, 14(1)*, 8–13. This article first appeared in *Journal of The Association for Persons with Severe Handicaps*. Visit http://www.tash.org or contact operations@tash.org for more information.).

For many adolescents in the United States, the postsecondary transition goal to attend college after high school is an unquestioned assumption. Part of habitus of the dominant U.S. Culture is the idea that postsecondary success is defined, in part, by attending college. Adolescents commonly articulate this goal regardless of the academic struggles they face as youth with disabilities and the financial constraints of living in poverty. (2008, p. 150)

Getzel and Wehman (2005) presented a sample form for determining an academic and career plan (see Figure 1.1). Anticipating which specific supports will be needed and planning ahead to ensure that these supports can be obtained can best achieve reaching postsecondary education and career goals.

Real Work for Real Pay

High-quality employment, career advancement, real work for real pay (Luecking, 2009; Wehman, Inge, Revell, & Brooke, 2007), and a viable career path are perhaps the strongest reasons for engaging in high-quality transition planning. In one of the best books on transition, Luecking clearly spells out a road map for diverse work experiences that can make a huge difference in the lives of young people with disabilities. He describes seven types of work experiences that can alter students' outcomes significantly (see Table 1.2).

Academic and Career Plan

Student Information

Name: _____   Social Security Number: _____

Address: _____   Telephone number: _____

_____   E-mail address: _____

Date of birth: _____   Date of intake: _____

How student learned of program: _____

Long-term career goal: _____

Previous Academic Information

Standardized test for admissions: Type: _____   Scores: _____

Transfer student: ___ yes   ___ no   If yes, name of college: _____

Previous Support Services

What is your disability (if willing to disclose)? _____

When were you first diagnosed with a disability? ___ Elementary   ___ Middle   ___ High school   ___ College   ___ Professional school

Did you receive support services prior to college/professional school? ___ yes   ___ no

If yes, check all that apply: ___ Resource center   ___ Private tutoring   ___ Speech therapy   ___ Collaborative teaching

___ Individualized classes: _____

Community Support Services

Have you received services or supports outside of the University? ___ yes   ___ no

If yes, check all that apply:

___ Department of Rehabilitative Services

　　Services received: _____

　　Current counselor: _____

___ Social Security Administration   ___ SSI benefits   ___ SSDI benefits

___ Central Virginia Independent Living Center

　　Services received: _____

___ Disability-specific organizations or support groups (e.g., Brain Injury Association of Virginia, Spinal Cord Injury Association, CHADD)

___ Job Accommodation Network or Virginia Assistive Technology System

___ Other _____

___ Information

Academic status: _____   Academic major: _____

Number of months/years at ___: _____   Current grade point average (GPA): _____

Current schedule: _____

Course	Credits	Grade	Date & Time

Supports/Services at _____

Have you formally disclosed your disability to the University? ___ yes   ___ no

What accommodations is the University *currently* providing?

___ Priority registration	___ Exam modifications
___ Notetakers	___ Extended time
___ Extended time on assignments	___ Proctor
___ Books on CD	___ Reader
___ Tape/digitally record lectures	___ Alternative testing room
___ Scribe	___ Other _____

Are you using these accommodations? ___ yes ___ no

Figure 1.1.   Sample academic and career plan.

What additional supports/services are you using on campus?
___ University Counseling Center   ___ Academic counseling   ___ Small-group study sessions
___ Tutoring   ___ Math Lab   ___ Writing Center
___ Support group for students with disabilities   ___ Other: _____
What type of assistive technology have you used while at the university? _____
_____

Which tasks do you find easy and difficult?

	Easy	Difficult		Easy	Difficult
Paying attention in class			Following directions		
Completing assignments			Spelling		
Taking notes			Finishing tests on time		
Memorizing			Writing		
Managing time			Proofreading		
Reading			Organization		
Understanding what I read			Being motivated		
Math			Asking for help		

Learning style: _____
_____

Strengths: _____
_____

Academic or career challenges: _____
_____

Career-Related Information
Are you currently employed? ___ Yes   ___ No
If yes, what type of work do you do? _____
_____
What types of jobs have you held in the past? _____
_____
Did you disclose your disability to your employer? _____
What kinds of accommodations, if any, did you use in your previous jobs? _____
_____
Does your course of study have any internship or field placement requirements? _____
If so, describe: _____
Are you eligible for work study? _____
Have you accessed the university career center? _____
If so, what services are you receiving? _____
Which of the following career-related services interest you?
___ information on ADA   ___ time management   ___ organizational skills
___ resume development   ___ interview skills   ___ internship
___ disclosure plan   ___ career exploration   ___ effective accommodations
___ informational interviews ___ job shadow/mentor   ___ evaluate technology
___ interpersonal skills   ___ stress management   ___ work experience
Are there any other career-related services that you would like? _____
_____

Academic and Career Action Plan
Short-term goal(s):

Immediate activities to implement:

Future/ongoing activities:

Next meeting date/time: _____

Plan Update
Date of contact:

Review outcome from previous activities

Activities initiated/changes to plan:

Next meeting date/time: _____

Table 1.2. Types of work experiences

Career exploration	Involves visits by students to workplaces to learn about jobs and the required skills. Visits and meetings with employers and people in identified occupations outside of the workplace are also types of career exploration activities from which students can learn. Typically, such visits are accompanied by discussions with students about what they saw, heard, and learned.
Job shadowing	Extended time, often a full workday or several workdays, spent by a student in a workplace accompanying an employee in the performance of his or her daily duties. Many companies have "take your child to work" or "job shadow" days.
Work sampling	Work sampling is work by a student that does not materially benefit the employer but that allows the student to spend meaningful time in a work environment learning aspects of potential job tasks and "soft skills" that are required in the workplace. It is important for transition specialists to be familiar with the Fair Labor Standards Act (PL 75-718) requirements for volunteer activity.
Service-learning	Service learning is hands-on volunteer service to the community that integrates with course objectives. It is a structured process that provides time for reflection on the service experience and demonstration of the skills and knowledge acquired.
Internships	Formal arrangements whereby a student is assigned specific tasks in a workplace over a predetermined period of time. Internships may be paid or unpaid, depending on the nature of the agreement and the nature of the tasks. Many postsecondary institutions help organize these experiences with local companies as adjuncts to specific degree programs. Internships are alternatively called *cooperative education experiences, cooperative work,* or simply *co-ops.*
Apprenticeships	Formal, sanctioned work experiences of an extended duration in which the apprentice learns specific occupational skills related to a standardized trade, such as carpentry or drafting. Many apprenticeships also include paid work components.
Paid employment	May include standard jobs in a company or customized work assignments that are negotiated with an employer, but these jobs always feature a wage paid directly to the student. Such work may be scheduled during or after the school day. Paid employment may be integral to a course of study or simply a separate adjunctive experience.

From Luecking, R.G. (2009). *The way to work: How to facilitate work experiences for youth in transition* (p. 12). Baltimore: Paul H. Brookes Publishing Co.; adapted by permission.

Luecking noted the major challenges still faced by thousands of young people:

- The latest national survey of youth with disabilities making the transition from public education to adult life indicates that these youth continue to experience employment rates that do not approximate that of their peers without disabilities (Wagner et al., 2005).

- Postschool employment support services are not sufficient to meet the demand from transitioning youth, and the quality of these services is widely variable (Mank, Cioffi, & Yovanoff, 2003; Wehman, 2006a, b).

- Youth with disabilities are much more likely than their same-age peers to drop out of school and to be unemployed and experience poverty as adults (National Organization on Disability, 2004).

- Community employment service agencies struggle to provide quality supported employment to youth and adults with intellectual disabilities (Boeltzig, Gilmore, & Butterworth, 2006; Braddock, Rizzolo, & Hemp, 2004; Conley, 2003).

- One study found that 75% of adult vocational services participants, most of whom have an intellectual disability, receive services in some type of segregated congregate setting (Braddock, Rizzolo, & Hemp, 2004).

- Subminimum wage and sheltered employment is the fate of thousands of people with intellectual disabilities (U.S. General Accounting Office, 2001). (2009, p. 3)

Living in communities and going to school where work is a priority is important to young people with disabilities. Hall, Butterworth, Winsor, Gilmore, and Metzel (2007) studied the 10 states with the most opportunity for integrated employment versus the 10 states with the least opportunity. The success of states such as Washington, Oklahoma, New Hampshire, and Vermont suggests that there is substantial untapped potential for supporting individuals in integrated employment.

Cobb and Alwell conducted a systematic review of research on transition planning. They also noted the perceived lack of efficacy of social skills curricula and reinforced the substantial role of vocational training with real jobs for students. Consider these important points they raised about interagency collaboration:

Since the mid-1980s, research has shown that students with disabilities who participate in work experiences, especially paid work, while in secondary school are significantly more likely than those who do not have these experiences to hold jobs after they exit school (see, e.g., Colley & Jamison, 1998; Hasazi, Gordon, & Roe, 1985; Luecking & Fabian, 2000; National Longitudinal Transition Study 2, 2006; Wagner, 1991). Simply stated, students benefit from frequent and continuous exposure to real work environments throughout the secondary school years and beyond.

> Many of the studies in our review highlight the need for flexibility in creating and providing individualized supports to youth with disabilities, rather than simply fitting them into existing service continuum options. For example, some even indicate the need for funding to go directly to individuals with disabilities (not programs) as young adults; this is most salient in the McColl et al. (1999) study, as money was a major concern for all three participants—a major barrier to their successful independent living. "Insurance would pay for a more expensive residential treatment facility for these young men, but it would not pay for them to live adequately in the community." (2009, p. 317)

In sum, growth and maturity, coupled with self-determination and self-advocacy, form the cornerstones to sound transition planning. A quality plan that addresses adult life goals related to going to college, gaining access to accommodations and supports, developing social competence, and going to work forms a critical foundation for crossing the bridge into adulthood.

ABOUT THE TRANSITION PLANNING TEAM

A transition planning team may consist of any of the following individuals: the student; family members; the school psychologist; general, vocational, and special education teacher(s); the school principal; vocational rehabilitation counselors; the speech-language pathologist; community agency representatives; and other related service personnel.

Research has shown that parental involvement is key to a successful transition (Morningstar, Turnbull, & Turnbull, 1995). Parents usually know their child best, can affect their child's values and decisions (e.g., career, residence), and typically have continual contact with their child throughout the transition process.

Student involvement is also essential to effective transition. Cobb and Alwell (2009) found that student-focused planning is critical; students should be invited and encouraged to participate in transition-related meetings. It is important for students to realize that

1) transition is a process, 2) self-advocacy skills are valuable, and 3) priorities and personal vision are important to the transition process.

The roles and responsibilities of the various participants in the transition IEP process are outlined in Table 1.3 (deFur, 2005) and discussed in greater depth in Chapter 6.

VOCATIONAL ASSESSMENT

Vocational assessment, a critical component of transition planning, helps students develop interpersonal and decision-making skills and ensures that students have the opportunity to explore vocations and careers. Some researchers have suggested that this process begin in the elementary grades and extend into middle school, when initial efforts can be made to formally assess students' interests, aptitudes, work habits, career maturity, and job exploration and interview skills. Career maturity is defined as the degree of development the individual reaches on a continuum of vocational development from exploration to decline. It involves the extent to which an individual possesses the skills and knowledge necessary to make realistic and informed vocational choices (Levinson, 1993). The period including the middle school years is also the time to begin to identify the types of supports students will need to obtain and hold work in the community. Once students have reached high school, transition planning should focus on acquiring work experiences and obtaining employment.

Self-evaluation tools that enable students to determine their own work performance and support needs can be very helpful. Becoming involved in making education and employment decisions, evaluating their performance, and providing input into their support needs can improve students' transition into supported employment. The Job Observation and Behavior Scale: Opportunity for Self-Determination (Brady, Rosenberg, & Frain, 2008) is an assessment designed to obtain such input from students preparing for—and employees participating in—supported employment.

Cobb and Alwell (2009) systematically reviewed the relationship between transition planning/coordinating interventions and transition outcomes for secondary-age students with disabilities. A total of 31 studies of 859 students with a wide variety of disabilities were reviewed. Using Kohler's taxonomy (Kohler & Field, 2003), Cobb and Alwell found support for the efficacy of student-focused planning and student development interventions in improving transition-related outcomes for students with disabilities.

THE PLANNING PROCESS

The objective of transition planning in high school is to promote a seamless transition to adulthood. In order that students make as seamless a transition to community living as possible, they should spend increasing amounts of time in the community each school year (Jefferson & Putnam, 2003; see Figure 1.2). By age 20, the transitioning student should be settled into the living arrangement, employment position, and community activities that he or she is expected to access at age 22. This goal can be accomplished by systematically including the student in community life early in the educational process (Thoma & Wehman, 2010).

The transition planning process is ongoing and can be thought of as a series of phases. The three major phases are 1) planning and development, 2) implementation, and 3) outcome evaluation. Chapter 4 describes this process in more detail.

Table 1.3. Roles and responsibilities of individualized education program (IEP) transition team members

Team Member	Required?	Role/responsibility
Student	Yes	Identify personal strengths and needs. Set personal goals; share interests and preferences for employment, adult living, and postsecondary education/training; assist in identifying transition strategies and activities; provide feedback.
Parent(s)	Yes	Share child's strengths and needs and long-term vision for employment, postsecondary training, and adult living options. Provide information on family supports. Participate in implementing plan; provide feedback.
Special educator	Yes	Prior to the meeting: Collect student interest information and prepare the student to be an active IEP participant; coordinate or oversee coordination of the meeting. At the meeting: Provide present level of performance information beyond that which the student and family share, facilitate participation of those present, record discussion and final decisions on the IEP. After the meeting: Provide follow-up to team members, monitor implementation of the transition and related services, and report progress toward annual transition goals and objectives/benchmarks.
General educator (a vocational educator is recommended)	Yes	Contribute to observations of the student's participation in the general curriculum and identify ways in which the student can access it. Provide instruction.
Administrator or designee	Yes	Identify the supports and services available within the school or school district. Make arrangements for supports and services that are not currently available.
Adult service provider (e.g., rehabilitation counselor, mental retardation services case manager, independent living center specialist)	Yes, if paying for or providing a transition service	Participate in the planning process and identify the services and supports available now and in the future through the adult service agency represented. Provide linkages to other adult services and community supports when appropriate. Provide or pay for transition services typically offered by the agency.
Related service provider (e.g., psychologist, speech-language pathologist, occupational therapist, physical therapist, assistive technology specialist, vocational evaluator, school nurse, job coach)	Yes, if providing a related service or interpreting assessment data	Assess the student when appropriate and communicate assessment data results. Share observations of the student's strengths and needs. Participate in the transition planning process, identifying options for developing transition-related skills. Identify the supports needed based on direct student observation and interactions. Collaborate, advise, and support team efforts and goals.
Transition coordinator	No	Coordinate interagency linkages and cooperative activities to promote the development of a continuum of transition services within the school division and community. Provide information on recommended practices and effective services related to transition. Develop systemic procedures to improve transition curricula, programs, and services for all students. Follow up on the student and service providers. Collaborate with employers and other community representatives to develop community-based work experience options. Provide the student with updated information regarding options within the school division and the community.
Guidance counselor	No	Provide the team with information regarding course of study options, career assessment options, scheduling and class placement options, and counseling support available through the guidance office (including career counseling, truancy and behavior challenges, personal development supports, etc.). Provide direct services, consultation, and coordination services within the school setting.

From deFur, S.H. (2005). Transition from School to Adulthood. In *Intellectual and Developmental Disabilities: Toward Full Community Inclusion* (3rd Ed.) (pp. 368–369), by P. Wehman, P.J. McLaughlin, and T. Wehman (Eds.), 2005, Austin, TX: PRO-ED. Copyright © 2005 by PRO-ED, Inc. Adapted with permission.

Planning and Development

Planning begins with establishing a transition team. The team is responsible for carrying out all three phases of transition. The initial task is to develop long-range community living goals, with the interests and preferences of the student and his or her family being given priority. Once goals have been established, comprehensive assessments of the student's needs in all goal areas (social, daily living, vocational) should be conducted in order to determine the student's present level of performance in these areas. School and community professionals and agencies that may be involved in the transition process should be identified.

When the student has completed all of the assessments, hold an IEP planning meeting that includes all team members. The purpose of this meeting is to develop functional and measurable goals and objectives. Clearly state in the body of the IEP what type of vocational experience the student will have and how many hours per week he or she will be working at the job site. Specify the natural environments to be used for training. Also specify which team members are responsible for implementing training in each of the goal areas (Bateman & Linden, 1997).

Implementation

Implementing the transition IEP is the responsibility of all team members. To the greatest extent possible, transition skills should be taught in the environments in which students will be expected to use them as independent adults. Throughout the implementation phase, progress toward transition goals should be measured daily, weekly, or biweekly. By monitoring progress at these short time intervals, team members will obtain the information necessary to adjust instructional programs to ensure that the rate of student progress is sufficient to meet the annual goals. Changes to transition goals may include increasing or decreasing the level of support given to the student, especially in the area of employment (e.g., supported employment or additional coaching at the current site). Transition goals and objectives should also be adjusted to meet the changing community living goals of the student and his or her family.

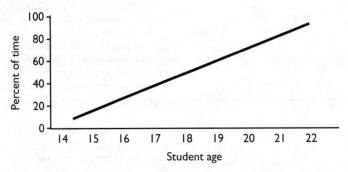

Figure 1.2.   Percentage of time students spend in the community. (From Jefferson, G.L., & Putnam, R.F. [2009]. *Understanding transition services: A parent's guide to legal standards and effective practices.* Norwood, MA: May Institute; reprinted by permission.)

Outcome Evaluation

Outcome evaluation is best accomplished through ongoing data collection on progress toward transition goals. Daily, weekly, or biweekly progress data should be used to inform instructional programming, modify goals, and establish new goals. Outcome evaluation should also include tracking progress toward the major milestones of effective transition services described in the next section. How quickly and effectively a program adjusts to the needs of a student is an indication of the quality of the program.

See Figure 1.3 for a Transition Planning Checklist and Chapters 4, 5, and 6 for more detail on individual transition planning.

PLANNING COMPONENTS

A smooth transition from school to adulthood requires 1) sound school programs and services in which useful learning takes place; 2) a comprehensive transition IEP; and 3) an array of employment, community, and residential choices for students and their families. These points are highlighted in the checklists here on 1) what should happen in school (see Figure 1.4 for a Checklist of Important Questions for a Teacher to Consider), 2) how transition planning should be conducted (see Figure 1.5), and 3) what happens after the student leaves school (see Figure 1.6).

These three basic transition components are necessary for every student with a disability regardless of the type or size of community in which the school is located. The chapters that follow provide many different examples of how to develop a blueprint addressing these components and how to include parents and students in the transition planning process.

CONCLUSION

In today's complex world, successful transition planning requires a dynamic, collaborative, integrated process. Years ago, Will (1984) and Halpern (1985) pioneered a model for transition from school to work and from school to community. Today more variables can affect outcomes, and there is greater need than ever for well-crafted transition IEP plans that take into consideration the academic, social, vocational, and personal preferences of each student. deFur and Korinek noted the following:

> The 21st century demands that employees have the skills that support job success— the academic competence, the employment attitudes and the job-specific aptitudes that enable ongoing and evolving career development. Employers identified advanced thinking and problem solving, professionalism and work ethic, communication skills, flexibility to adapt to change, and interpersonal skills for teamwork as critical skills for the modern workplace (Cassner-Lotto & Barrington, 2006; Thornburg, 2002). These skills are consistent with self-determination curricula for students with disabilities that focus on self-awareness, goal setting and attainment, social skills, self-advocacy, and problem solving (Martin, et al., 2003). (2008, p. 187)

Checklist for Supporting Transition Planning and Review

Instructions: Read over and refer to this checklist of important considerations and factors that will need to be addressed in the transition planning and review processes. Space is provided to fill in names, if needed.

Starting the Transition Process

- Who will tell the student about the transition planning process and work out with the student whom to involve in the process?

- Who will tell the parents or caregivers about the process, discuss how the parents can support the student, and ask whom the parents would like to involve in the process?

- Who will organize dates for transition plan meetings and review for the year?

- Who will inform and invite other professionals with at least 3 months' advance notice?

Organizing and Planning the Meeting

- Who will chair the meeting?

- How and when will the student and family be introduced to the questions to assist him or her with thinking about the visions for the future or life after secondary school, and how will he or she be supported to find the answers?

- How will the meeting be made a relaxed, person-centered, and positive experience for the student and the family (e.g., in terms of layout, refreshments, venue, music, timing)?

- Has someone organized supplies (e.g., flipchart, pens) and designated a notetaker?

- How will families get to and from meetings? Will they need help?

Follow-Up on the Transition Meeting

- Have the student and family agreed that colleges or other support agencies can see the transition plan?

- Who will ensure that all people involved in the plan or review have been given copies of the documents?

- Who will ensure that all necessary agencies are sent a copy of the plan or review?

- Who will follow up and make sure that people are taking the actions agreed to in the plan?

- Who will contact agencies that were not able to attend the meeting to inform them of the agreed-on actions?

- Have dates been agreed on for subsequent reviews over the coming year?

Figure 1.3. Checklist for Supporting Transition Planning and Review.

Checklist of Important Questions for a Teacher to Consider

Instructions: Check the items that indicate sound school programs and services in which transition planning can flourish.

		Yes	No	Notes
1.	Does the student have opportunities to access the general curriculum and learn side by side with students who do not have a disability?			
2.	Does the student have ongoing access to information about the process of transitioning to postsecondary education, including the documentation requirements of various 2- and 4-year colleges and universities?			
3.	Does career/vocational planning begin at the elementary level and continue smoothly and logically across grade levels? Are teachers from all grade levels involved in program development?			
4.	Is a functional vocational curriculum in place that reflects skills required in local employment sites for instruction on job skills, completing work in a timely manner or reaching production standards, and interpersonal skills?			
5.	Are collaborative efforts with postsecondary education disability support services in place to ensure a smooth transition to 2- or 4-year college settings?			
6.	Do special and general educators, including career/technical educators, work together to provide services and collaborative teaching?			
7.	Do the student's desired postsecondary goals identify meaningful jobs and appropriate training strategies that are implemented before the student graduates?			
8.	Is there parental involvement in career planning?			
9.	Have agencies and individuals been identified before the student graduates to provide follow-up training on the job?			
10.	Is there administrator and program supervisor support for community-based instruction, coordination of services with community agencies, and staff and resource allocation to permit job placement and training?			

Figure 1.4.   Checklist of Important Questions for a Teacher to Consider.

Transition Planning Checklist

Instructions: When planning, a teacher should consider the following questions:

	Yes	No	Notes
1. Have the student and his or her family provided input into, made choices about, and participated in identifying postsecondary education, employment, community living, and other postschool options?			
2. Has there been participation from well-informed parents and guardians?			
3. Has a plan been developed for the student that includes annual goals and the steps necessary to attain the goals?			
4. Does the plan specify who is responsible for each aspect of the transition process, including referral to appropriate agencies, job placement, on-the-job training, and job follow-up?			
5. Have there been coordinated efforts on the part of all appropriate agencies, including vocational rehabilitation counselors, community rehabilitation providers, developmental disabilities service providers, disability support personnel at 2- and 4-year colleges/universities, and postschool vocational education programs?			
6. Is the plan user-friendly; that is, is it easy for the student and parents to understand and take ownership of?			

Figure 1.5. Transition Planning Checklist.

What a Student Will Need Post–High School Checklist

1. What skills will the student need to access support services on college and university campuses?

2. Will the student have regular competitive employment opportunities?

   Yes_____   No_____

3. Will competitive employment programs offer ongoing employment supports?

   Yes_____   No_____

4. Will various transportation options (e.g., drivers, public buses) be available?

   Yes_____   No_____

5. Will residential alternatives, such as supported living, group homes, and in-home companions, be available in the community?

   Yes_____   No_____

6. Will various leisure activities, such as a cycling club, ballroom dancing, and YMCA membership be available, and will the student be encouraged to check out these recreational options?

   Yes_____   No_____

Figure 1.6.   What a Student Will Need Post–High School Checklist.

FOR FURTHER INFORMATION

Perceptions of High School Staff

Carter, E.W., & Hughes, C. (2006). Including high school students with severe disabilities in general education classes: Perspectives of general and special educators, paraprofessionals, and administrators. *Research and Practice for Persons with Severe Disabilities, 31,* 174–185.

Explores how general and special educators, paraprofessionals, and administrators converge and diverge in their evaluations of different aspects of general education participation for adolescents with severe disabilities.

The Summary of Performance

Izzo, M.V., & Kochhar-Bryant, C.A. (2006). Implementing the SOP for effective transition: Two case studies. *Career Development for Exceptional Individuals, 29,* 100–107.

Two excellent case studies of how the Summary of Performance (SOP) helped to facilitate one student into supported employment and another into a college program.

Madaus, J.W., Bigaj, S., Chafouleas, S.M., & Simonsen, B.M. (2006). What key information can be included in a comprehensive summary of performance? *Career Development for Exceptional Individuals, 29,* 90–99.

Delineates what specific key information needs to be part of a comprehensive SOP.

Ward, M.J. (2006). Incorporating the summary of performance into transition planning. *Career Development for Exceptional Individuals, 29,* 67–69.

Describes the interaction between two teachers in terms of how the SOP can work.

Teaching Self-Advocacy Skills

Wehmeyer, M.L., & Palmer, S.B. (2003). Adult outcomes for students with cognitive disabilities three years after high school: The impact of self-determination. *Education and Training in Developmental Disabilities, 38,* 131–144.

Highlights strategies for teaching self-advocacy skills to students with disabilities.

2

Individual and Community Transition Planning

Melissa is an outgoing and active young woman who is eager to experience living on her own. She would like to move from her parents' home into an accessible apartment within the next 2 years. Her team envisions her living with one other woman. She would have 24-hour supports for meals, housekeeping, and daily living care. Melissa's family and occupational therapist agree that she could be fully independent in her daily self-care routines as long as her bathroom and bedroom were fully accessible. Melissa's family indicates that although she likes to spend time in the kitchen, Melissa needs a lot of support to prepare meals. They also note that she does not enjoy housekeeping and finds many such tasks physically challenging.

Maurice is an intelligent, soft-spoken, and self-determined young man. He would like to live at home next year and attend college as a part-time student. He plans to study child psychology and ultimately earn a doctorate. Because he uses a ventilator to breathe, he and his mother want his vocational rehabilitation counselor and a representative from the university to be actively involved in both choosing appropriate assistive technology for schoolwork and medical care and touring the university to check for necessary physical accommodations. Maurice hopes to live in a dorm on campus during his junior and senior years of school and become involved in university social life. His mother is fearful of this and worries about Maurice's safety and his medical needs.

Melissa and Maurice are excellent examples of students who require individualized transition planning. The first step is to build a team that includes those who can assist the student with identifying goals, needs, and future services. The earlier those discussions can take place and a blueprint for the future can be designed, the more likely Melissa and Maurice will experience a good outcome.

As the personal goals and aspirations for Melissa and Maurice begin to come into focus, a community transition plan and the essential supports required to implement it will be needed to make these individual dreams a reality. Individualized transition planning leads to the building of a community transition plan with appropriate supports that are customized to the individual student's needs.

Thoma (1999) presented an excellent overview of how various strategies can be used for both individual and community transition planning. Emphasis needs to be placed on holding high expectations for students, being prepared, ensuring student decision making in the individualized education program (IEP) process (Thoma & Wehman, 2010), developing portfolios of skills, and building supports for students with challenging needs.

23

Table 2.1 presents excellent examples of these strategies along with the rationale behind the strategies.

This chapter presents an overview of individual and community transition planning as a lead-in to the more in-depth discussion on these topics in Chapters 4, 5, and 6. It also targets several specific areas, such as transition supports, self-determination, and inclusion in the school and community.

Table 2.1. Strategies for effective transition planning

Strategy	Rationale	Example
Hold high expectations for students.	Students truly shine when working on goals that matter to them. If perceptions of students' abilities are based on students' performance on goals unrelated to their own visions for the future, then these perceptions are probably not accurate. When a student says that he or she wants to work toward a desired goal, the transition team needs to expect the best because they most likely have not seen what the young person is capable of achieving.	Elaine's dreams for the future included going to college. Most of her teachers were quick to believe that this was an unrealistic goal for her because her performance on most achievement and aptitude tests demonstrated that she had a moderate cognitive disability. Elaine's mother, however, believed that Elaine could go to college. Through the efforts of the coordinator in the Office for Students with Disabilities, Elaine was accepted on a provisional basis. The accommodations that were put in place allowed her to succeed in a way that others had not expected.
Prepare students for their transition planning meetings.	Student presence does not necessarily ensure student involvement in the individualized education program or individualized transition plan process. Students need to understand their roles in the process. They need opportunities to role-play, to participate in the information gathering that takes place before these meetings, to discover their options, and to talk with possible support providers.	Jack's transition coordinator met with Jack and his mother at their home before the transition meeting. They discussed Jack's plans for his future and the ways in which he could discuss those issues during the meeting. They assigned priorities to the goals for the coming year so that he could talk about those that were most important to him. They brainstormed possible objections to working on these chosen goals as well as Jack's rebuttals to those objections. The role playing even helped him redefine certain goals. Jack was well prepared to discuss his own goals and not answer, "I don't know" during the meeting itself.
Involve community members as participants on transition planning teams.	The planning for students' transition from school to adult life should involve identifying necessary supports that will ensure that students' dreams become a reality. Who is better able to provide information about what supports are available than someone who is already a member of the community?	Amy was interested in helping others and wanted to find an agency that would accept the help she was offering. An employee at the local United Way office was invited to attend Amy's transition planning meeting. Before the meeting, Amy called the employee, introduced herself, and told her what she would like to do. The employee offered to call some of the agencies that she thought might need Amy's help so that she could bring that information to the planning meeting. At the meeting, the employee shared information about three local agencies, and Amy was able to make a decision about which agency met her needs.
Use a portfolio-based assessment process to document student achievement.	A portfolio-based assessment process can accomplish two important goals: 1) It allows students to demonstrate what they know and what they have learned in a manner that best demonstrates that knowledge, as opposed to trying to make assumptions about students' progress based on their ability to take a test, and 2) it provides an opportunity for students to be more active participants in the meeting by sharing the portfolio with team members as a way of addressing current level of performance.	Sue wanted to go to college and learn skills to be a teacher or teaching assistant. Her writing skills were poor, which might have prevented her from being admitted to a college program. Sue and her team worked with a college admissions counselor to determine which skills she needed to be accepted into the college, and the team then discussed Sue's strengths to determine how to demonstrate that she had these competencies. Sue took the SAT just like other college applicants, but she also included a portfolio of her best work from school. This portfolio included a videotape of Sue teaching a group of first graders as part of a school-sponsored work experience.

Focus on supports rather than programs.	When transition planning focuses primarily on matching students with pre-existing programs, the possibility of students attaining their adult lifestyle goals decreases dramatically. When teams first determine what students' goals are and then determine the level of support necessary to make them a reality, new possibilities can emerge.	Steve knew that he wanted to be an auto mechanic like all of the other men in his family. A local auto mechanics class at the vocational/technical school had never accepted anyone with a disability. Instead, students with disabilities entered a community transition program and were taught in fast food restaurants or retail settings. Steve's transition planning team determined that his physical disability would not prevent him from participating in the auto mechanics class. Because he had good upper body strength, he was able to transfer in and out of his wheelchair, and he could use tools once he was under the car. His limited reading ability meant that he would need modifications to the written manuals and the written tests that were part of the program. The auto mechanics teacher agreed to work with the special education teacher to make such modifications, and Steve became the first student with a disability in that large urban school district to enter a vocational education program.
Provide opportunities for students to explore their communities and their career interests.	Students need to be exposed to lots of experiences to make informed choices regarding their dreams for an adult lifestyle. Until they know what choices are available, they may make decisions that are based on limited information.	John wanted to be a pilot. A family friend who was a pilot arranged to give John a tour of an airport and introduced him to many people who worked there. They answered John's questions and showed him what they did, giving John a clearer picture of the job possibilities in the airline industry as well as the education and other requirements needed to obtain and keep these jobs. John realized that being a pilot was not the best decision for him. He secured a part-time job helping to refuel airplanes and load customer baggage, which provided him with additional hands-on experience to help him make a more definite career decision.

From *Supporting student voice in transition planning* by C.A. Thoma, *Teaching Exceptional Children, 31*(5), 4–9. Copyright © 1999 by The Council for Exceptional Children. Adapted with permission.

INDIVIDUALIZED TRANSITION PLANNING

When young people grow up, they must make decisions and set goals in areas such as career planning, nutrition, fitness, financial and estate planning, vocational training, employment, transportation, postsecondary education, and independent living. Through individualized transition planning, adults can show young people how to make decisions, set goals, plan, and organize their futures. When done correctly and comprehensively, individualized transition planning assists students in learning about themselves, developing statements of their future goals, and negotiating with their IEP team members for a plan of objectives and activities that are necessary to accomplish their goals. Table 2.2 gives some idea of some questions to think about when developing the vocational component of a student's plan.

Goals of Planning

Individualized transition planning has two goals. The first goal is to identify which outcomes students and their families desire and expect, along with the services and supports that

Table 2.2. Questions to generate student profile data

Interests and preferences	What are the student's favorite things to do at home?
	What does the student dislike doing at home?
	Describe your dream job for the student.
On-the-job supports	What accommodation(s) does the student use at home?
Ideas for future work (most suitable for students in their last year of school)	Name some businesses in which you would like to see the student employed.
	Do you have a connection at any of these businesses?
	What days of the week and times of day is the student available to work?
	What transportation options are available to assist the student in getting to and from work?
Student evaluation and curriculum development	Does the student have insight into what type of work he or she would like to perform?
	What skills can be taught or practiced to promote a successful vocational future?

students will need to achieve these outcomes. This process usually draws on a person-centered planning approach (Holburn, 2002), which will be discussed in more detail in the following section.

Using needs data to drive local systems change is another goal of individualized transition planning. This information can be used to increase a state's capacity to improve and expand its transition services and programs. Such data may assist in the development of the necessary services, supports, and opportunities for youth and young adults with disabilities so they may reach their personal desired quality of life. This development may also include improving cooperation and coordination of many stakeholders including state agencies, employers, families, local schools, and the general public and other changes in programs to effectively improve transition services for all students.

Being informed of the law, best practices, and what to expect in terms of youth, family, and community involvement and interagency collaboration are also key to driving systems change. Although recognizing the necessity of this goal is extremely important, discussing it further is beyond the scope of this book. However, we will touch on community participation and collaboration, both key outcomes from positive systems change.

The transition planning process provides transition IEP teams with an understanding of each student's unique desires and needs along with an individualized plan or blueprint showing how to achieve the desired outcomes. (Cameto, 2005)

Person-Centered Planning

Wehman noted the close association between person-centered planning and student-directed planning. Although the two approaches may appear synonymous, "person-centered planning emphasizes the role of significant others, whereas student-directed planning processes emphasize building student capacity" (2001, p. 77). After reviewing 31 published studies, Cobb and Alwell found that student-directed planning was very important for discerning successful outcomes. In addition, they noted,

> These studies also indicate that vocational training should include work experiences in real jobs, particularly work experiences that focus on socialization with coworkers, and access to adult role models and mentors in meaningful work roles.

Furthermore, they add support for a focus on career planning and development that encompasses and builds on specific job skills. Both the studies with participants with identified mild/moderate disabilities and those with more severe disabilities suggest that having a job is not enough—without extensive and seamless transition supports; for example, students with moderate and severe disabilities can lose jobs as quickly as 2 to 3 months after graduation. (2009, p. 78)

Student Involvement

The goal of all person-centered approaches is to learn about people with disabilities in more effective and efficient ways in order to plan and create supports that can assist these individuals in participating in and experiencing self-directed lives (O'Brien, 2002). Let's examine how Rochelle, her parents, and her teachers began the brainstorming process.

Rochelle is a 15-year-old student at a high school located in the mountains of rural Colorado. At a very young age, Rochelle began to express an interest in becoming a chef. Today, when the subject comes up, you can see the excitement in her eyes and hear it in her voice.

Rochelle was involved in a motor vehicle accident when she was a toddler and experienced a traumatic brain injury as a result. Rochelle enjoys school but often struggles with learning new things. Sometimes she has difficulty completing daily tasks because she cannot remember the steps involved, or, after completing the first step, she does not remember the original goal. Her special education team is committed to supporting Rochelle in the general education curriculum, including providing assistance with impulsive behaviors.

Soon after her 15th birthday, in early spring, Rochelle is preparing for her first transition-planning meeting. She and Ms. Appleton, the special education teacher, meet to talk about her vision for life after high school. Rochelle states that she wants to enroll in culinary school. This will require a move to the city. Later that afternoon this vision is discussed with Rochelle's mother along with other possible goals to help Rochelle prepare for the future. Her mother voices concerns about Rochelle moving out of the area to attend school. She states that plans have been made to add on a garage apartment for Rochelle to live in. She goes on to say that Rochelle can also earn an income by helping take care of her aunt's children after school and on weekends. Rochelle's mother notes that this will also include the chance to prepare meals for the children.

At the end of the meeting Rochelle, her mother, and Ms. Appleton agree to explore the possibilities further so that they can prepare for the planning meeting scheduled in the fall. For the remainder of the school year, Rochelle completes assessments designed to gather more information about her needs and interests. Over the summer, Rochelle and her mother attend a recruitment event at a school and look into various living arrangements and support services.

When school begins in the fall, the planning team corresponds via e-mail and telephone to relate information and discuss additional ideas and concerns. Ms. Appleton works with the school faculty to determine which general educators will be teaching the classes that Rochelle will be taking so that they may attend the meeting. When the planning meeting is held, the entire team is able to use the report from the planning team to establish a coordinated set of activities and support services that will enable Rochelle to achieve her dream of entering the food industry.

Values and Beliefs

Rochelle's case study reflects the importance of substantial involvement from the student. Individuals with disabilities must be placed in respected positions and even leadership positions during the assessment, planning, and service delivery process. To accomplish this, all person-centered approaches share some common values or beliefs. Schwartz, Holburn, and Jacobson (2000) identified eight hallmarks of person-centered planning (see Table 2.3).

Basic Steps in Person-Centered Planning

In general, person-centered approaches require teams to follow five basic steps that fit within the traditional model used by most IEP team members:

1. The team is convened around the transition-age student, and leadership roles that the student can assume within his or her team are identified.

2. The team reviews assessment data and conducts additional assessment activities.

3. The team develops service and support plans, in this case IEPs or statements of transition services.

4. The team updates the IEP or transition IEP annually and implements follow-up procedures.

5. The team holds an exit meeting for the student during his or her last year in school.

    It is clear that transition teams must initially focus on students' needs, wishes, and dreams. This requires thoughtful planning and involvement from the student (Thoma & Wehman, 2010). But is this enough? Or does meeting these needs and achieving these wishes require further external planning? To find out, let's turn now to community transition planning.

Transition planning that is driven by the needs and preferences of the student results in better postschool outcomes (Benz, Lindstrom, & Yovanoff, 2000; Frank & Sitlington, 2000; Merchant & Gajar, 1997) and higher levels of student and parent satisfaction with the educational program (Colleg-Klingenberg, 1998; McDonnell & Hardman, 2010; Miner & Bates, 1997).

COMMUNITY PARTICIPATION AND COLLABORATION

High-quality transition planning also requires that a major emphasis be placed on strong community participation. All too frequently, transition IEPs fail to effectively involve and link to the resources that can help students be successful working and living in the com-

Table 2.3. The hallmarks of person-centered planning.

1. The person's activities, services, and supports are based on his or her dreams, interests, preferences, strengths, and capacities.
2. The person and people important to him or her are included in lifestyle planning and have the opportunity to exercise control and make informed decisions.
3. The person has meaningful choices with decisions based on his or her experiences.
4. The person uses, when possible, natural and community supports.
5. Activities, supports, and services foster skills to achieve personal relationships, community inclusion, dignity, and respect.
6. The person's opportunities and experiences are maximized and flexibility is enhanced within existing regulatory and funding constraints.
7. Planning is collaborative and recurring and involves an ongoing commitment to the person.
8. The person is satisfied with his or her relationships, home, and daily routine.

From Schwartz, A.A., Holburn, S.C., & Jacobson, J.W. (2000). Defining person-centeredness: Results of two consensus methods. *Education and Training in Mental Retardation and Developmental Disabilities, 35,* 238; reprinted by permission.

munity. Why? Special education is an entitled service, and the local school system is the single agency that coordinates it. Yet many educators, family members, and students with disabilities do not recognize that most adult services have their own eligibility criteria related to access.

Community Resources

During the transition planning process, it is important to look at resources within the school and also target community agencies and organizations that can provide students with support. Each of these organizations can play a unique and vital role in a student's successful transition from school to work and independence in the community. Successful students with disabilities will receive services and support from a variety of public and private programs. However, the exact mix of programs will vary depending on the student's needs, his or her family's economic resources, and each program's eligibility requirements (Wittenburg, Golden, & Fishman, 2002).

Planning for transition will necessarily involve the entire community, so an extensive analysis of the community must be completed to ensure that all programs and services are identified. Examples of community organizations that are important transition resources include Community Work Incentive Coordinators for Social Security Administration projects, federally funded state vocational rehabilitation programs, community rehabilitation service providers, social services agencies, community colleges, centers for independent living, One-Stop Career Centers coordinated by the U.S. Department of Labor, community service boards, and local businesses. Each of these community organizations brings its unique set of services and supports to students with disabilities (see Table 2.4). The roles and functions of each of these organizations are discussed in more detail in Chapter 8.

Community Program Development

Many different community organizations are available to provide transition support. Yet Hartman (2009) outlined how to pull all of these components together to develop a community-based transition program (see Table 2.5). She noted that planning, hiring, selecting students, and managing details are key in partnering with community organizations and agencies. Hartman's very practical guidelines address some of the challenges that may be faced during the transition process and outline possible solutions.

The organizations listed in the previous section and in Table 2.4 are only some of the more typical ones available to provide assistance in the transition planning process. Many other local resources may also be accessed. It is important to involve community agencies early in the process so that entire transition team can become familiar with the resources they offer (Wehman, 2001).

Interagency Collaboration

Interagency collaboration is a huge part of the community transition process. According to Wehman (2006b), although some families and students can do all of the transition work on their own and have the time to do so, addressing the essentials of comprehensive

Table 2.4.   Community organizations that support youth in transition

Organization	Role and function
Local rehabilitation services	Determine eligibility; provide assessments, guidance, counseling, and job placement services under an individualized plan for employment
Community rehabilitation providers	Provide assessments, counseling, job placement, and follow-up services
Social services agencies	Assist with housing, financial, health, and transportation issues
Community colleges and technical schools	Provide assistance with the application process and financial aid; provide information on accessibility and accommodations
Social Security Administration	Provides financial assistance in the form of Supplemental Security Income; provides other work-related benefits (e.g., Plan to Achieve Self-Support, Impairment-Related Work Expenses [IRWE])
Centers for independent living	Provide information for self-advocacy and understanding one's rights; provide training programs dealing with money management, sexuality, leisure activities, and socialization
One-Stop Career Centers	Assist students with career and vocational counseling; help with occupational training and job placement
Local community service boards	Coordinate services and assistance for counseling, family planning, nutrition, health care, and transportation
Local businesses	Assist with mock interviews and development of job-seeking skills; provide career information and work experience opportunities
Work Incentives Planning and Assistance programs	Provide financial analysis and information on work incentives and disability benefit programs operated under the Social Security Administration

From Brooke, V., Green, J.H., Revell, W.G., & Wehman, P. (2006). Transition planning in the community: Using all of the resources. In P. Wehman, *Life beyond the classroom: Transition strategies for young people with disabilities* (4th ed., p. 99). Baltimore: Paul H. Brookes Publishing Co.; adapted by permission.

planning usually requires a team of community agencies working together. Noonan, Morningstar, and Erickson used an evidence-based approach to study the strategies used by high-performing local school districts and communities. They noted,

> In a time of such poor outcomes for youth with disabilities, interagency collaboration remains a fundamental challenge for educators. Indeed, some have argued that, by definition, transition planning is an interagency endeavor, and that without high levels of collaboration, transition services and planning are jeopardized (Agran et al., 2002). (2008, p. 132)

Although several researchers have looked at collaboration (e.g., Agran et al., 2002; Benz, Lindstrom, & Halpern, 1995; Morningstar, Kleinhammer-Tramill, & Lattin, 1999), none have looked at the components that make interagency collaboration most effective. Thus, Noonan et al. (2008) conducted focus groups with 29 high-performing districts and state-level transition coordinators from five diverse states. The results were used to develop 11 key strategies or evidence-based examples of what can be done to enhance interagency collaboration. This not only has important implications for professionals in the field but ultimately it can help improve postschool outcomes for students with disabilities. The strategies include the following:

Strategy 1: Flexible Scheduling and Staffing: Formalize the role of the transition coordinator to work closely with multiple agencies and often parents to initiate and secure adult services for youth with disabilities before they exit high school. Coordinators should possess extensive levels of knowledge of eligibility requirements, services, and funding.

Table 2.5. Developing a community-based transition program: Challenges and solutions

Challenge	Solution
Transportation	Include supervisors and bus drivers in the planning phase. Research local public transportation in relation to job sites.
Stakeholders	Get support from key players (the ones with the power to provide money, staff, etc.) up front.
Communication	Make sure everyone in the program has a cell phone. Teachers need to communicate with each other, the bus drivers, and the students on work sites.
Teacher access to school mail, materials, and so forth	Set up a home base for the teacher at a school near the community site. The teacher will need to receive school mail, student information, make copies, and so forth.
Free and reduced lunch and medication	Pick up meals at the student's home school. The teacher will have to be in charge of medications.
Access to technology	The teacher should be provided with a laptop so he/she can access e-mail and Internet resources for students. (It would be great if the students had laptops also!)
Choosing a "home base" site	The site should be as close to the community the student lives in as possible. Public libraries, local mall, community center, and various service organizations may be willing to share space. When choosing a space, make sure it is open on school days. Look at closing policies and hours of operation. Ask about access to the space, keys, storage, restrooms, and so forth. Have a back-up plan in the event the site is closed on a school day.
Contracts	Create a student and parent contract that is approved by your risk management personnel. This protects you and your program in the event something goes wrong or you need to remove a student from the program.
Interagency agreements	Agreements should be in writing and denote responsibilities of each member.
Attendance	Report attendance to the student's home school on a weekly basis via e-mail.

From *Step by step: Creating a community-based transition program for students with intellectual disabilities* by M.A. Hartman, *Teaching Exceptional Children, 41*(6), 6–11. Copyright © 2009 by The Council for Exceptional Children. Reprinted with permission.

Strategy 2: Follow-Up After Transition: Transition coordinators continue to assist families and students even after they have exited school services.

Strategy 3: Administrative Support for Transition: Administrative support is provided at the local level that allows flexible scheduling, compensation time, paid summer training, and substitutes. Furthermore, interagency collaboration should also occur at the administrative level, such as between the special education administrators and the adult agencies.

Strategy 4: Use of a Variety of Funding Sources: Tap into a variety of funding sources at the local level. Also share funding with a variety of agencies to improve services and training.

Strategy 5: State-Supported Technical Assistance: Technical assistance can be obtained from the State Education Agency (SEA) to effectively collaborate with adult agencies; value local input when designing resources and training.

Strategy 6: Ability to Build Relationships: Work closely with a spectrum of adult agencies. This includes developing a high level of awareness and interaction with outside agencies, including development of personal relationships with staff from those organizations.

Strategy 7: Agency Meetings with Students and Families: Transition coordinators facilitate meetings between adult agencies and students and families, above and beyond the annual IEP meetings.

Strategy 8: Training of Students and Families: Provide information and training to students and families regarding adult agency services, employment, and postsecondary education.

Strategy 9: Joint Training of Staff: Participate in joint training opportunities.

Strategy 10: Meetings with Agency Staff and Transition Councils: Hold regularly scheduled meetings between the Local Education Agency and adult agency staff, (e.g., VR, mental health, developmental disability) to ensure ongoing collaboration, sharing of information, and individualized student planning.

Strategy 11: Dissemination of Information to a Broad Audience: Provide information to parents, students, teachers, and others using a variety of approaches such as products, up-to-date web site linking to state-of-the-art resources, mailings, presentations, and sponsoring attendance at conferences.

Noonan et al. (2008, p.135) also recommended a list of focus group questions to target specific areas of interagency collaboration, including professional roles, practices, policies, attitudes, and information that both inhibit and enhance interagency collaboration:

Questions around gaining adult services involvement

- How do you collaborate with your local vocational rehabilitation (VR) services? Let's go around and each comment briefly.
- Besides VR [vocational rehabilitation], which outside agencies are typically invited to IEP (Individualized Education Program [IEP] meetings? Let's go around and each comment briefly.
  - What strategies did you use to get outside agencies involved?
  - What strategies have you used to get outside agencies to attend IEP meetings?
- When do you start contacting them?
- How easy or difficult is it to get their involvement? What barriers get in the way?
- If this wasn't always the case, who were the critical players in making this happen (e.g., special education director, agency director, transition coordinator, guidance counselor)? What did they do? (e.g., Special ed. director, agency director, transition coordinator, guidance counselor)
- Were any products created to increase outside agency involvement? (e.g., family transition guide, resource guide)?
- Did any school or agency policies (e.g., interagency memoranda of understanding) change? How?
- What changes have you seen in the attitudes of practitioners or agency staff?
- What about other agencies (not just VR)?
- What do you do if agency representatives cannot attend?

Questions around the IEP

- How are the interagency responsibilities and linkages reflected on the IEP?
- Who were the critical players (e.g., special education director) in making the change on the IEP? What did they do? (e.g., special ed. director)
- Did any school or agency policies change? (e.g., how the IEP meeting is conducted, who creates the IEP, third-party IEP reviews)?
- Were any products created?
- How do parent invitations include information about adult services participating?

- How were teachers prepared to add interagency linkages and responsibilities (e.g., extra training) into the IEP? (e.g. extra training)
- Did you see any change in the attitudes of practitioners or agency staff regarding their new roles?
- How do you create a coordinated set of activities in the statement of needed transition services?
- Are outside agencies included in this coordinated set of activities? How?
- Has this always been the case, or if not, what did you do to change this?
- Have you ever had an instance where an adult agency failed to provide the agreed-upon services contained in the IEP, and if so, what did you do?[1]

Understanding Adult Services

Moving from the public education system to the adult services system involves learning about a new set of community resources, each with its own unique rules, regulations, eligibility guidelines, and procedures. For individuals interested in obtaining competitive employment, a variety of opportunities and potential challenges exist in working with the adult services system (Wehman, Revell, & Brooke, 2003).

Once students with disabilities reach age 22 or have completed high school and received a regular diploma, they no longer have a legal right to the variety of services covered by the Individuals with Disabilities Education Act (IDEA) of 1990 (PL 101-476; U.S. Department of Education, 2005). For the most part, services in the adult system are not based on entitlement. Most postsecondary employment and related service agencies (e.g., those providing postsecondary education, counseling, rehabilitation, therapy, residential services, and recreational services) have their own eligibility requirements. Different laws and policies govern each of these programs. Some families of individuals with autism have reported that identifying, gaining access to, and paying for needed adult-oriented services involves working through a complex public and private service system (Sullivan, 2001). Therefore, all students with disabilities and their family members must gain a strong understanding of these community programs to ensure a smooth transition.

TRANSITION SUPPORTS

One approach to establishing a community transition plan is taken from Hughes and Carter's (2000) model of transition supports, which focuses heavily on improving student competence. By blending what researchers know about supports, about how to use an ecological model, and about how to tie supports to individual transition needs, Hughes and Carter (2000) presented a model that encompasses hundreds of different transition supports that might be useful for students with special needs. Consider the case of Angelo:

Angelo Rust entered high school at age 15. He had no work experience when he walked in the office of Ms. Gustafson, the high school vocational counselor, early in September. Ms. Gustafson explained to Angelo that besides taking his regular academic courses, he could enroll in the school's

---

[1]From Noonan P. M., Morningstar, M. E., & Erickson, A. G. (2008). Improving interagency collaboration: Effective strategies used by high-performing local districts and communities, p. 135. *Career Development for Exceptional Individuals, 31*(3), 132–143. Copyright © 2008 by SAGE Publications. Reprinted by Permission of SAGE Publications.

job experience program if he wanted to. The job experience program would give Angelo the chance to try out or sample different kinds of jobs. Counselors in the program would help Angelo find jobs and would make sure that he had the opportunity to explore a variety of work experiences so that he could begin to figure out what career areas he was most interested in. By targeting a particular area, Angelo could learn what skills he needed. The counselors would also keep a record of his job experiences to help him identify his career preferences and to begin to develop a résumé for potential employers.

The job experience program sounded like a good idea to Angelo. He could use some part-time work while he went to school, and he really did need some help trying to find a job. Also, he wasn't sure what kind of jobs were "out there" and what he really wanted to be when he finished school. Angelo knew that he liked being with little kids, such as his nieces, and he knew he wanted to show his nieces that they could have a better life than he had had. However, he didn't know if there even was a job where you could work with little kids all day. Maybe he could find out in the job program.

During the next few years, Angelo tried out new jobs when he wasn't in school. He liked some jobs—such as the day care program—but there were some jobs he didn't like at all—such as the auto body shop. Each time he sampled a new job, his vocational counselor would complete his student job history. By the time he entered his senior year, Angelo had quite a long job history! Besides the day care and the auto body shop, Angelo had also held jobs in an office, a landscaping business, and an advertising company. The job Angelo liked best and at which he performed best was being an aide at the day care center. Because of his interests, Angelo enrolled in child care classes at school. His instructor, Ms. Chickie, was thrilled with his exceptional performance in class and was overjoyed that a man was interested in going into preschool teaching! Male teachers were desperately needed in preschool, but Angelo was the first young man to enroll in her child care classes in the 8 years she had taught at Walt Whitman High School.

Angelo was grateful for the job sampling he had had in the job experience program. He learned what career he wanted in life by having the chance to go out and try different jobs. By comparing his jobs and how he performed on them, Angelo learned that child care was the best job match for him. Now he has some real career plans. When Angelo finishes high school, he plans to go on to Central State College to complete his certification as a preschool teacher.

A philosophy of transition support accepts that *all* people need support to develop competence—just in varying degrees and in differing areas of life. Enabling students to develop competence to the maximum extent possible requires individually designed support programs that address student-specific strengths, needs, preferences, and interests. For example, transition support might include a coworker giving a student a ride to work, a peer helping a student who has limited use of her hands to eat lunch, or a vocational rehabilitation counselor assisting a student with developing a functional résumé. Transition support can include any assistance or help provided directly to a student to promote a successful transition from school to adult life. It is also important to look at how students and families can choose these supports and what knowledge and control they need to effectively gain access to them.

SELF-DETERMINATION

In discussions about person-centered planning, transition IEPs, and how to maximize the use of supports in the community, we have to ask: How much does self-determination play a role, and how can self-determination be taught to students with disabilities? Self-determined students tend to be more competent and have a greater capacity to move through the transition period with fewer problems. For example, research has shown that students with learning and intellectual disabilities who are high in self-determination often have higher postschool employment rates (Wehmeyer & Palmer, 2003; Wehmeyer & Schwartz, 1997).

Self-determination provides additional control and capacity for students to become more employable.

Student Leadership and Self-Determination

Given the link between self-determination and employability, it is essential that activities during the high school years focus on teaching self-determination through student leadership of the IEP process. Consider the example of Martin:

Martin, Mithaug, Oliphint, Husch, and Frazier (2002) compared employment outcomes for almost 600 workers with disabilities who participated in a systematic self-determination assessment and job placement program with 200 workers who completed only the job placement program. Those who completed both the self-determination assessment and the job placement program kept their jobs significantly longer than those who did not complete these programs.

Martin actively participated in his IEP meetings and collaborated with his educators to develop goals, interventions, and self-evaluation strategies in both elementary and middle school. Now a high school student, Martin needs to further develop the self-determination skills he will need after leaving school.

The IEP process provides the perfect opportunity for Martin to learn these crucial skills. At the start of the school year, Martin's IEP team reviews his day and activities for both school and home. The team realizes that he needs more time to learn self-determination behaviors. The IEP team thus creates two annual goals and suggested activities for Martin.

Goal 1: Martin will express his employment and post–high school education interests, skills, limits, and goals at his next IEP meeting.

Sample Activities:

a. In his transition class and community work experiences, Martin will complete employment goals lessons. These lessons will provide Martin with the opportunity to learn which job characteristics he likes and to determine whether various community job sites are a match for him.

b. In his learning strategies class, Martin will complete education goals lessons. Among other skills, Martin will learn to identify the classroom characteristics he likes best (e.g., lecture or hands-on, small-group activities) and compare them with the characteristics of classes available next semester.

Goal 2: Martin will take on a leadership role during the IEP process.

Sample Activities:

a. Martin will complete self-directed IEP lessons. For example, Martin will learn 11 steps needed for him to lead his own IEP meeting.

b. Prior to his IEP meeting, Martin will videotape a role play using the 11 steps needed to lead his own IEP meeting. Martin and his teacher will each assume various roles. After the role play, Martin will review his performance with assistance from his peers and teacher.

Wood, Karvonen, Test, Browder, and Algozzine (2004) presented an in-depth set of strategies for promoting student self-determination in IEP planning (see Table 2.6).

Academic Performance and Self-Determination

Fowler, Konrad, Walker, Test, and Wood (2007) reviewed six major studies to synthesize intervention research on the effects of self-determination interventions on academic skills for students with cognitive disabilities. They analyzed the strength of the research results, analyzed the quality of the research designs, and discussed implications of the findings for

Table 2.6. Promoting student self-determination (SDD) skills in individualized education program (IEP) planning

SDD skills	Student description	IEP annual goal	IEP objectives
Goal setting and attainment	Carl is a 14-year-old student served in a classroom for students with learning disabilities. He is not a good student and says that he wants to leave school and get a job. His teacher has convinced him that the school can help him improve his job skills and that he should be making the decisions and setting his goals for getting a job that he wants.	I will develop a goal and action plan to get the job that I want when I leave school.	1.1. I will develop a career interest portfolio that addresses my job strengths and interests. 1.2. I will select 5 community-based work experience sites that I will go to and learn about different jobs. 1.3. I will analyze my skills and interests in relation to the job duties and responsibilities on the 5 different community based work experiences. 1.4. I will set goals for work skills that I will need to succeed in the employment field I have chosen. 1.5 I will develop action steps to achieve my employment goal. 1.6. I will monitor my progress in taking the action steps and make changes as needed.

From Promoting student self-determination skills in IEP Planning by W.M. Wood, M. Karvonen, D.W. Test, D. Browder, & B. Algozzine, *Teaching Exceptional Children, 36*(3), 14. Copyright © 2004 by The Council for Exceptional Children. Reprinted with permission.

researchers and practitioners. Findings indicated that the majority of self-determination interventions affected skills that directly support academic performance (e.g., organization of academic assignments); however, traditional academic skills such as math productivity and spelling accuracy were also positively affected. Students learn self-determination skills best when educators use interventions that systematically teach goal setting and attainment skills (Fowler et al., 2007). Increased self-determination skills improve in-school and postschool outcomes for students with disabilities. Fowler et al. found that increased self-determination skills are associated with increased academic performance. Martin et al. (2003) also found significant increases in academic performance as students increased their self-determination skills.

SCHOOL AND COMMUNITY INCLUSION

Transition planning at the individual and community levels cannot and should not operate in a vacuum. The stronger the school and community sites are in terms of providing practice for a successful move to adult living, the better the outcomes. In addition, the more students with disabilities can interface daily in classrooms

Teachers and parents were asked to assess the self-determination prospects of 135 youth with severe intellectual and developmental disabilities. Teachers typically reported that youth evidenced limited knowledge about self-determined behavior, ability to perform these behaviors, and confidence regarding the efficacy of their self-determination capacities. However, teachers agreed that opportunities to engage in self-determined behavior were available both at school and at home. Also, social skill and problem behavior ratings were both significant predictors of teachers' ratings of students' self-determination capacity, opportunities at school, and opportunities at home. In addition, problem behaviors were negatively correlated with ratings of students' self-determination capacities and opportunities (Carter, Owens, Trainor, Sun, & Swedeen, 2009).

with their peers without disabilities, the greater the likelihood of positive transition outcomes.

Prerequisites to Inclusion

Successful inclusion requires that school administrators and teachers make changes in the ways in which they assign students to classrooms, schedule classes, set up teams, allocate resources, design curricula, deliver instruction, and assess student progress. However, change must go beyond simply reallocating resources and implementing new teaching methods. Villa and Thousand (1992) found that change is deeply embedded in the systemic structure of an organization. Although programs and materials can support change, the beliefs and actions of individuals are most important.

Five essential prerequisites to change are 1) a vision, 2) the knowledge and skills needed to implement the vision, 3) an incentive to change, 4) the necessary resources to implement the change, and 5) an action plan. Schools that take on the challenges of inclusion must recognize that change occurs slowly and that the process requires all stakeholders to make a long-term commitment to providing ongoing support and addressing problems as they emerge.

Transition-focused educators have long advocated for a vision of postschool life for young adults with disabilities that includes preferred community and social activities in addition to employment and continuing education. Although social and community outcomes are critical to the quality of life of young adults, the National Longitudinal Transition Study–2 (Wagner, Newman, Cameto, & Levine, 2005) found that students with disabilities are less likely than their peers without disabilities to participate in community activities after leaving school. Students with intellectual disabilities who have exited the public school system often experience isolation and have limited social interactions. It is important for students with disabilities to participate in community and social activities to enhance their social interactions and to build a social network outside of school.

Eisenman, Tanverdi, Perrington, and Geiman (2009) conducted semistructured interviews with family members of 45 young adults with significant intellectual disabilities who were enrolled in or had graduated from transition-focused programs designed for students aged 18–21. They examined the types of community and social activities in which the young adults engaged and explored the resources and supports the youth used to participate in the community. In general, families reported that the young adults participated in a wide variety of typical and specialized activities. There were few differences with the outcomes among those students who were still enrolled in school and those who had graduated. Families provided the primary supports for students' participation, and activities in which the youth participated tended to be those in which the family also engaged. Families reported that they and the young adults were mostly satisfied with their community and social situations.

Systemwide Planning and Evaluation for Inclusion

Increasing the quantity and quality of inclusive education in schools requires comprehensive systemwide planning and ongoing evaluation. Common barriers include the lack of a common understanding and awareness of supporting inclusion, the lack of planning for step-by-step implementation of inclusion, limited personnel preparation, and scarce human and material resources.

Conducting a needs assessment is the most important step in preparing for inclusion. Walther-Thomas and Bryant (1996) identified district-, building-, and classroom-level planning issues for key stakeholders to address. Inclusion planning teams must begin by assessing several areas: the district or school's current implementation of inclusive service delivery models and the potential for change; the readiness of teachers, parents, and students to change; the availability of resources to support inclusion; and student needs for support across school activities and the general education curriculum.

Administrative Support

Administrative support is another meaningful variable associated with successful inclusion (Mastropieri & Scruggs, 2001; Walther-Thomas & Bryant, 1996). Administrators at the district and building levels can provide leadership and vision to effect school change. Kennedy and Fisher (2001) found that teachers were more willing to consider alternative service delivery models when administrators created an atmosphere that was supportive of inclusive education. Involving the administration can ensure that the inclusion planning team consists of willing and capable participants who are representative of all key stakeholders, including general and special education teachers, resource and related services personnel, and families. Collaborative efforts are facilitated when administrators provide opportunities for teachers and teams to meet and plan together on a regular basis. Administrators also play an important role in addressing many of the issues that arise with inclusion, such as allocating resources, teaching assignments, and student assignments; scheduling classes; and supporting professional development for teachers.

CONCLUSION

The purpose of this chapter has been to present how individual and community transition planning needs to be designed in order for desired outcomes to occur. Each student should identify his or her individual dream(s) and goal(s) for adulthood. School and community inclusion and self-determination skills can enhance these dreams. The transition IEP must reflect a model of interagency collaboration and supports that can make a difference in the implementation phase.

FOR FURTHER INFORMATION

Individualized Transition Plans

Alwell, M., & Cobb, B. (2009). Functional life skills curricular interventions for youth with disabilities. *Career Development for Exceptional Individuals, 32,* 82–93.

This systematic review of 31 studies of 859 youth with all types of disabilities is an excellent resource for teachers and transition specialists to use to evaluate how various approaches have been used.

Inclusive Practices

Smith, P. (2007). Have we made any progress? Including students with intellectual disabilities in regular education classrooms. *Intellectual and Developmental Disabilities, 45*(5), 297–309.

A historical overview on the progress of inclusion in schools.

Transition Supports

Hughes, C., & Carter, E.W. (2000). *The transition handbook: Strategies high school teachers use that work!* Baltimore: Paul H. Brookes Publishing Co.

Identifies more than 500 supports that can be used when implementing a transition IEP.

3

Developing the Transition Curriculum

DiAnne B. Davidsen and Karren D. Streagle

Jonathan, an auditory learner, remembered everything that was presented to him orally. He achieved almost perfect scores on any academic assignments or tests that were administered orally. During his senior year, Jonathan had active leadership roles in football, basketball, and track. His peers had great respect for his athletic ability and his academic success and fully expected him to attend college on an athletic scholarship. Jonathan knew he could be successful in college if he received the accommodations necessary to access the general education curriculum while still in high school. He required books on tape; oral presentation of tests, quizzes, and exams; a scribe; and notetakers.

One day Jonathan was taking a college-level oceanography test with a read-aloud accommodation in the resource room. A freshman athlete came into the special education office to see the teacher who was administering the test. The freshman laughed at Jonathan and asked why he was in the special education office having a test read to him. Very slowly, rising to his full height, Jonathan said to the student, "I am an auditory learner. I know the material well and can tell you where the teacher was standing in the room when she taught the information. I have difficulty reading. If I take this test by myself I will fail it, but if I allow someone to read it to me and I have a chance to dictate my answers, I can get a perfect score or close to it. I want to maintain my 3.0 grade point average so I can go to college. If I don't get this help, I will not make it to college. Have you got a problem with that?" Needless to say, the freshman had nothing to say. The next day, the freshman, also a student with a disability, came in and asked the teacher if he could have his tests read aloud. He had aspirations for an athletic scholarship to play ball at college.

Sam, a student with intellectual disabilities, wanted to be a doctor. When his teachers explained the academic classes he needed to take to attend college, he was fond of reminding them he could not read or do the math. He wanted to remain in the functional curriculum program. However, he persisted in wanting to be a doctor.

Finally his teacher asked the right question: "Why do you want to be a doctor?"

Sam answered, "I want to wear a white coat and work in a hospital." Sam successfully completed his high school requirements with a certificate. By including Sam and his parents in the transition planning meetings, the team worked to help Sam navigate the public transportation system independently to get to and from his job at the hospital. While he is not a doctor, Sam is very happy wearing a white coat and name tag while he delivers necessary food and nutrients to patients in the hospital.

The purpose of this chapter is to help educators design a curriculum to prepare students such as Jonathan and Sam to make the transition from high school to adult life.

Many model curricula have proven successful for some students with disabilities (Karpur, Clark, Caproni, & Sterner, 2005). However, not every school can afford expensive programs. It takes time for special and general educators to develop a transition curriculum for their students, but it can be done. It is important that students participate at every juncture in planning the transition curriculum. Identifying the critical academic and functional skills students need for the future helps to individualize the program.

This chapter discusses resources and information that can be used to develop a transition curriculum that any teacher can implement. It also touches on learning styles and their impact on future careers, goal setting, self-determination skills, and accessing the general education curriculum. It provides related information on high-stakes testing, diploma decisions, and learning environments. In addition, it reviews how to incorporate career exploration and college decisions and suggests topics to approach in any classroom that lead to seamless transition for all students.

HOW TO DETERMINE A STUDENT'S CAREER GOALS

When exploring a student's career goals, it is imperative for teachers, parents, and service providers to ask the right questions: "*What* do you want to do after finishing high school? *Why* do you want to do that?" These questions should be asked of all students with disabilities who are preparing to make the transition from high school. No matter their cognitive ability, students have dreams that need to be explored. The student's preferences and interests need to be identified.

According to deFur and Taymans (1995), important components of seamless transition planning are coordination, communication, and collaboration. Wehman (2006a) described how partnerships between school service providers and community professionals facilitate opportunities for students with disabilities to be competitively employed before exiting high school. These job experiences also lead students to better answer the "what" and "why" questions asked by teachers when developing a transition curriculum.

Research by Greene and Kochhar-Bryant (2003) supports Wehman (2006a) and deFur and Taymans (1995) in proposing recommended practices for transition, some of which are pertinent to curriculum development. These include interagency collaboration, use of a functional life skills curriculum and community-based instruction, career and vocational assessment and education, business and industry linkages with schools, and student voice and self-determination in the development of the transition curriculum.

Talk to Students

It is imperative to talk to students individually. Communication between teachers and students is critical in determining the what and why of students' future goals. A great time to discuss these questions is when students are working on transition individualized education programs (IEPs). It is critical that teachers make it a priority to have these important discussions with their students.

Provide Students with Experiences

Providing students with career-related experiences helps them answer the what and why questions for themselves. Armstrong (2007) pointed out the need for students to experience career opportunities as early as middle school to get a feeling for careers they might be interested in pursuing. Armstrong also recommended that high school students have real-world experiences. If the high school curriculum includes reading, writing, science, and math related to life after high school, students can develop competencies needed in the areas of interest to them, which will in turn support their future independence (Armstrong, 2007). Students with disabilities need to be taught the skills needed to be successful adults as well as the academic skills required for graduation. The transition curriculum must address graduation requirements, academic content assessed in high-stakes testing, and work- and community-related experiences.

Jonathan, the young man in the opening vignette, once said that students with disabilities need to know all there is to know about their disability and be able to articulate their strengths and areas of challenge, because that disability will be part of who they are for the rest of their lives. Jonathan had well-developed self-determination skills and was confident in who he was. These skills enabled him to reach his goals and become a successful, independent adult.

Conduct a Personal Interest Inventory

A personal interest inventory is a good starting point for answering the what and why questions related to future goals. Personal interest inventories are found in every school district and are typically conducted by guidance counselors. Unfortunately, the completed inventories often end up buried in a folder, of little use to anyone. Yet this information is important! Collaborating with guidance counselors will take the inventory out of the folder and put it in the hands of teachers and students to stimulate discussions that will drive the development of a transition curriculum. However, as students participate in real-world experiences, their interests and skills may change. The transition curriculum needs to be flexible enough to accommodate students' evolving interests. A transition curriculum needs to be revisited annually as new students with new interests and future goals come into the classroom.

Create a Skills Summary

The Individuals with Disabilities Education Improvement Act (IDEA) of 2004 (PL 108-446) requires schools to provide students with an academic and functional skills summary when they move to another school district or exit high school. Transition teams need to be proactive in collecting data and setting goals throughout a student's high school career to produce a meaningful exiting Summary of Performance. It is imperative for schools to design a form for collecting and compiling relevant information that will transfer with students as they move to other communities or postsecondary environments.

Neubert and Moon (2000) advocated for schools to develop an academic and functional skills summary form that would be useful to students and other school districts. Two exiting student information forms are shown in Figure 3.1 (Career and Vocational Transition Worksheet) and Figure 3.2 (Postsecondary Education Transition Worksheet).

Career and Vocational Transition Worksheet
(page 1 of 2)

Student name _____   Date of birth_____

Address_____   Phone (home)_____

_____   Phone (cell)_____

Parent/guardian _____

High school _____

Anticipated graduation date_____   Diploma type _____

Disability category _____   Date of last eligibility _____

Employment/career goals _____

Community participation goals_____

Independent living goals _____

Leisure and recreation goals_____

Academic and vocational strengths _____

Academic and vocational challenges_____

Adult services agencies	Name of agency	Services provided
Already in use		
Anticipated		

Work competencies _____

_____

_____

Essentials of Transition Planning, by Paul Wehman
Copyright © 2011 Paul H. Brookes Publishing Co., Inc. All rights reserved.

Figure 3.1. Career and Vocational Transition Worksheet.

44

Career and Vocational Transition Worksheet
(page 2 of 2)

Student name _____

On-the-job supports _____

_____

_____

Self-advocacy skills in place _____

_____

_____

Self-advocacy skills needed _____

_____

_____

Employment experience

Place of employment	Dates of employment	Job description and responsibilities

Other relevant information

_____

_____

_____

_____

_____

_____

_____

_____

Postsecondary Education Transition Worksheet

Student name _____ Date of birth _____

Address _____ Phone (home) _____

_____ Phone (cell) _____

Parent/guardian _____

Anticipated graduation date _____ Diploma type _____

Disability category _____ Date of last eligibility _____

Grade	GPA	Class rank	Credits
9		/	
10		/	
11		/	
12		/	

	Date	Verbal	Nonverbal	Writing	Composite
SAT scores					
	Date	Reading	Science	Composite	
ACT scores					

Woodcock–Johnson	Date of test	Grade	Age
Test	Grade equivalent	Age equivalent	Age standard scores
Broad Reading			
Broad Math			
Broad Written Language			
Broad General Knowledge			

Employment/career goals _____

Postsecondary education goals _____

Independent living goals _____

Leisure and recreation goals _____

Results of Personal Interest Inventory _____

Academic strengths _____

Academic challenges _____

Accommodations for success in class _____

Accommodations for success on tests _____

Results from Learning Style Survey _____

Essentials of Transition Planning, by Paul Wehman

Figure 3.2. Postsecondary Education Transition Worksheet

Conduct a Vocational Assessment

Many school districts pay private organizations to conduct vocational assessments for students with disabilities, whereas some districts have developed their own assessment centers. There are several steps to the vocational assessment process. Students are assessed through surveys and questionnaires to evaluate their interests and skills in a variety of vocational areas. Based on the results of these surveys and questionnaires, students move through simulated job experiences over a 2- or 3-day period. Individual vocational assessment reports developed by the on-the-job supervisors describe students' job performance, including aptitude, work habits, employee–employer interactions, and recommendations for possible future employment and other areas of competence.

The vocational assessment report is a wonderful source of information about possible vocational pursuits for students. However, they are rarely reviewed with the students and their teachers. Teachers need to ask questions about these vocational assessments, locate them if they have been completed, or request them for students with disabilities when they have not been completed.

Neubert and Moon (2000) found that having personal information, interests, and preferences in one place is valuable in transition planning. In addition, having this information readily available streamlines the development of a transition curriculum, ensuring that relevant vocational competencies are addressed.

Complete a Personal Learning Style Survey

All students are usually administered a personal learning style survey by the school guidance counselor at some point during their middle or high school years. This information is often placed in students' cumulative folders. Teachers should request to see the results and then review them with students and their parents. Because different learning styles lend themselves to different careers, knowing a student's personal learning style can help guide choices about that student's future. See http://www.learning-styles-online.com for a handy reference for how learning styles affect career possibilities.

Identify Goals

When a special education teacher's youngest son, Ryan, was preparing to enter high school, his older brother was months away from graduating and going off to college. Ryan's older brother was eager to help Ryan plan his course of study and shared the importance of taking advanced placement courses to prepare for college. Ryan sat quietly during the whole discussion. When the session was over, his enthusiastic brother asked, "Well, what do you think?" Ryan got up and left the room, saying, "I feel like my whole life was just planned for me and I had nothing to say about what I wanted."

This scenario mirrors what special educators often do to their students when they begin the transition process. So often, teachers and parents, service providers, and counselors develop goals for the future and make decisions for students with disabilities, and the students have no voice in the outcomes. Ryan's mother prepared a worksheet that enabled him to clearly state his goals and why he had set them.

What are students' goals for their futures? The My Future worksheet (see Figure 3.3) can help students identify their postsecondary goals. It can be completed at school with teachers or at home with parents. But again, this worksheet will be useless if it is not discussed with students individually and used to inform the development of the transition curriculum.

Develop a Vision

Many students do not have a clear vision for their futures. Consider the following example:

Yuri was a quiet, soft-spoken 17-year-old 11th grader getting ready to attend his transition IEP meeting. His mother, Mrs. North, feared her son had no skills or interests that would lead to a career. At past IEP meetings, Mrs. North never felt she could ask questions. As a result, she did not understand her son's disability or how it affected his schooling or future goals.

Mrs. North asked a friend, a special educator, Ms. Bennett, to review and explain Yuri's eligibility assessments. After going over the documents, Ms. Bennett was able to describe Yuri's specific learning disabilities and how they affected his academic performance by interpreting the findings into strengths and challenges. Yuri and his mother were glad to know how to tell people about his disability, and for the first time they understood his strengths and challenges.

Mrs. North invited Ms. Bennett into Yuri's bedroom to show how responsible he was about taking care of his personal space. Ms. Bennett noticed a bookcase filled with books about animals and animal care, books about dogs, and dictionaries of animals. When asked about the books, Mrs. North passed them off as stuff Yuri had bought when he had some extra money. Ms. Bennett pointed out that Yuri's interest in animals could lead to a possible career. This made Mrs. North very happy, and they immediately shared this with Yuri. That week, Yuri led his transition IEP meeting. Added to the IEP was an internship experience with a veterinary clinic.

Like Yuri, students with disabilities often do not have a clear idea of a potential career path. The transition curriculum should include career planning that can lead students to develop a vision for their future. Over the course of a school year, students can broaden their understanding of possible career opportunities by researching multiple occupations. Young adults often change their minds about their future as they explore the wide range of opportunities available. It is also important to remember that people often change careers over their lifetime.

Students need to be reminded that they have many skills, interests, and preferences. When exploring career options, students should be encouraged to reflect on their likes and dislikes and their needs and wants. As people themselves grow and change, so do their skills, interests, and preferences. Identifying students' strengths may help at this point. Encourage students to reflect on the hobbies and activities they engage in at home and in the community. These leisure activities may provide insight into future careers.

During the research process, students can begin to narrow their career goals and then identify the steps they will need to take to achieve them. What do they need to be doing in the next 1 to 5 years? Writing goals for 1 year from now and 5 years from now can help students identify the steps necessary to reach their goals and see their potential for achieving them. Good resources for researching careers are state employment commission web sites.

My Future

Instructions: The future is yours. It begins now. You are making decisions every day that will affect your future. This worksheet may help you better decide what choices to make concerning your future. Think about your preferences and interests. Discuss this worksheet with your parents and teachers. It's your future; you have a voice in where you are headed.

My goals	Why?
Others' goals for me (or what I think others want me to do)	Why?
Why I do not want to do what others want me to do	Why I think I will be successful in the future with the goals I have picked
Prioritize your goals list here	Steps I must take to reach my goals

Figure 3.3. My Future worksheet. (*Source:* Garner, Bartholomew, & Thoma, 2007).

HIGH-STAKES TESTING AND DIPLOMA DECISIONS

Transition activities of any kind should not be conducted in isolation. Transition assessment, planning, and curriculum development are interdependent with other activities in both the school and community. Participation in high-stakes testing and diploma decisions cannot be left out of the equation, and it is critical that teachers understand how high-stakes testing, alternative assessments, and graduation requirements are considered. This holds true regardless of the types of assessments that students with disabilities take or the types of diplomas they pursue.

Realities of High-Stakes Testing

The No Child Left Behind Act (NCLB) of 2001 (PL 107-110) requires that schools assess student achievement in reading and mathematics annually in Grades 3 through 8 and at least once between Grades 10 through 12. In addition, student achievement in science must be assessed at least one time during elementary, middle, and high school. The 1997 and 2004 amendments to IDEA (PL 105-17 and PL 108-446, respectively) require that students with disabilities have access to the general curriculum and be included in state and district assessment accountability systems.

Most states administer three main types of high-stakes tests at the high school level: comprehensive assessments, minimum competency tests, and end-of-course tests or exams at the completion of the semester (Zabala, Minnici, & McMurrer, 2008). It is important for teachers of students with disabilities who are implementing a transition curriculum to work closely with general education teachers, guidance counselors, and school test coordinators to ensure that students with disabilities are adequately prepared for the required high-stakes tests without neglecting transition activities. Coordinating with these teachers and service providers will ensure that students are enrolled in appropriate classes and that they receive adequate instruction to prepare for the high-stakes tests while also participating in meaningful learning opportunities for transition.

Alternative Assessments

Alternative assessments for students with significant intellectual disabilities were first mandated by IDEA 1997, which included these students in high-stakes assessment accountability systems. NCLB requires that alternative assessments be based on general education academic content standards in reading, math, and science. However, the academic achievement standards to which students with significant intellectual disabilities are held to demonstrate proficiency in those content areas have been reduced in complexity (U.S. Department of Education [DOE], 2005). These alternative academic achievement standards are intended to address all domains within the grade-level content areas of reading, math, and science, but meeting them does not necessitate having the depth or breadth of knowledge required of students in the general curriculum. DOE has also placed a 1% cap on the number of students with disabilities whose passing scores may be included in adequate yearly progress calculations. These assessments are known as alternative assessments based on alternative achievement standards (AA-AAS).

Embedding AA-AAS components into daily instruction correlates highly with student alternative assessment scores (Kampfer, Hovarth, Kleinert, & Kearns, 2001). This recommended practice makes AA-AAS an integral part of academic and transition instruction instead of an add-on component. Also, similar to grade-level high-stakes testing, different states implement different types of AA-AAS (performance based, comprehensive rating scales, portfolio assessments; Elliott & Roach, 2007). It is essential for special education teachers to fully understand the AA-AAS processes and procedures required by their school division.

Involving students in the transition IEP process and embedding alternative assessment components into daily instruction correlate positively with student alternative assessment scores. (Kampfer et al., 2001).

Alternative assessments based on modified achievement standards (AA-MAS) are another alternative for assessing students with disabilities under NCLB and are intended for use with up to 2% of the total school population or 18% of the special education student population. Although AA-MAS are not required by DOE, several states are in the process of developing them. These assessments must be aligned with grade-level academic content, but the achievement expectations are modified (DOE, 2007). Special education teachers, general educators, guidance counselors, and school test coordinators should stay informed of the progress of AA-MAS development in their state.

Graduation Expectations

Graduation requirements vary widely from state to state. Most states enforce minimum requirements, although there has been a decrease in the number of diploma options available to students other than the traditional standard diploma (Johnson, Thurlow, & Stout, 2007). States vary on whether they offer allowances for students with disabilities who are unable to meet graduation requirements, with some states offering modified or IEP diplomas or certificates of attendance (Johnson et al., 2007). Although NCLB does not require that high-stakes test scores be included in graduation criteria, it does require that graduation rates be included as another academic indicator in adequate yearly progress calculations.

In 2007, Johnson et al. found that 28 states had increased their standard graduation requirements for students with and without disabilities over the past 3 years. In addition to the standard diplomas offered by all 50 states and the District of Columbia, 33 states offer alternative diploma options such as advanced/honors, IEP/special education, occupational/vocational, certificate of attendance, and certificate of achievement.

Although guidance counselors are not mandatory members of the transition IEP team, their inclusion in the IEP development process is key to ensuring that students are enrolled in the necessary courses, pass requisite assessments, and make adequate progress toward the diploma option identified by the student and the transition IEP team. It is also important that special educators be informed about the assessment and graduation requirements of their school division. It is heartbreaking for any student—with or without a disability—to discover the week before graduation that he or she has not met the requirements of graduation and will not receive a diploma with his or her peers.

The Assessment and Diploma Options Form shown in Figure 3.4 can serve as a powerful resource for promoting collaboration among special and general education teachers, guidance counselors, and school test coordinators. It is intended for use as a single form that follows a student's progress throughout high school to facilitate discussions about graduation and assessment options. It can also be used to track a student's course enrollment to ensure that graduation requirements are anticipated and completed.

ACCESS TO THE GENERAL EDUCATION CURRICULUM

Johnson, Stodden, Emanuel, Luecking, and Mack (2002) described the challenge of ensuring that students with disabilities have access to the full range of academic curricula while participating in transition-related activities such as postsecondary education, employment, independent living, and community integration. Instruction in academic content and transition need not be mutually exclusive. Balance can be achieved by embedding transition-related activities into academic instruction for all students. Students with disabilities deserve the same opportunities as their peers without disabilities to develop the knowledge and skills to be successful after high school (Bouck, 2009). A way to provide equal opportunities for students with disabilities is to ensure that they have access to the same academic curricula as their peers without disabilities.

Of the different types of diplomas available to students with disabilities, employers considered occupational diplomas and standard diplomas most desirable. Students who received certificates of completion or attendance are more likely to be considered for menial jobs. However, employers were willing to take into account the individual characteristics of prospective employees—not just the type of diploma they held—when considering them for a job (Hartwig & Sitlington, 2008).

Postsecondary academic success for students with disabilities hinges on their success in the general education classroom in high school (Hitchings, Retish, & Horvath, 2005).

Functional Curriculum

A functional curriculum has traditionally been used with students of all levels of intellectual disability. Components of a functional curriculum include "functional application of skills from the core subject areas (academics), vocational education, community access, daily living, finances, independent living, transportation, social/relations, and self-determination" (Bouck, 2009, p. 4). However, with the emphasis of NCLB and IDEA on academic achievement and access to the general curriculum, the use of a functional curriculum for most students with disabilities has fallen out of favor. Although the components of a functional curriculum are relevant to the needs and interests of many special education students who are making the transition from high school, there is a conflict of interest between the academic and assessment requirements of NCLB and IDEA and the nonacademic domains related to transition (Bouck, 2009).

However, functional and general curricula do not have to be mutually exclusive. Implementing a functional curriculum for students with significant intellectual disabilities is a natural fit and dovetails easily into many academic requirements. With careful planning, the transition team can easily incorporate opportunities for special education students to work on transition-related goals in general academic classes, in career or technical education classes, or in the community. Including elements of a functional curriculum in the general academic curriculum for students with mild to moderate disabilities requires balancing the academic demands of high-stakes testing and diploma requirements with the functional domains associated with transition.

Assessment and Diploma Options Form
(page 1 of 3)

Section 1: General Information

Student name: _____

Student number: _____

Date of birth: _____

Projected graduation year/cohort: _____

Guidance counselor: _____

Service coordinator: _____

Transition specialist: _____

School test coordinator: _____

Section 2: Diploma Goals (check all that apply)

____ Advanced Diploma
____ Standard Diploma
____ Career/Technical Diploma
____ Modified Diploma
____ IEP Diploma

Section 3: Assessment Requirements

	General academic state assessments		AA-MAS		AA-AAS	
	Tests	**Score**	**Tests**	**Score**	**Tests**	**Score**
Grade 9						
Grade 10						
Grade 11						
Grade 12						

(continued)

Figure 3.4. Assessment and Diploma Options Form. (*Key:* IEP, individualized transition program; AA-MAS, alternative assessments based on modified achievement standards; AA-AAS, alternative assessments based on alternative achievement standards.)

Figure 3.4. *(continued)*

Assessment and Diploma Options Form
(page 2 of 3)

Section 4: Course Projection

Grade 9: School year _____ - _____

Content area	Course	Grade
English		
Math		
Science		
History		
Elective		
Elective		
Community Integration		

Grade 10: School year _____ - _____

Content area	Course	Grade
English		
Math		
Science		
History		
Elective		
Elective		
Community Integration		

Grade 11: School year _____ - _____

Content area	Course	Grade
English		
Math		
Science		
History		
Elective		
Elective		
Community Integration		

Assessment and Diploma Options Form
(page 3 of 3)

Grade 12: School year _____ - _____

Content area	Course	Grade
English		
Math		
Science		
History		
Elective		
Elective		
Community Integration		

Additional school year: School year _____ - _____

Content area	Course	Grade
English		
Math		
Science		
History		
Elective		
Elective		
Community Integration		

Additional school year: School year _____ - _____

Content area	Course	Grade
English		
Math		
Science		
History		
Elective		
Elective		
Community Integration		

Universal Design for Learning and Universal Design for Transition

Universal design for learning (UDL) and universal design for transition (UDT) are two valuable principles to consider when developing and implementing a transition curriculum for a student with disabilities. The Center for Applied Special Technology (2009) web site describes UDL as "a framework for designing curricula that enable all individuals to gain knowledge, skills, and enthusiasm for learning. UDL provides rich supports for learning and reduces barriers to the curriculum while maintaining high achievement standards for all."

UDL uses multiple means of instructional material, student expression during learning activities, and engagement to maximize student learning in all content areas and settings. One aspect of UDL is the use of technology in the education process. A transition curriculum should include the use of technology (or, if necessary, assistive technology) in the learning process for students with disabilities.

The Center for Applied Special Technology web site (http://www.cast.org) includes numerous resources for understanding the principles of UDL, resources for developing lesson plans, publications, and professional development tools. This web site is worth bookmarking and visiting on a regular basis.

UDT involves the application of UDL principles to transition (Thoma, Bartholomew, & Scott, 2009). At its core, UDT is all about embedding transition domains into the general academic curriculum. This provides an opportunity for all students to be actively engaged in the learning process. The value-added element of UDT is real-world application of lessons learned in the general curriculum. Like UDL, UDT provides multiple means and opportunities for students to demonstrate an understanding of transition skills and apply them in a variety of settings relating to postsecondary outcomes.

Providing for the proper technology and assistive technology needed by individuals with disabilities positively affects their independence and their access to and success in postsecondary education and employment (Scherer & Craddock, 2002).

COMMUNITY-BASED INSTRUCTION

Students with disabilities who are making the transition from high school need learning opportunities beyond what are offered in the school building. Community-based instruction takes place in natural settings in which students will live, work, play, and go to school as adults. One goal of incorporating community-based instruction into the transition curriculum is to foster generalization of skills and independence. With individual students in mind, teachers can develop excellent, authentic learning experiences that will improve student outcomes after graduation.

Community Resource Mapping

Community resource mapping (CRM) is a strategy described by Crane and Mooney (2005) to identify the resources available in a local community by facilitating collaboration with area businesses and agencies to provide career opportunities to students. It is one of the "Essential Tools" publications developed by the National Center on Secondary Education and

Transition. CRM is an invaluable resource for developing a community-based transition curriculum. For more information about CRM, visit http://www.ncset.org/publications/essentialtools/mappingdefault.asp.

Community Integration

A transition curriculum that includes community integration activities provides opportunities for students to increase their independent living, transportation, recreation, and leisure skills. Some examples of community integration activities include taking a walking field trip or having students ride and understand public transportation. These trips into the community broaden students' knowledge base, empowering them to consider the variety of options available for independent living, transportation, recreation, and employment.

The interests and needs students identified in their personal interest inventories as being relevant to their future goals should inform what community resources need to be explored. School and community service providers help with supervision, make connections to adult services, and supply expertise about potential sites. Collaborating with business owners sets the tone for "buy in" from those professionals to facilitate positive community integration learning experiences.

Once potential community sites have been identified, teachers can identify necessary skills students will need to be successful in those environments, such as appropriate social behaviors or skills specific to the business. These skills can be taught and practiced in the classroom in preparation for community visits. However, they must also be taught and practiced in the natural environment of the community to promote generalization and independence.

Community-Based Vocational Activities

Community-based instruction for career opportunities includes vocational activities such as job shadowing, job sampling, and after-school and summer work experiences. As with community integration, collaboration is the key to successful career exploration. Special educators and school service providers should be familiar with the businesses and services in the community that are open to working with individuals with disabilities to ensure positive encounters for all involved. Coordinating with job coaches and community business partners will provide insight for the development of a transition curriculum to address issues related to successful employment.

POSTSECONDARY EDUCATION

Wilton, a student with a learning disability, had challenged himself by taking general education classes while in high school because he knew he wanted to attend college. He had not realized that his excellent math skills would translate into a computer science degree because he had never sat down with his high school teachers to discuss his interests, strengths, and areas of challenge. Had he taken computer classes in high school, he would have been better prepared for a computer science major in college. His success in the area of math led Wilton into computer science, and upon graduating from college he was hired by an internationally recognized computer company. When he reflected on his high school and college experiences, he wished he had received more guidance and been encouraged to take more technology classes in high school to lay a better foundation for his career.

Both Jonathan from the opening vignette and Wilton had goals that included postsecondary education. Both successfully completed college and are now living their dreams—Jonathan by coaching college sports and Wilton by working for a computer firm.

Informed Decision Making

When future goals include attending college, students are empowered to make informed postsecondary education choices if they understand their disability and how it affects their academic achievement (Garner, 2008). When discussing the possibility of postsecondary education, begin with questions that may help students and their parents determine whether the decision to attend college is realistic. The College Discussion Worksheet (see Figure 3.5) provides a format for this discussion.

It is important for students to include a career goal as part of their reason for wanting to attend college. If students are planning to attend college for social reasons, they will not be set for success. A well-thought-out curriculum will help students make real-world connections between the academic rigors of college and their career aspirations.

Research postsecondary programs and find one that will match the needs and career goals of each individual student (Garner, 2008). In some cases a community or junior college may be the best fit. Attending a local community college will allow students to remain connected with familiar supports, such as teachers, peers, and parents. It is crucial for teachers, students, and their families to be made aware of programs that support educational options beyond high school. Each college and university has its own system of assisting students.

Additional Considerations

Once students have been accepted into a college program, they need to identify themselves as a student with a disability to ensure proper supports are in place once they begin classes. Students who use assistive technology in high school must be prepared to discuss their needs and advocate for the use of these supports in college; they must be aware that colleges are not required to provide assistive technology devices. However, some university offices of disabilities services do provide devices on loan. There are many other differences between high school and college (Table 3.1) in terms of skills needed and disability services provided, and it is important to discuss them with students throughout the transition process.

ACHIEVING SOCIAL COMPETENCE

The term *social competence* has been a part of the vocabulary of special education for some time. It is often used interchangeably with the terms *social skills, personal–social skills, life skills,* or *social awareness.* Odom and McConnell (as cited by Black & Langone, 1997) described social competence as the ability to effectively and appropriately use specific social skills when interacting with others. It involves the ability to understand the nuances of

College
Discussion
Worksheet

Instructions: Think about the student's strengths and challenges and help the student and parent look realistically at their options. How have they prepared for college? Have the student fill this out or help him or her fill it out, answering "Yes" or "No" to each of the following.

Ask the student the following questions:	Yes	No
Can you successfully make it in your inclusion or general education classes with accommodations and modifications?		
Have you taken Algebra I, Geometry, Algebra II?		
Have you taken a foreign language or an approved program in American Sign Language?		
Do you have good study habits?		
Have you taken or do you plan on taking the SAT or ACT?		
Do you need to request testing accommodations?		
Are you willing to put forth the effort to realize your dreams and goals of completing college?		
Where do you want to attend college? A 2-year college?		
A 4-year college?		
A vocational or technical program?		
What do you plan on majoring in once you go to college?		
List five colleges you would like to research to help make your decision. Write their names and whether they have a program for students with disabilities. 1.		
2.		
3.		
4.		
5.		
Are you planning on playing sports in college? Complete the NCAA Clearinghouse application to be cleared to participate in college sports. Ask your guidance counselor to walk you through the process.		
Talk to students with learning disabilities who have attended the colleges you have on your list.		

Essentials of Transition Planning, by Paul Wehman

Figure 3.5.   College Discussion Worksheet.

Table 3.1.   Differences between high school and college in skills needed and disability services provided

High School	College
Guidance counselor organizes the student's class schedule.	The student organizes his or her own class schedule.
Good study skills may not be taught and may not be necessary for success.	Good study skills are necessary for success.
Teachers give frequent and regular feedback.	Feedback may be infrequent.
The semester is typically 18 weeks long.	The semester is typically 15 weeks long.
The student has a full year (36 weeks) to master course information.	The student must master content in a single semester (15 weeks).
Use of a computer may not be necessary for written assignments.	Computer skills are a must for all assignments.
A few hours of study each week are required.	From 10 to 15 hours of study per week per class is required.
The school provides proof of disability.	The student must provide proof of disability.
Special education services are an entitlement.	Special education services are provided at the discretion of the institution.
Services are IEP driven.	Services are disability driven.
A resource teacher is available for daily help.	Limited help is available through the campus disability office.
Special educators automatically give help.	Help must be requested by the student.
Regular progress reports are given to parents.	The student has to inform his or her parents of progress.
IDEA and Section 504 provide protection for services.	ADA provides protection for services.

Key: IEP, individualized education program; IDEA, Individuals with Disabilities Education Improvement Act of 2004 (PL 101-476); ADA, Americans with Disabilities Act of 1990 (PL 101-336).

different environments and to make decisions as to the most appropriate way to behave in different situations. Not only must students possess appropriate personal–social skills and an awareness of social cues from others but also they must be able to generalize the use of those skills across home, school, work, and recreational environments. In some cases a person's social competence can determine his or her success in the community, at work, or in postsecondary education. Social competence is vital to the success of young adults with disabilities as they make the transition from high school to adult life, and thus it should be included in the transition curriculum.

Getting Along in the Community

For young adults with disabilities making the transition out of high school, the goal is to participate in the community as independently as possible. Many young people are able to develop social competence through extracurricular activities, employment, recreational activities, independent living, shopping, banking, leisure activities with friends, or postsecondary education. Other students, especially those with more significant disabilities, need explicit instruction to acquire and generalize social competence. It is important to identify the community settings students plan to be in after graduation and the type of skills they will need to function successfully in those environments.

Charting the social competencies required in the community environments identified as important by students can be an essential component of helping students be successful in those environments. The Social Competencies Worksheet in Figure 3.6 can help students

Social Competencies Worksheet (Page 1 of 3)

Student name: _____

Date: _____

Location: _____

Location type: Community   Work   School
(circle one)

Instructions:
1. The student brainstorms social competencies required at this location with the teacher. The student writes these competencies in the table below.
2. The student rates him- or herself on the social competencies required at this location by checking the appropriate box.

Social competency	Do I have these skills?				
	Always	**Mostly**	**Sometimes**	**Seldom**	**Never**

3. The student highlights his or her strengths—the social competencies that he or she always or mostly always has.

Figure 3.6.   Social Competencies Worksheet (blank).

Figure 3.6. *(continued)*

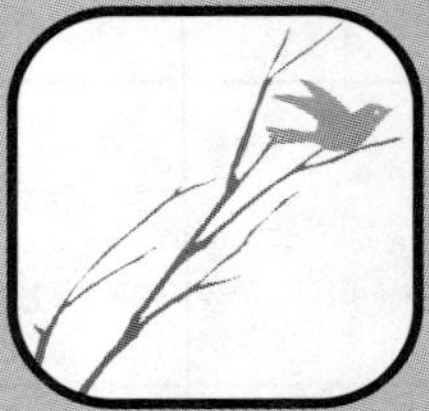

Social Competencies Worksheet
(Page 2 of 3)

4. The student prioritizes and transfers the social competencies that need improvement to the table below.
5. The student explains how to improve these competencies.

Social competency I need to improve	How am I doing with this competency now? What does it look like?	How will I improve this competency?	How will I know I have mastered this competency? What will it look like?

Essentials of Transition Planning, by Paul Wehman

Social Competencies Worksheet (Page 3 of 3)

6. The student rates his or her progress by circling S, I, or M.

Social competency I need to improve	Date Competency	Date Competency	Date Competency	Date Competency	Date Competency	Date Competency	Date Competency
	S I M	S I M	S I M	S I M	S I M	S I M	S I M
	S I M	S I M	S I M	S I M	S I M	S I M	S I M
	S I M	S I M	S I M	S I M	S I M	S I M	S I M
	S I M	S I M	S I M	S I M	S I M	S I M	S I M
	S I M	S I M	S I M	S I M	S I M	S I M	S I M
	S I M	S I M	S I M	S I M	S I M	S I M	S I M
	S I M	S I M	S I M	S I M	S I M	S I M	S I M

Note: S = My competency is the same, I = My competency is improving, M = I have mastered this competency.

Essentials of Transition Planning, by Paul Wehman

identify needed social competencies, rate their own performance, and develop a plan of action to improve. If students participate in this process from the start, they will be more engaged in evaluating their own performance on those skills, developing intervention strategies, and tracking their progress. Consider Sam, the student described at the beginning of the chapter who wanted to work in a hospital setting. Sam and his teacher worked together to complete the Social Competencies Worksheet for when he goes to the movies with his friends (see Figure 3.7).

Remember, generalizing social competencies can be a challenge for many students with disabilities. Many students are able to internalize and generalize new social competencies through role play, discussion, and other traditional types of instruction. However, some students may need direct instruction and practice with these competencies through community-based experiences in the settings in which they will use those skills as adults.

Getting Along at Work

Carter and Lunsford (2005) described social skills as one of four sets of skills (along with personal–social skills, life skills, and social awareness) that significantly influence the successful employment of students with disabilities. Lacking social competence can make it difficult for young adults with disabilities to negotiate the changing demands of work relationships with supervisors, coworkers, and customers. "A poor fit between student skills and employer expectations inevitably leads to problems in the workplace, including job frustration, lack of promotion, or termination" (p. 64).

As with community settings, it is important to identify possible work environments for students and the social competencies vital for success in those locations. Once the necessary skills have been identified, it is important to provide instruction and practice at school and in the actual environments in which the skills will be used. This process can be facilitated by using the Social Competencies Worksheet (see Figure 3.6). Sam's completed Social Competencies Worksheet for his job at the hospital is shown in Figure 3.8.

Getting Along in College

Social competence, in the form of social integration, self-esteem, and social support, is important in postsecondary education as well (Napoli & Wortman, 1998). It is sometimes easy to become too focused on preparing students academically for college. Even self-determination skills can be overly concentrated on self-advocacy skills related to academic performance and accommodations. However, it is essential that college-bound students with disabilities also hone their social competencies. Identifying and enhancing the social skills important to success on a college campus is every bit as valuable as academics in terms of preparing for college. The Social Competencies Worksheet (see Figure 3.6) is versatile enough to use with students preparing for college.

PUTTING IT ALL TOGETHER

When it comes time to put the transition curriculum into practice, it is important to operationalize the skills and knowledge discussed in this chapter. How you do this will vary

Social Competencies Worksheet (Page 1 of 3)

Student name: _Sam_

Location: _Regal Cinema_

Date: _9/5/09_

Location type: (Community) Work School
(circle one)

Instructions:
1. The student brainstorms social competencies required at this location with the teacher. The student writes these competencies in the table below.
2. The student rates him- or herself on the social competencies required at this location by checking the appropriate box.

Social competency	Do I have these skills?				
	Always	Mostly	Sometimes	Seldom	Never
Waiting in line/taking turns			X		
Initiating communication (greeting ticket clerk)		X			
Making and communicating choice (choosing movie)		X			
Saying "please" and "thank you"			X		
Ignoring distractions				X	
Following theater rules (no talking or using cell phones during movie)		X			
Using self-control			X		

3. The student highlights his or her strengths—the social competencies that he or she always or mostly always has.

Figure 3.7. Sample completed Social Competencies Worksheet for Sam: Going to the movies.

(continued)

Figure 3.7. *(continued)*

Social Competencies Worksheet (Page 2 of 3)

4. The student prioritizes and transfers the social competencies that need improvement to the table below.
5. The student explains how to improve these competencies.

Social competency I need to improve	How am I doing with this competency now? What does it look like?	How will I improve this competency?	How will I know I have mastered this competency? What will it look like?
Waiting in line/taking turns	Sometimes I get out of line to talk to my friends. People get mad at me.	I will practice keeping in line at school. My friends will remind me. Then I will do it myself.	I will keep my place in line until I get to the ticket lady.
Saying "please" and "thank you"	I forget to say "please" when I ask for something.	I will practice saying "please" when I ask for stuff at home and school. My teachers and mom will remind me when I forget.	I will remember to ask the ticket lady, "May I please have a ticket?
Ignoring distractions	I yell at people if they talk or make noise during my movie or other times that people disturb me.	I will put my finger over my lips when someone else is talking or when the movie is playing to remind me not to yell.	I will sit through the whole movie without yelling at people for talking. I might need my friends to remind me sometimes.
Using self-control	Sometimes I cut in line because I am excited about being with my friends on a Friday night.	I will practice starting at the end of the line at school. My friends will help me.	I will walk to the end of the line and wait my turn at the movies.

66

Social Competencies Worksheet (Page 3 of 3)

6. The student rates his or her progress by circling S, I, or M.

Social competency I need to improve	Date	Competency	Date	Competency	Date	Competency	Date	Competency	Date	Competency	Date	Competency
Waiting in line/taking turns	9/20/10	S Ⓘ M	10/18/10	S Ⓘ M	11/15/10	S I Ⓜ		S I M		S I M		S I M
Saying "please" and "thank you"	9/20/10	S Ⓘ M	10/18/10	S Ⓘ M	11/15/10	S I Ⓜ		S I M		S I M		S I M
Ignoring distractions	9/20/10	Ⓢ I M	10/18/10	Ⓢ I M	11/15/10	S Ⓘ M		S I M		S I M		S I M
Using self-control	9/20/10	Ⓢ I M	10/18/10	S Ⓘ M	11/15/10	S Ⓘ M		S I M		S I M		S I M
		S I M		S I M		S I M		S I M		S I M		S I M
		S I M		S I M		S I M		S I M		S I M		S I M
		S I M		S I M		S I M		S I M		S I M		S I M

Note: S = My competency is the same, I = My competency is improving, M = I have mastered this competency.

Social Competencies Worksheet (Page 1 of 3)

Student name: _Sam_

Location: _Memorial Hospital_

Date: _9/9/09_

Location type: Community (Work) School
(circle one)

Instructions:

1. The student brainstorms social competencies required at this location with the teacher. The student writes these competencies in the table below.
2. The student rates him- or herself on the social competencies required at this location by checking the appropriate box.

Social competency	Do I have these skills?				
	Always	**Mostly**	**Sometimes**	**Seldom**	**Never**
Talking in a quiet voice				X	
Staying on task			X		
Asking for clarification				X	
Using kind greetings with patients and staff		X			
Ignoring distractions				X	
Using self-control			X		
Following directions		X			

3. The student highlights his or her strengths—the social competencies that he or she always or mostly always has.

Figure 3.8. Sample completed Social Competencies Worksheet for Sam: Hospital job.

Social Competencies Worksheet
(Page 2 of 3)

4. The student prioritizes and transfers the social competencies that need improvement to the table below.
5. The student explains how to improve these competencies.

Social competency I need to improve	How am I doing with this competency now? What does it look like?	How will I improve this competency?	How will I know I have mastered this competency? What will it look like?
Talking in a quiet voice	I yell out to people I know when I see them in the hall.	I will practice whispering at school and home. My white coat will remind me to talk quietly at work.	The nurse will not fuss at me for yelling in the hospital.
Staying on task	Sometimes I forget to deliver all the meals before I take a break. I stop my work to talk to friends in the hall.	My "watch" (timer) will beep every 5 minutes to remind me to keep working.	I will deliver all my trays and take the cart to the cafeteria before my break to visit with friends.
Asking for clarification	I stop working when I forget what to do. I sit down if I don't understand directions.	I will tell my supervisor to ask me what I don't understand if she sees me sitting down.	I will ask for help when I don't know what to do.
Ignoring distractions	I stop working when I see people I know. I make comments about smells in patients' rooms.	My white coat will remind me that I am a professional. I must keep my comments to myself and keep working when I see people I know.	I will remember to speak kindly to patients. I will wave to my friends in the hall but keep working.
Using self-control	I talk too long to patients, friends, and nurses when delivering trays.	I will ask my friends and the nurses to remind me to finish my work. My watch will help me keep working.	I will deliver all my trays while the food is still warm.

(continued)

Figure 3.8. *(continued)*

Social Competencies Worksheet (Page 3 of 3)

6. The student rates his or her progress by circling S, I, or M.

Social competency I need to improve	Date Competency	Date Competency	Date Competency	Date Competency	Date Competency	Date Competency
Talking in a quiet voice	S I M	S I M	S I M	S I M	S I M	S I M
Staying on task	S I M	S I M	S I M	S I M	S I M	S I M
Asking for clarification	S I M	S I M	S I M	S I M	S I M	S I M
Ignoring distractions	S I M	S I M	S I M	S I M	S I M	S I M
Using self-control	S I M	S I M	S I M	S I M	S I M	S I M
	S I M	S I M	S I M	S I M	S I M	S I M

Note: S = My competency is the same, I = My competency is improving, M = I have mastered this competency.

depending on students' goals for the future. Young adults preparing to make the transition to college will have different needs and will require a different curriculum from those planning to go straight to work. Students with significant intellectual disabilities will have different needs from those with more mild to moderate disabilities. The transition curriculum implemented for each student must be driven by the student's strengths and interests as identified by the transition IEP team. "Putting it all together" requires dedicated education professionals who are willing to take the time to identify and prioritize key activities essential to the successful transitioning of their students.

Table 3.2 gives examples of transition-related activities that are linked to general education core content curricula. This list is intended to be a starting point for designing a dynamic transition curriculum. Activities will change each year based on the strengths and needs of the students. Remember, as students become more self-aware and acquire firsthand experiences with work and other transition-related activities, the curriculum should be fluid enough to accommodate their changing interests.

TEN PRECIOUS MINUTES

Often there are 5 to 10 minutes left in the class period when students are allowed to talk to their peers. If those minutes were multiplied by the number of days in the teaching year, it would equal from 15 to 30 hours of teaching time that could be spent working with students on the transition curriculum.

So many items of interest can be discussed with students in the precious minutes at the end of core content classes. Making real-world connections to core content classes is important. Students want to know how the lessons will affect their futures. Discussing transition-related ideas will get students more interested in the lesson because they will see the positive outcomes related to job and future independence. The following are suggestions to facilitate transition-related discussions with students in those few precious moments.

- Using the My Future worksheet (see Figure 3.3), discuss at least one of the career goals students have selected each day at the end of class. Have students brainstorm what they think the job will require in the way of education, training, and other demands.
- Identify, locate, and use the abundant resources available on the Internet and in the community to further explore careers.
- Explore newspaper employment ads (most schools have classroom sets of newspapers delivered daily), the Internet, libraries, materials from job placement agencies, materials from vocational programs in the district, and materials from school guidance counselors.
- Discuss positive and professional attitudes needed for workplace success.
- Plan field trips (walking if possible) to visit businesses or agencies to experience actual work environments.
- Have guest speakers from local businesses come to share about their businesses and job requirements and the training necessary to be successful.
- Have students interview a family member or a friend in the community who is working. Then have the students share what they learned with the class. (The interview can be as detailed as you want. Students can develop an interview protocol for all to use for these interviews.) This activity increases occupational awareness.

Table 3.2. Transition-related activities linked to general education core content curriculum

Class	Assignment	Objective
English/Integrated language arts	Letter writing	Students will research a job in the newspaper ads and write a cover letter to the employer 1) explaining why they should be hired, 2) explaining their qualifications, 3) making reference to their résumé, 4) requesting an interview, and 5) providing their contact information.
	Résumé writing	Students will use a chronological format: 1) Name/Address/Phone, 2) objective (kind of job student expects to do, greatest strengths, results student expects to produce), 3) background summary, 4) professional experience (including selected accomplishments), 5) education/professional training, and 6) personal interests/memberships (optional).
	Discussions	Teachers will use open-ended question format to discuss college and career topics with the class.
	Paragraph writing	Students will write a paragraph on the reason they want a particular job. Students will write a paragraph to accompany their college application (many colleges require an essay). Students will search out these topics and work on them in English class.
	Interviewing techniques	Students will learn proper interviewing techniques, how to prepare for an interview, and types of questions that may be asked. Students will role-play job interviews.
	Journal writing	Students will write in their journals on topics related to careers and college decisions and reasons why they want to pursue a particular postsecondary option.
	Job search kit	Students will collect a folder of items they may need when applying for a job or preparing for an interview. Items may include their birth certificate, Social Security card, work permit, driver's license, diploma, previous employment information, copies of their résumé, copy of a job application, letters of introduction and/or recommendation, an ink pen, and paper for taking notes.
Research: Use of technology	Career exploration: Internet	Students will use the Internet and selected web sites to explore careers or colleges.
	Microsoft Office	Students will develop brochures about career findings and distribute them as they discuss career exploration.
Math	Budget planning	Students will select an occupation and determine its income.
Summer math programs: *http://www.ams.org*		Students will determine the cost of living independently in their future neighborhood.
		Students will develop a budget of expenses, including rent, utilities, loans (car, home, college), insurance, taxes, entertainment, etc.
	Paying bills	Students will learn to write checks or pay bills online. Students will learn to read a pay stub. Students will learn to calculate their pay per number of hours worked or per their contract.
	Purchasing a car or home	Students will research the cost of purchasing a car or home, calculate the interest on the loan, payments, and realistically determine what type of car or home they can afford.

Core content classes: Science, social studies, and so forth	Web sites for job searches:	Web sites of interest for core curriculum:
	http://www.snagajob.com/	http://www.sciserv.org
	http://www.coolworks.com	http://www.gettech.org
	http://www.studentjobs.gov/	http://www.teachervision.com
	http://www.jobprofiles.org/	http://www.odysseyofthemind.com
	http://www.careeronestop.org	http://www.homesofourown.org
		http://www.need.org
		http://www.nsta.org
		http://www.awim.org
		http://www.glogerm.com
		http://www.nlm.nih.gov

- List topics students feel they need to discuss and include them in the curriculum, such as key occupational skills, needed educational preparation, technical training or professional requirements, how to research salaries and fringe benefits, and opportunities for promotion or job advancement within the company once hired.
- Role-play to practice basic office skills and business etiquette. Discuss employee rights and employer expectations.

Remember, teachers inspire students to greatness. Students with disabilities often find it hard to communicate their wishes or they lack the knowledge about how to develop goals. The time put into transition discussions during these precious minutes at the end of classes can enable students to make informed career decisions. Embedding transition-related topics into instruction enables all students, not just those with disabilities, to acquire the skills necessary for successful transition (McConnell, Johnson, Polychronis, & Risen, 2002).

CONCLUSION

An effective transition curriculum enables students with disabilities to dare to dream and to realize that they are people of worth who have much to offer the world. Collaborating with all stakeholders and creatively embedding transition components into the general curriculum leads to a dynamic transition curriculum that can empower students with the skills they will need to reach their goals. Establishing a well-developed transition process allows students with disabilities to graduate from high school and realize positive outcomes for postsecondary education, employment, independent living, recreation and leisure, and community integration. Yet a transition curriculum can be developed only after a team identifies the critical academic and functional skills students need. The time it takes to develop a tailor-made transition curriculum—with student participation at every juncture in the planning—is worth it for students, their families, and the community.

FOR FURTHER INFORMATION

Accessing the General Curriculum

National Center on Accessing the General Curriculum (NCAC) (http://www.cast.org/publications/ncac/index.html)

Materials provide support to educators interested in learning about policies and practices related to improved access to the general curriculum. Most are available as web site pages and as downloadable Word and PDF documents.

Alternative Assessment

National Alternate Assessment Center (http://www.naacpartners.org)

A federally funded research project to gather data and disseminate information regarding the design, implementation, and effectiveness of alternative assessments.

Supporting Students with More Significant Support Needs

Wehman, P., Smith, D.M., & Schall, C. (2009). *Autism and the transition to adulthood: Success beyond the classroom.* Baltimore: Paul H. Brookes Publishing Co.

Provides hard-to-find information on how specific social, behavioral, and cognitive characteristics of people with autism affect the transition to adulthood, exploring potential challenges and traits that can be powerful assets; walks readers through every aspect of transition planning, including planning for employment and postsecondary education.

4

Planning for the Future

One Student at a Time

Pamela Sherron Targett and Paul Wehman

The school year was off to an exciting start for 14-year-old Stella. It all began just a few weeks ago when Ms. Brighton, Stella's special education teacher, talked to Stella's mother. During the conversation, Ms. Brighton suggested that Stella, her family, her friends, and some select service providers get together to discuss Stella's future.

Ms. Brighton went on to explain that this kind of meeting, called *personal futures planning,* could be instrumental in helping Stella plan for her adult life. Using this organized approach to life planning, a group of people who know and care about a student come together to share information and provide ideas to help shape his or her future. Afterward, a number of assessments take place to help evaluate the student's current level of performance related to meeting his or her various adult life goals. As a next step, a date was set for the following month. Then a list of invitations was made. Stella's mother invited family members and the neighbor's daughter who had grown up playing with Stella.

Each time someone agreed to attend the meeting, Stella was shown where to place a check next to his or her name on the list. At the same time, Ms. Brighton extended the invitation to some key school personnel and community service providers. While making contacts for the meeting, Stella's mother realized the lack of connections she and her daughter had with the community. Then suddenly she began to feel anxious about her daughter's future. She thought, "Stella is lonely now; what will happen when she leaves school?" Then she recalled Stella's reaction to things that she did not want to do. Stella could be very stubborn, such as the day she did not want to leave her favorite fast-food restaurant without getting ice cream. Stella's mother could not make her understand that the machine was out of order and that they would have to come back another day. She literally had to drag Stella out of the lobby. Stella's mother wondered if Stella would be able to work in the future. She was not sure whether an employer would consider hiring Stella. These and other thoughts flooded her mind.

Finally, the day of the big event arrived. The meeting was scheduled for 5 p.m. in the large conference room at Ms. Brighton's office. The time and place were selected because they were the most convenient for the attendees. Stella and her mother arrived early to set up some light refreshments. As the guests arrived, Stella and her mother welcomed each person. Stella waved and sometimes said, "Hi yep" (her hello greeting) as she handed out a nametag.

Stella's mother knew everyone in attendance except for the meeting facilitator, who had been hired by the school to lead the process. Ms. Brighton often felt that bringing a meeting facilitator was the best way to proceed, particularly for her students with more significant support needs. Having a facilitator lead the meeting freed Ms. Brighton up to focus on and support her student's involvement in the meeting. It also gave her time to observe the student's abilities related to self-advocacy, communication, and other topics.

After everyone arrived, Ms. Brighton motioned Stella to come stand at the front of the room and said, "Let's make it quiet." This was a verbal cue she was using to teach Stella to get another person's attention. Then, just as they had practiced in the classroom on a number of occasions to get her classmates settled in, Stella said, "Make quiet please" in a loud voice. This did not initially get everyone's attention, so Ms. Brighton then pointed to the handheld bell that was sometimes used to command attention in the classroom. When prompted, Stella picked up the bell and shook it, shouting, "Make quiet please!" Soon the audience's attention was captured, and Stella sat down at the head of the table next to Ms. Brighton. Ms. Brighton welcomed the group to Stella's personal futures planning. Ms. Brighton explained that this organized approach to life planning included a circle of support (i.e., people who knew and cared about the student). She told the group that they would define what they saw working for Stella now and in the future. The ideas and dreams would be captured using descriptive graphics or maps. The end result would be a vision for the future along with an action plan. At a later date, this important information, combined with results from other assessments, would be used to help guide Stella's transition individualized education program (IEP) planning efforts.

With the explanation complete, Ms. Brighton looked at Stella and said, "Let's go." With that prompt, Stella stood up and, with a big smile on her face, said, "Let's go, start me." Everyone in the audience smiled, and a few people clapped. With that the facilitator stood up and said, "Let's start talking about Stella's dreams for the future."

Individualized student transition planning starts by helping a student such as Stella clarify her goals for the future. To some this may sound simple enough, but for a student with a disability it can be very challenging unless he or she is given the supports, accommodations, training, and coordination of services necessary to make his or her future life vision a reality. This process begins by asking about or helping the student to define his or her vision for the future. Some students and their families may be able to describe this; others, such as Stella, will benefit from person-centered futures planning.

Often transition assessments take place with an initial vision for the future already in the student and family's mind. These assessments guide the formulation and prioritization of measurable postsecondary goals across various adult life domains. The results from the transition assessments are also incorporated into the student's present level of educational performance. The student's present level of performance assists the team with developing annual goals and accommodations that support achieving the measurable postsecondary goals. In turn the student's annual goals lead to the identification of various transition services, which include courses of study, linkages, and activities that are needed to move him or her closer to achieving the measurable postsecondary goals.

This chapter takes a close look at individualized student planning for the transition IEP. It begins with a look at the basic elements that make up a student's transition IEP. The major adult life domains and other essential parts of the transition IEP are described. Next we review some considerations associated with starting transition IEP planning early on. Then we take a look at the importance of assessment and consider some examples of formal and informal methods. An overview of the various transition IEP team members, their roles, and their responsibilities follows. The chapter concludes with some suggestions and strategies for getting families and students involved in transition planning.

WHAT TO ADDRESS IN THE TRANSITION
INDIVIDUALIZED EDUCATION PROGRAM

The foundation for adult life should be established while a student is still in school. For some students with restrictive disabilities, building this foundation may require being in a secondary school program that focuses heavily on developing the practical life skills necessary for some level of independence in adult life. Students' education should focus on their strengths and challenges in these adult life domains.

Adult Life Domains

Major adult life domains associated with transition planning include employment, postsecondary education or training, independent living, and community participation. These domains and other areas that may need to be addressed in transition planning are listed in Table 4.1. In addition, some examples of knowledge, skills, and attitudes that students may need to acquire to function in each realm are provided. It is important to keep in mind that every student is different, and thus every transition IEP must be individualized to the student. In addition, the knowledge, skills, and attitudes listed in Table 4.1 should not be considered exhaustive of those that may be needed to lead a successful adult life.

Some students will require instruction in only one or two of these adult life domains; however, others may need instruction across the board. Some areas, such as transportation and self-determination, require the use of skills that cut across several domains. For example, a student can learn to cross the street from the bus stop to the workplace or while walking to the grocery store. Or he or she can learn decision-making skills while comparison shopping in a grocery store or self-advocacy skills when lodging a complaint about poor service from a specialized transportation provider.

Key Elements

The transition planning mandate in IDEA 2004 guides how the IEP process for transition is structured. The following are the key elements that should be addressed in the plan.

Measurable Postsecondary Goals

An inspection of a student's future desires, interests, and preferences should lead to the creation of measurable postschool goals related to adult life. These goals state what the student plans to do upon exiting from secondary education. The goals must come from the student and his or her family and should point directly toward their vision for the future. Information needed to form these statements comes from assessment. At the meeting the assessment results will help formulate postsecondary goals that provide the framework to develop annual goals and transition services.

In some instances additional assessment may be warranted to further inform the student's plan for transition. By reflecting on the student's long-range adult life goals, the team should be better positioned to plan and create additional meaningful assessments.

Transition assessment should guide the development of measurable postsecondary goals. These goals are required in the areas of education and training, employment, and independent living where appropriate. Here are some examples:
- *Employment:* Austin will work in a full-time job that pays above minimum wage and offers medical benefits. He will travel to and from work by walking or using the subway.
- *Postsecondary education:* Ellen will attend a community college to become employed in a field that will take advantage of her mathematical and computer skills.

Table 4.1. Transition focus domains and other areas

Domain	Associated knowledge, skills, and attitudes
Employment	Defining employment-related interests, preferences, and support needs; locating work opportunities; requesting accommodations; choosing an employment support service; completing an application; interviewing for a job; performing job tasks; getting along with others; communicating with coworkers; communicating with management; taking a break; clocking in and out of work; checking the schedule; picking up a paycheck; practicing work safety; traveling to work; managing time
Postsecondary education training	Defining a study track, choosing a postsecondary education or training program, completing an application, making appointments, requesting accommodations, managing time, using study skills, getting around campus
Independent living	Practicing self-care (e.g., toileting; grooming; dressing; caring for hair, nails, and teeth; bathing; eating), preparing food, performing household maintenance (e.g., housekeeping, lawn care), participating in home leisure activities, developing lasting relationships with others, being safe at home, setting appointments, managing time, managing money (e.g., banking, paying rent, paying bills, shopping), asking for help, expressing the value of independence, getting along with others, showing sensitivity to the needs of others, expressing gratitude
Community participation	Attending recreational activities alone or with a group, participating in clubs or team sports, performing hobbies, going to appointments (e.g., doctor, dentist, service coordinator), visiting friends or family, traveling, using services (e.g., bank, restaurant, grocery store, beautician), being safe in the community, managing time, managing money, asking for help
Transportation	Driving a vehicle, riding a bike, walking, using public transportation, taking a taxi, riding with friends or family, accessing disability transportation services, traveling safely, managing time, managing money
Self-determination	Understanding one's disability, advocating for oneself, setting goals, making informed choices, making decisions, expressing a desire to work, making positive statements about contributing to society through work, taking pride in one's work, staying on task and not giving up
Communication and social skills	Communicating needs and wants, making conversation, making eye contact, smiling, keeping personal space, greeting others, handling frustration and anger, making friends, developing relationships, getting along with others, asking for help

- *Independent living:* Gareth will live either alone or with one roommate in an apartment that is located on the bus line and is close to his brother's house.
- *Community participation:* Briana will go shopping at the mall and out to eat, and will attend a movie at least once a month. She also will attend religious services at her family church once a week.

The goals should be stated as an outcome that occurs after high school rather than a process. This means results-oriented terms such as those in these examples should be used. As in the case of Stella, sometimes information about the student and family's vision for the future is obtained in advance. When the IEP transition meeting takes place, the vision is presented to the team. As always throughout planning, the measurable postsecondary goals must be based on each student's strengths, preferences, and interests.

Present Level of Performance

In addition to measurable postsecondary goals, a measure and statement of the student's current level of performance is needed. A summary of the student's present level of performance should be presented during the meeting and written in to the plan. Information on the students' current level of performance is obtained through reviewing information from previous IEPs and using a variety of assessments that are designed to reveal the student's current abilities and support needs.

Assessment information should be obtained from multiple sources. Once obtained, all of the information should be reviewed to make a more accurate determination about the student's abilities, needs, and goals (Neubert, 2003; Sitlington & Clark, 2007).

Both formal and informal approaches may be used within the various areas associated with adult life domains; however, typically, information is gathered through informal means such as review of previous IEPs, personal interviews, surveys, observations in natural environments, and situational assessments. Information can also be gleaned from person-centered planning meetings. Although person-centered planning is not usually referred to as a type of assessment, the information gathered during this group meeting can greatly influence transition planning.

The results of a comprehensive assessment should lead to an understanding of the student's present levels of performance. An analysis of where the student is performing now (current level of performance) and where the student desires to be in the future (vision statement) helps clarify potential areas for instruction. In addition, the assessment results establish a baseline of the student's performance. At a later date this can be used to measure the effectiveness of the student's educational program. Excerpts from some students' current level of performance summaries are provided in Figure 4.1.

Again, it is the discrepancy that exists between the student's current level of functioning in a particular area and the vision of where he or she needs or wants to be in the future that signals the need for education, activities, skills training, services, and supports to move him or her in the desired direction.

Transition Services

Transition services include courses of study and coordinated activities, including linkages to other services as needed. The courses of study are designed to help the student make a successful transition to postschool adult life. This long-range plan is designed to make the student's educational program relevant. It may include classes, experiences, or activities that directly relate to the measurable postsecondary goals. It should also be meaningful and help motivate the student to complete school.

The coordinated set of activities includes strategies or steps in the long-range plan. It also documents the effort between the student, family, school, and other appropriate postschool support programs to work together in assisting the student with reaching his or her postsecondary goals.

The annual academic or functional goals must logically link the postsecondary goal(s) of education, training, and employment and—if appropriate—independent living. Together the course of study, coordinated set of activities, and annual IEP goals should lead the student closer to his or her measurable postsecondary goals.

Dates for Implementation

It is important to establish a time frame to observe and measure a student's goals and objectives. Some teachers prefer to establish the dates when all activities will start and end,

---

Employment

Austin is not employed, although he has participated in some work experiences through the school community-based vocational education program. This included trying out some retail tasks in the front (stocking) and back (processing) of the store and working at an apartment complex (cleaning and caring for the grounds). He seemed to prefer working inside performing tasks requiring his hands and movement around the workplace. He required frequent bathroom breaks and had difficulty staying on task without instruction.

Austin's parents report that he often wanders off when they do not keep a close eye on him. Fortunately, they have always been able to find him. They usually find him in the family garage unloading and then reloading boxes of junk or in the flower garden pulling weeds. On a few occasions he was at the neighbor's house watching television. When asked why he was there instead of home, he would say "TV." He was also enjoying popcorn.

Postsecondary Education

Ellen is taking the courses needed to enter the community college. She currently uses assistive technology and other supports in the classroom. She does not ask for assistance, but when her work is waning and assistance or support is recommended, she accepts it.

Independent Living

Gareth performs a variety of chores at home. For example, he cleans his room, unloads the dishwasher, sets the table, takes out the trash, and vacuums. He does not complete tasks that require using household products with chemicals that may be hazardous if ingested or sprayed in the eyes. He can prepare soup in the microwave and make a sandwich.

He is able to perform basic activities associated with getting ready for school. However, he requires reminders from his parents to bathe and use soap. His mother selects the clothes he wears to school. He cannot tie his shoes and instead uses Velcro hooks.

In the classroom he frequently expresses an interest in helping the teacher and others. However, often when he offers to help, help is not needed. When told that no help is needed at the time, he gets upset and sometimes has to leave the room until he is able to calm down.

Community Participation

Briana has basic independent living skills. She goes shopping with her parents. She pushes the cart in the grocery store, helps select items for her school lunch and dinner desserts, and helps bag the groceries. She does not push the cart in the parking lot but does help her parents load and unload the groceries from the car. Briana does not participate in any community activities without her parents. She seems to enjoy shopping and going to the movies. She also likes to eat out with her parents. Briana goes to church with her parents. Briana has a savings account but does not handle money. She buys things from vending machines that require exact change (i.e., bubblegum dispenser at the grocery store, drink vending machine at church).

Figure 4.1.   Excerpts from present level of performance summaries.

whereas others only indicate the approximate date for completing all steps. Sometimes a specific date is included in the objective.

Person(s) Responsible

The student's transition IEP should state the primary person responsible for overseeing implementation and list all others who are involved. The documentation should reflect coordination among general educators, special educators, family, community service providers, and any other team members. The teacher should specify the service that each agency will provide. For example, the state vocational rehabilitation office rehabilitation counselor will provide job coach services, or the community services board service coordinator will assist with completing the eligibility process for vocational rehabilitation services.

In addition, the student and parents will have their own responsibilities. For example, the mother will get the student's medical records to the Social Security representative, or the student will participate in a series of situational assessments in various businesses to determine what types of work tasks and settings he or she prefers. Much more detail on the roles of different members of the transition team is provided in Chapter 6.

Summary of Performance

The local education agency has to provide the student with a summary of academic achievement and functional performance that includes recommendations on assistance needed to meet his or her postsecondary goals. The time line for completing the summary will vary depending on the student's transition goals. For example, a student who is applying to college may need this documentation during the application process. Although the team decides when to complete and update the summary, it must be included in the student's plan in his or her final year of high school.

Rights

The student's transition IEP should include any rights that will transfer from the parent to the child when the child reaches the age of majority. The student must be notified 1 year prior of any rights that will transfer to him or her upon reaching the age of majority. The plan should include a statement that indicates that the student has been so informed.

Organization and Time Frame

A student's transition IEP plan provides a framework for the team to identify, plan, and carry out activities that will help the student make a successful transition from school to adult life. The format for an individualized student transition IEP varies. Some school districts may have a preferred style on file, or it may be up to the teacher to choose. Regardless of format, some basic elements must be included, such as a long-range outcome or vision statement; a summary of the student's present level of performance, annual goals, objectives or steps needed to accomplish these goals (if needed); time frames; and responsible parties. When appropriate, a Summary of Performance and transfer of rights statement are included.

WHEN TO BEGIN PLANNING

Transition planning should begin as soon as the transition team determines that it is appropriate. Many students can benefit from transition activities years before they reach the mandated age of 16. As soon as the team can meet to do some futures planning, examine present level of performance, and determine goals for postsecondary experiences, planning can begin by convening a meeting with the student, parents, special and general educators, vocational rehabilitation personnel, and any other team members. It is important to discuss academic abilities, self-advocacy, employment goals, and independent living skills because all of these things play an important role in adult life.

When the team gets together to begin planning—as early as seems reasonable, considering the individual student—several topics are important to consider. Some questions to ask include the following:

Is it time to start planning for transition? Why or why not?

Is the student on schedule to accomplish goals (associated with work, postsecondary education, and community living) that will affect his or her ability to lead as independent an adult life as possible?

What skills are needed to optimize the student's independent functioning as an adult in the community?

If the student could perform (insert X function here), would it allow him or her to be more independent both now and in the future?

What experiences and skills will help the student become a more productive and independent member of society?

Is the student's educational experience making the best use of limited time by moving the student closer to maximizing his or her independence in the future?

Personal goals should be discussed to determine educational and vocational programming, and the team should review the steps necessary for the student to achieve those goals. Over time, the goals and objectives must be monitored to be sure that the student is on schedule to achieve them. If not, adjustments must be made! Remember that transition planning is an ongoing process that requires input from a number of critical team members: For example, the student and his or her family help personalize the goals, the classroom teachers deliver instruction and monitor progress, and vocational rehabilitation counselors help ensure reliable contacts with community businesses.

The transition IEP generally starts in middle school and continues until the student exits school. Some students will need more time to develop the basic skills associated with the transition to adulthood, so it is important to start planning as early as possible. In other cases, it may be acceptable to begin planning as the student is preparing to enter high school. As with every aspect of transition planning, each student's IEP must be looked at individually, and decisions must be made specifically for each student.

Carter, Trainor, Sun, and Owens (2009) examined the transition-related strengths and needs of 160 students with emotional and/or behavior disorders or learning disabilities from the perspectives of special educators, parents, and students. They found that student ratings were significantly higher than those of teachers and parents. The study also highlighted the importance of incorporating multiple perspectives into transition planning.

SOME STRATEGIES FOR PLANNING

The ultimate goal of transition IEP planning is for a student to leave the educational system with a certain body of knowledge or set of skills to lead as full an adult life as possible. Conducting assessments about the student's current levels of performance allows the team to focus directly on learning needs. As a result, specific instruction can be planned to help each student reach his or her long-range adult life goals. It is important to assess the behaviors (knowledge, skills, and abilities) that the student brings to the planning table. For example, the team cannot just assume that each student is ready and able to enter into an adult life. It would be very unusual for any student with or without disabilities to possess all of the necessary skills associated with successful employment or independent living at age 16. Yet assuming that each student is starting at ground zero would be naïve. Each student arrives at transition planning with a variety of life experiences, so before planning that student's transition IEP, the team must take time to get to know him or her. As with any other type of instruction, the recipient of that instruction (i.e., the student) must be considered from the beginning of the instructional planning process if appropriate goals are to be established. Before the team can get started with a plan, they have to know where they are going.

Determine Current Levels of Performance

Transition assessments reveal a student's current level of performance in various adult life domains and help ensure that the student receives the right instruction. After reviewing the assessment results, the team should be able to begin designing educational activities and training experiences as well as coordinating the relevant adult services to help the student achieve his or her desired postschool outcomes.

Evaluating a student's current level of performance may be done using a variety of informal methods, such as interviews, surveys, or checklists. Or it may require a much more intense or formal approach, such as collecting performance data of the student's abilities while observing him or her in school and community-based environments. It is common to use a mix of formal and informal assessments to collect this information.

Regardless of the approaches used, the results of the transition assessments should provide the team with a better awareness of the student's characteristics, which in turn will influence the design and development of the measurable postsecondary goals. A student's characteristics include intellectual skills, prior knowledge or experience in adult life domains, physical skills, language ability, and motivation level (among other things). Instructional decisions made without this information will not necessarily be relevant to the student. Time will most likely be wasted, and the education program will probably fall short of providing the student with the skills necessary for an adult life in the community. Methods of assessing a student's present levels of performance differ from the techniques used to obtain information about the student's expectations, interests, and preferences. The information that is highlighted in the student's postschool outcome or vision statement typically comes from conversations with the student and his or her family and/or from person-centered planning, not from an assessment of the student's current levels of performance.

Identify Different Types of Assessment

At the secondary level the use of age-appropriate transition assessments is mandated by IDEA 2004. Schools may use formal (standardized) or informal (nonstandardized) procedures to assess students' attributes and potential support needs. Standardized instruments use evidence to document an acceptable level of validity and reliability. Some instruments are norm referenced,

Some students have a negative perception of the relevance of their school experience to their current life and future desires (Scanlon & Mellard, 2002; Whitney-Thomas & Moloney, 2001). Students who do not make a connection between their current educational program and their future needs may be prone to drop out of school or may not be motivated to work on goals (Sinclair, Christenson, & Thurlow, 2005; Wagner, Newman, Cameto, Levine, & Marder, 2007).

whereas others are criterion referenced. Examples of standardized or formal assessments include achievement tests, aptitude tests, intelligence tests, adaptive behavioral scales, and interest inventories. Only a few published standardized assessment instruments are specifically related to transition, for example the Transition Planning Inventory (Clark & Patton, 2006).

Informal assessments—such as curriculum-based assessment, personal interviews, surveys, portfolios, observations in natural environments, vocational situational assessments, adaptive behavioral or functional skill inventories, and environmental or ecological assessments—are just as legitimate and often more informative than formal assessments. They are often the preferred method of gathering information for transition planning, particularly as the student gets older. For example, a wealth of data can be accumulated by observing the student as he or she participates in various academic and work experiences, talking with the student about his or her likes and dislikes, and setting up experiences that will allow the student to try something that he or she thinks may be of interest. This type of assessment is subjective and often teacher-made.

A lot of time has been devoted to testing and assessing individuals with disabilities in the name of planning their "best future" at work, at home, and in the community. The team needs to work closely with the student and his or her family to determine their perceived needs and goals, set objectives, and choose educational and training activities to make these plans a reality. Although no one assessment measure is recommended over another, serving a student with a severe disability may require more explicit and extensive assessment and transition planning.

> *Transition assessment should build on a student's existing skills and strengths (Epstein, Rudolph, & Epstein, 2000). This was emphasized in IDEA 2004, which added that transition services be "based on the individual child needs, taking into account the child's strengths, preferences and interests" (300.43[a] [1]).*

Avoid Standardized Testing for Students with Severe Disabilities

A team that is working with a student who has a severe disability should avoid using standardized tests. These measures usually compare the performance of individuals with disabilities to that of students without disabilities. Because some tests do not include individuals with disabilities in their standardization samples, use of these instruments could lead to inappropriately labeling people as unable to do something. Instead, assessment should focus on surveying the student's current and future environments to identify existing skills and abilities and using an ecological evaluation process and situational assessments. Although this approach is more tedious, precisely measuring the behavior to be taught is critical. A functional assessment might even be necessary to obtain information about a student's current levels of performance. The steps involved in designing a functional assessment are included in the checklist in Figure 4.2.

Deciding what to assess and how to collect and use data to plan transition are important steps in establishing meaningful postschool outcomes for all students. Assessment results are used to help determine the student's annual goals and objectives and decide what educational and training activities and what related services are necessary to prepare the student for adult life in the community. Assessment should help the team answer the following questions: What does the student need to learn this year, how will it be taught, by whom, and by when? Finally, remember that each student's assessment must be individu-

Checklist of Steps in Designing a Functional Assessment

Instructions: Check off each step as you complete them for each student needing a functional assessment.

Inventory the community

____ Identify the environments in the community (e.g., grocery store, bank, apartment, gym) in which the student expects to function in the future, and take an ecological inventory of subenvironments (e.g., home subenvironments include the living room, kitchen, bathroom, bedroom, and yard) to determine the activities and skills associated with participation in those areas.

Determine student and parent preferences

____ Interview the student and those who know him or her best, observe the student in various environments, and/or review the results from the person-centered planning meeting.

____ *Gather information about student skills and abilities:* Interview those who have had an opportunity to observe the student in various environments; if there is no evidence of ability, then further assess the student in the environment to gather information on performance.

____ *Prioritize student goals and objectives:* Use outcomes to determine instructional priorities; consider areas that have the greatest potential to increase independence in the future, that are chronologically age appropriate, and that reflect strengths and interests.

Figure 4.2. Checklist of Steps in Designing a Functional Assessment.

alized and must take into account his or her particular desires, strengths, and needs.

In summary, transition assessment helps identify postsecondary goals and is incorporated into the student's present levels of performance. This information is then used to help the team plan the student's annual goals and accommodations that support postsecondary goals. This, in turn, leads to identification of transition services, including courses of study linkages and activities. This information may be obtained using a variety of formal and informal assessments. Sometimes a variety of assessments will be needed before useful information is found. For students with the most significant disabilities, a functional approach to assessment is recommended.

KEY PLAYERS ON THE TRANSITION TEAM

When it is time to leave the public school system, the student and his or her family will face a complex array of service options and resources. Each organization will have its own unique roles, funding sources, and eligibility requirements. A key function of transition planning is to provide students, families, and service providers with information that will facilitate service use. The transition IEP helps the student and family connect with supports and services before the student leaves the school system. As the student progresses through his or her secondary school years, the IEP planning team expands to include personnel from adult service agencies who will form a new broad-based support system for the student when he or she leaves school.

The transition IEP is developed by a team. At the center of the team are the student and one or both parents. If the student does not have a parent, then his or her caregiver should be involved. Representatives from the school are on the team, too. These representatives include the student's special education teacher, who may take on a myriad of roles, from gathering assessment data to planning instruction. If the student is in a general education class but also receives special education services, both teachers are required to participate. A representative of the school district who is qualified to provide or supervise special education may also be required to attend team meetings. Chapter 6 provides more detail on the logistics involved in building the team.

The transition planning process has gained renewed attention since the early 2000s (Martin, Van Dycke, Christensen, et al., 2006; Martin, Van Dycke, Greene, et al., 2006; Test et al., 2004). IDEA 2004 increased the emphasis on linking assessment with transition goals in an effort to increase accountability and improve educational results (Bassett & Kochhar-Bryant, 2006; Sitlington & Neubert, 2004). IDEA 2004 requires "appropriate measurable postsecondary goals based upon age appropriate assessments related to training, education, employment and where appropriate independent living skills" (300.320[b]). However, there is limited empirical research on transition assessment. There are limited databased findings that can inform educators about what they may learn or encounter in the assessment process (Morningstar & Liss, 2008). Additional research is needed.

Research has shown that implementing some form of student-led IEPs with students with disabilities leads to positive outcomes regarding self-knowledge, self-determination, and self-advocacy (Konrad & Test, 2004; Mason, McGahee-Kovac, Johnson, & Stillerman, 2002). Involving students and parents in transition planning is a recommended practice (Kohler & Field, 2003).

Transition planning is typically done by an interdisciplinary team composed of special educators, general educators, vocational educators, vocational rehabilitation specialists, and representatives from postsecondary education settings and other adult service agencies (Eckes & Ochoa, 2005; Skinner & Lindstrom, 2003).

In addition, the school is responsible for bringing in representatives from other agencies, such as vocational rehabilitation service agencies or postsecondary education settings, to be part of the student's transition IEP planning process. Such agencies may also be responsible for delivering some of the services the student needs.

Table 4.2 lists some adult service agencies and describes the role they may play in a student's transition planning. Should agencies fail to provide the agreed-on transition services, schools must find alternative ways to meet the transition goals and objectives for that student.

Table 4.2. Adult service agencies involved in transition planning

Agency	General description
Information and advocacy service agencies	These organizations, which may include disability-specific groups, state legal advocacy services, and groups that support parents of children with disabilities, offer valuable information and assistance in various areas.
County human services agencies	Counties may offer services for individuals with developmental disabilities who have an IQ score of 70 or less and who have adaptive behavioral needs. Service coordinators help individuals design a plan and identify the supports that may be needed to implement the plan. They may contract with private not-for-profit agencies in local communities that are designated as community service boards. These organizations typically provide a range of services related to employment, independent living, and community participation.
Residential service agencies	Various residential programs are designed specifically for individuals with disabilities. In addition to supplying housing, the programs may provide supervision and guidance for residents and provide access to community experiences, including other supportive services needed to live and work in the community.
State vocational rehabilitation service agencies	State vocational rehabilitation counselors work in cooperation with educators and other service providers to assist students in making a successful transition to work. Services available through vocational rehabilitation agencies may include service coordination related to employment, guidance, counseling, job placement assistance, purchase of services related to postsecondary education, supported employment, and transportation to work. Cost and no-cost service options may be available. Individuals may need to meet eligibility requirements for cost services.
Social Security Administration	The Social Security Administration provides information related to Social Security and Medicaid benefits. Additional services include medical benefits through Medicaid. A youth with a disability can apply 6 months before they turn 18. The enrollment process can take up to a year.
Postsecondary education/ college disability service representatives	After some initial investigation of acceptance into a postsecondary setting, disability service personnel from a trade school, community college, or university may join the team. These professionals can assist students with disabilities to select courses and obtain the supports necessary to succeed in the postsecondary education setting.
Consultants with specialties related to specific disabilities	Examples include mobility or orientation specialists, speech-language therapists or audiologists, psychologists, or rehabilitation engineers.
Work force centers	Operating under state departments of labor and employment, these centers (sometimes referred to as *One-Stop Career Centers*) offer vocational services such as work registration, job referrals, career guidance and counseling, employment-related skill development (e.g., interviewing, networking, résumé writing), and more. The centers work closely with state vocational rehabilitation divisions as needed to obtain more intensive services for some individuals with disabilities.
Independent living centers	These centers provide a variety of services to people with disabilities to help them function more independently in their home, workplace, and community. There may be a small fee for some services. Contact the state vocational rehabilitation office for the independent living center nearest you.

WAYS TO INVOLVE FAMILIES

Having a child with a disability requires important communication, research, and advocacy skills. However, some parents lack skills and knowledge in these areas. Moreover, some parents are not able to obtain the skills or retain the knowledge necessary to be completely effective in these areas. These parents and their children may not know their rights or how to exercise them.

Provide Information

One of the first orders of business may be to provide families with information about transition and their rights related to special education. Here is a list of the type of information families need to know:

- Understand your child's disability and how it will affect you now and in the future.
- Be familiar with accommodations and support services and how these can help your child be successful now and in the future.
- Teach your child self-advocacy skills. Promote your child's use of these skills in the home.
- Learn the basics about the laws and rights associated with your child's transition.
- Contact representatives from advocacy organizations who are well versed in disability rights issues. Simply sharing information from a web site or a handbook may not be enough; some family members may need support to acquire and use this knowledge. Just be considerate of each family's background and try to use direct and jargon-free language when communicating with families.

Encourage Participation

Family members have valuable insights about the student. Some will be active members of the team, but others will not. It may be difficult to get some parents to attend the student's meeting, but it is important to try. Ways to increase the likelihood of parent participation include complimenting parents on how well they know their son or daughter, describing the format of the meeting, and discussing how they can contribute. It may also be helpful to think about ways you and the other team members might react to parent responses to questions during the meeting. Reactions to responses can either encourage or discourage further participation. It is important to consider not only what you say in the meeting but how you say it.

Body Language

Positive body language encourages participation. Smiling, making eye contact, and nodding the head not only encourage the person speaking to continue but may also signal others to join in. If a response to a question does not make sense, consider the fact that some people are not good at articulating their feelings or opinions. They may need patience and help paraphrasing what they have said.

For example, a father might say, "I never had much need for education. We do just fine; we have plenty to eat and a roof over our head, but I do wonder what my son will do when he gets older. My employer would not consider hiring someone like him." In such an instance, you can paraphrase this in a more positive way to confirm what you heard: "If I understand you correctly, you're saying that you would like for your son to pursue some type of work so he can earn a decent income and have a home of his own."

If a response to a question seems unintelligent, consider rephrasing the response to find some merit in it and apply the response to the question. For instance, in response to a question about where her son may want to work in the future, a mother could say, "I don't want my son working in the paper manufacturing plant. He may fall in a machine and get ground up." A positive response may be "Yes, I can see how working in an environment with dangerous machinery could lead to concerns. What steps could we take to make him safe at work?"

It is also important to comment on a good response. Genuinely acknowledging a concern should encourage participation.

Some parents just may not feel comfortable participating in a meeting. They may lack the nerve to speak out or may not perceive the value of what they have to contribute and thus just leave it to the "experts." If parents still seem hesitant after ample encouragement, avoid asking specific questions and putting them on the spot. However, it is important to keep an eye out for a spark of interest and draw them into the discussion if possible. After the meeting, try asking how the parents feel and inquire whether something can be done differently to get them more involved; this may provide an insight into how to engage them in the future.

Effective transition planning takes into account the multiple perspectives of people who know the student well, such as parents. Their contribution to the process is extremely important (Geenen, Powers, & Lopez-Vasquez, 2001; Hogansen, Powers, Geenen, Gil-Kashiwabara, & Powers, 2008).

Other Tips

It is hoped that most students' parents will want to attend the transition IEP planning meeting. Skillful planning, sensitivity, and good communication can all help persuade reluctant parents to get involved. A checklist of tips for engaging family members in the transition IEP planning process is offered in Figure 4.3.

Whenever a parent chooses not to attend a meeting, you should keep detailed records of efforts made to arrange a meeting at a mutually agreeable time and place. Regardless of whether the parent attends the meeting, afterward the school must inform the parent about any decisions that were made.

WAYS TO INVOLVE THE STUDENT

Students can get involved in transition planning through a number of means. Ideas for involving students with less significant support needs may immediately come to mind, whereas it may be more difficult to figure out how to actively involve students with more severe disabilities. No matter what the situation, each student should be involved to the greatest extent possible. Sometimes new and creative ways to promote involvement will be required.

Checklist of Steps for Including Parents in the Transition IEP Process

Instructions: Check off each step as you complete it to ensure that you are including parents in the transition IEP process.

Before the meeting

___ Schedule the meeting at a time and place that are mutually agreeable.

___ Make the setting friendly (not formal).

___ Offer alternative means of participating (e.g., through conference calls).

___ Make sure the parent understands English. Get an interpreter if needed.

___ Offer multiple ways for the parent to share information about the child's strengths and needs as well as about what the parent thinks the child can accomplish during the school year.

___ Invite the parent to visit the school to observe the child.

___ Explain the importance of the parent attending the meeting.

___ Inform the parent of who else will be attending the meeting.

At the meeting

___ Encourage the parent to speak up by using language the parent can understand.

___ Make concepts easy to grasp by using key words or icons.

___ Ask questions; for example, ask what the parent knows about the child and what the parent would like others to know (be more specific, if needed).

___ Present information in a way that is more visual than verbal, as needed.

___ Provide examples of successful students as illustrations. Do not reveal the students' identities.

___ Listen.

After the meeting

___ Schedule times to talk to the parent about the child's progress over the telephone, by e-mail, or in person.

___ Encourage the parent to drop in and observe the child in action.

___ Thank the parent for attending, and reinforce the importance of the meeting.

Figure 4.3. Checklist of Steps for Including Parents in the Transition IEP Process.

Person-Centered Planning

As mentioned in earlier chapters, the term *person-centered planning* refers to any number of approaches that can be used to help both the student and his or her team members explore, identify, and better understand the student's personal interests, preferences, and needs. A variety of people are invited to help the student identify his or her vision for the future through this process.

Personal futures planning is one specific set of practices for guiding teams in defining and achieving goals. During this process, the student and his or her chosen support network meet and discuss their vision for a positive future. The team can then compare that vision with the student's current situation and from there develop an action plan to move closer to the desired vision for the future. The plan serves as a guide for future actions and choices (Mount, 2000). Although there are many ways to conduct personal futures planning, one of the tools most often used with students is the Making Action Plans System (Pearpoint, Forest, & O'Brien, 1996).

Person-centered planning may take place before or after information is gathered about a student's present levels of performance. For example, the process may be used to clarify the student's dreams or vision for the future and to identify personal interests and preferences, abilities, and support needs. This information may be referred to during the planning meeting to ensure that the transition IEP is designed to move the student closer to his or her desired future. Or the results of a student's assessment across various adult life domains may reveal a number of skills that need to be addressed. In short, person-centered planning may be used to help personalize and prioritize the student's goals and objectives.

A person-centered plan will help individualize and maximize the effectiveness of the student's transition plan. During the student's transition IEP planning meeting, the student, with the support of family or a teacher, can present a summary of the results to the team. The team members can reflect on this and on assessment results to formulate student-centered goals and objectives. This information is vital for establishing a suitable direction for the student's future education.

Active Role

The student must be invited into his or her transition IEP planning process and encouraged to be as active a participant as possible (Thoma & Wehman, 2010). A large body of research on self-determination and self-advocacy supports having students take ownership of this process and perform a lead role (Wehmeyer, Palmer, Agran, Mithaug, & Martin, 2000).

A study examined the effectiveness of the self-directed IEP to teach students the skills necessary to lead IEP meetings. The self-directed IEP had a strong effect on increasing the percentage of time students started, led, and talked during the meetings. The findings add to the growing literature demonstrating the effectiveness of the self-directed IEP (Martin, Van Dycke, Christensen, et al., 2006).

CONCLUSION

Students with disabilities can successfully make the transition to adult life when sound planning leads to the development of a relevant transition IEP. This chapter has presented information to assist educators who help students plan for the future. Adult life domains, key elements of the transition IEP, and formal and informal approaches to assessment were described. The members of the transition team and ways to promote family and student involvement were also examined.

It is important to remember that the transition to adulthood is an ongoing process. It starts at birth for parents, and in the world of special education it begins when the student enters school. However, by law it becomes formalized during the secondary school years and intensifies as the student moves closer to exiting school and assuming an adult life. Taking the time to plan is the first step to designing and implementing a transition IEP that helps ensure a student becomes as competent an adult as possible.

FOR FURTHER INFORMATION

Building Capacity to Support and Improve Transition Planning, Services, and Outcomes

National Secondary Transition Technical Assistance Center (NSTTAC) http://www.nsttac.org/
NSTTAC is a national Technical Assistance and Dissemination center directed and staffed by the Special Education Program at the University of North Carolina at Charlotte, in partnership with the Special Education Programs at Western Michigan University and Appalachian State University.

Curricula

ChoiceMaker Curriculum (Martin and Marshall, 1995)
This curriculum uses an 11-step process to promote active participation and facilitation of the IEP meeting. After direct instruction, students assume a role in the IEP meeting. A pretest and posttest is available.

Next S.T.E.P. (*Student Transition and Education Planning*; Halpern et al., 2000)
This curriculum helps students become motivated in transition planning, engage in self-evaluation, identify transition goals and activities, monitor their transition plans and adjust if needed, and conduct the transition planning meeting. It also includes an assessment component that helps evaluate a student's strengths and weaknesses associated with personal life, jobs, education, training, and living on one's own.

Parent Information

Technical Assistance Alliance for Parent Centers (http://www.taalliance.org)
Includes a listing of parent training and information centers and community parent resource centers in every state.

Transition Planning

Wehman, P. (2006). *Life beyond the classroom: Transition strategies for young people with disabilities* (4th ed.). Baltimore: Paul H. Brookes Publishing Co.

Includes updated information throughout the book on transition planning, ensuring access to the general education curriculum, pursuing postsecondary education, helping individuals secure housing, meeting the specific needs of young people with a range of disabilities, and navigating the complex challenges of transition.

5

Writing the
Transition Individualized
Education Program

Wendy Parent and Paul Wehman

Judy is 21 and is getting ready to exit high school this year. Both she and her mother are ready for the transition and eager for Judy to replace her school activities with paid employment. The transition coordinator at Judy's school prepares her well to be ready for the big day. As outlined in her transition individualized education program (IEP), Judy will start her own business, opening a kiosk in a coffee shop selling university logo items, magazines and newspapers, gift baskets, and coffee products. The coffee shop is lined up, the small business development center assists with developing a business plan, and linkages with the vocational rehabilitation counselor and the case manager (also known as a service coordinator) are made. Judy's transition coordinator arranges for Judy to participate in a work experience at the coffee shop during her last year of school while the business is in development, giving Judy the opportunity to become familiar with the people and the setting. Judy receives training and support from her school paraprofessional, including learning how to straighten and stock the condiment area, interact with customers, and become a team player with other coffee shop employees. In addition, Judy and her paraprofessional create a brief written survey asking customers which magazines and newspapers they would like to have available for purchase in the coffee shop. The rehabilitation counselor arranges a speech assessment and purchases start-up materials. Medicaid dollars are used to purchase a device to allow Judy to communicate verbally. The details are arranged. Judy will continue to maintain the condiment bar once her business is started in exchange for the coffee shop ringing up her sales, because she is unable to count money. Judy's service coordinator and mother will keep the records and order the merchandise. The customers and coffee shop employees have already gotten to know and like Judy, and everyone is prepared to offer her support. Yet in the end, Judy decides to exit school and attend a sheltered workshop instead of starting her own business.

What could have happened to create this unexpected outcome? An employer was ready and willing to enter into this new business endeavor. The rehabilitation counselor was prepared to provide the funding necessary for start-up and job coach support. Other agency and natural supports were in place to assist with business needs and long-term support. The missing piece in this community was an adult-supported employment provider with skilled job coaches who would provide training and accommodations for Judy. Without transitioning from the paraprofessional to adult job coach support, Judy will not receive the assistance she needs to learn how to run her business and the ongoing follow-along support to help her keep her business. The smaller adult-supported employment providers refused services; the largest provider recommended that Judy would be better suited at its sheltered workshop. After months of sitting at home and repeated attempts to arrange adequate job site support, Judy's mom agreed that the sheltered workshop would be the better way to go.

Molly attends the same school as Judy and, at the age of 21, is also preparing to exit school. Molly's transition IEP has a similar goal of self-employment as a postschool outcome; however, her steps to achieve this goal are quite different from Judy's. Molly's mom and transition coordinator always knew that Molly had a talent in the fun, colorful, "happy" art she did. The three of them get together and decide on the art pieces that would be best to print and sell. A business plan is developed with assistance from Molly's team, including a vocational rehabilitation counselor, service coordinator, transition coordinator, small business development center representative, benefits specialist, and Molly's mother. Molly starts her business while still in school with start-up funds from her rehabilitation counselor and job coach support from her school paraprofessional. In her school courses Molly learns helpful skills for her business, such as coloring techniques, organization, and record keeping. The transition coordinator provides opportunities on weekdays for Molly to practice making presentations to expand her customer base. At art fairs and craft shows, Molly receives support from her mother. Her paraprofessional, who is also a job coach vendor approved by vocational rehabilitation, is hired by her rehabilitation counselor on weekends to teach Molly how to do her own shows at local events. In addition, Molly's transition coordinator helps her obtain paid employment at an art store and arranges job coach training and support from the school paraprofessional. This gives Molly an opportunity to obtain work and social skills and will provide an income and daytime activity once Molly leaves school. An unexpected benefit is an employee discount on art products that Molly can use when buying her business materials. Her team assists with developing an updated business plan that outlines Molly's road map for expansion after leaving school. Molly's transition coordinator helps her create a PowerPoint presentation that describes her business and path to self-employment.

Now Molly has exited school. She is working part time at an art store and part time as a small business owner. She gives a presentation to a group of young women with disabilities. One woman remarks that she has learned this lesson from Molly: "If you make your own business, you make a lot of money and can be proud of it. It was so awesome. I wish I could be just like Molly when I grow up." In addition, Molly is a role model, mentor, and volunteer with middle school students and donates a portion of her sales to disability organizations.

How can Molly's life after school be so different from Judy's? The transition IEP for both students met the letter of the law in that they detailed, as stated in the Individuals with Disabilities Education Improvement Act (IDEA) of 2004 (PL 108-446),

- Appropriate measurable postsecondary goals based upon age-appropriate transition assessments related to training, education, employment, and where appropriate, independent living skills
- The transition services (including courses of study) needed to help the student in reaching those goals. (34 CFR 300.320[b] and [c]) (20 U.S.C. 1414[d][1][A][i][VIII])

Both Judy's and Molly's transition IEPs were guided by the essential elements of successful transition, including early transition planning, interagency collaboration, family and student involvement, appropriate curriculum and instruction, school inclusion, and adult services and community involvement (Beach Center on Disability, n.d.). However, only one of the young women successfully achieved her targeted postschool outcome. The advantage for Molly was that her annual IEP was adjusted to compensate for those pieces in her transition planning that were less than adequate, namely a lack of supported employment job coach services.

Transition is an outcome-oriented process that is driven by the vision of an adult life as identified by each student and his or her family (Bambara, Wilson, & McKenzie, 2007;

Cameto, 2005; Certo et al., 2008; Wehman, 2006b). Postschool goals drive the transition planning process, creating a blueprint with which to achieve them. When developing goals for the transition IEP, a good rule of thumb is to ask, "Does each step contribute to the overall goal of a more inclusive adult life?"

The annual transition IEP provides the mechanism to take action and outlines the specific steps needed to achieve goals. By starting early and revisiting the IEP annually, the transition team can make plans to help students reach their goals and modify these plans to address any bumps in the road along the way.

A 10-year study of 13- to 16-year-olds with disabilities found that 45% attended postsecondary education and 72% were employed at some time in the first 4 years out of school. However, compared with their peers without disabilities, they were less likely to enroll in postsecondary education or graduate from college, were less likely to be employed, and worked for a shorter period of time (National Longitudinal Transition Study-2, 2009).

WHERE TO BEGIN

It is important to have high expectations for every student and to develop postsecondary goals accordingly. This is the time to explore options and not rule out possibilities. Rather than think about what this student can do, think about what he or she likes or wants to do. Even if you cannot envision how a student with significant support needs will go to work, aim high with that goal in mind and work backward to determine the steps to get there. You have years to work toward reaching a student's postschool goals. During this time, teach as much skill acquisition as possible, implement supports to promote independence, and make modifications in how activities are completed. Here are some other things to consider.

Avoid Artificial Limitations

All too often, artificial limitations are set and time is lost because of developmental approaches that require a student to meet certain criteria before an employment goal is considered. For example, Johnny's annual IEP goal states that once he masters shredding documents in the classroom he will participate in a community-based work experience to prepare for employment. Unfortunately, what is not taken into account is the fact that Johnny does not need to know how to shred documents to be able to complete most job duties. Instruction provided in one environment often does not generalize to another, and community-based instruction is the most effective strategy for achieving employment outcomes (Wehman, 2006b).

Embrace Student and Family Desires

The services or funding resources available rather than the preferences of the student and his or her family frequently dictate postschool goals for adulthood. For example, Donna's family had always thought she would go to work after school; however, her transition IEP meeting did not reflect this. Following the announcement that there was a waiting list for services and agency budget cuts across the board, it seemed unlikely Donna would ever be a recipient of adult services. It is simply not acceptable to settle for placement on a waiting list for services or placement in a sheltered workshop as a student's transition outcome. In fact, the steps designed to achieve employment can also help reduce the need for adult services or help develop alternative strategies to bypass service shortages. For example, as a result of some individualized planning, one student started his own laundry service business and hired an employee who also provided support to the small business owner. Another student, with assistance from her benefits specialist, was able to use Social Security Work Incentives to purchase transportation and job coach support for her job in a legal office.

Remember: Employment First

Conveying a message of "employment first" (Niemac, Lavin, & Owen, 2009) by considering employment the first option for postsecondary goals can have a powerful impact on the attitudes and practices of the transition team and can ultimately improve employment outcomes. Introducing the topic into the transition planning meeting can result in an incredible exchange of creative energy and group brainstorming that promotes innovative employment exploration (Parent, 2009). In addition, the idea that employment is the intended outcome implies that "can't" or "won't" are not options and challenges the group to figure out another way to make it happen when traditional approaches are not viable.

WHAT TO DO IF MORE INFORMATION IS NEEDED

It is not uncommon for the transition team to be uncertain about which areas of employment a student might like to pursue. A student who has no work experience and limited community participation may not know how to respond to a question about what kind of work he or she would like to do. Many adolescents think that life after graduation is too far off to think about. A good place to start is to identify the student's passions. What does he or she like to do? What does the student typically do? What has he or she shown an interest in? What excites the student? People are more apt to work at something they enjoy or are interested in rather than something they do not like.

Explore Jobs and Careers

The transition IEP can help you explore jobs and careers in areas of a student's passions. One option for an annual goal might be to conduct employment exploration activities both in the classroom and in the community by looking at web sites, talking to different people (e.g., a friend, relative, or individual employed in a particular line of work), visiting businesses in the community (e.g., a bank, hospital, museum), learning about different job requirements (e.g., through videos, visits, or interviews), and job shadowing at community businesses. Figure 5.1 shows the Employment Exploration Activity form, a useful tool to help students evaluate their experiences and contribute to choosing a job.

Another goal might be to explore different types of businesses within a specific job area or passion. For example, the student may have a love of animals. Activities may include touring a service dog-training center, a veterinarian office, a pet wash, a pet store, the Humane Society, a doggie day care and resort, or a nature center. Using a student self-assessment form (see Figure 5.2) can help reveal likes and dislikes and what the student considers important in a job.

Employment Exploration Activity:
What Did I Do? What Did I Learn?

Teacher instructions: After conducting an Employment Exploration Activity either in the classroom or in the community, have the student (with any needed support) indicate his or her area of interest at the top of the page and then respond to each of the items that follows. For the last item, have the student circle the symbol that best represents his or her overall feelings. Responses can be used to facilitate individual or small-group discussions about work by asking, "What did you learn about yourself by completing this activity?" The student should also refer back to this information when determining what type of work options to pursue.

Student instructions: Think about what you just did and learned about work. Then rate your overall feelings about this work experience by circling the picture that best represents your thoughts. File these in your work folder.

Area of interest _____

People I visited or talked with:
1.
2.

Places or web sites I visited:
1.
2.

Classes I took, or things I learned:
1.
2.

Work experiences or job shadowing experiences I had:
1.
2.

What I learned about myself and this career area:

I like:

I don't like:

I learned:

Rate this area (circle one):   ♥ I loved it   ✌ It was OK   ☹ It was not good

Essentials of Transition Planning, by Paul Wehman
Copyright © 2011 Paul H. Brookes Publishing Co., Inc. All rights reserved.

Figure 5.1. Employment Exploration Activity form. (*Source:* Girls at Work Project, Kansas University Center on Developmental Disabilities, University of Kansas, 2009.)

Self-Assessment Form

Teacher instructions: During or upon completion of a work exploration activity, have the student (with any needed support) complete this self-assessment by indicating the name of the business at the top of the page and then placing a mark in the box that best represents his or her feelings about each item listed. Then have the student indicate whether he or she would like to work in that particular business, adding comments to explain why. It is important for students to understand why they like and dislike certain situations. The information provided may be used to hold individual or group discussions about work by asking the student what he or she liked or disliked and why. Completed forms should be referred back to when the student is considering work options.

Student instructions: Think about what you just experienced. What did you like or dislike? Write the name of the business at the top of the page. For each item listed, check the box that comes closest to how you feel. Then indicate whether you would like to work there by circling yes or no; add comments if you want to. File these in your work folder.

Think About What You See

Business: _____

	Liked	It was okay	Didn't like	Would you like to work here?
The workplace				Yes No
The people				Comments:
The job duties				
Overall job				

Figure 5.2. Job observational self-assessment form. (*Source:* Girls at Work Project, Kansas University Center on Developmental Disabilities, University of Kansas, 2009.)

Build and Teach Self-Determination Skills

Teaching self-determination skills is critical to enable students to actively participate in their transition process (Wehmeyer, Gragoudas, & Shogren, 2006; Wehmeyer & Palmer, 2003). Goals can be established that create opportunities for students to make decisions and evaluate different options contributing to their postschool employment success (Fowler et al., 2007; Getzel & Thoma, 2005; Wehmeyer & Palmer, 2003). Several curricula promote self-determination and can be integrated into a student's course of study, as is noted in Chapter 4. (Wehmeyer et al., 2004; Wehmeyer et al., 2009). Students can be assisted in preparing for and leading their transition IEP meetings in creative ways, such as by using collages, PowerPoint presentations, worksheets, and videos. See Figure 5.3 for an example of a PowerPoint presentation that one student developed to illustrate the problem-solving process that led to her vocational decision.

Focus groups conducted with 34 post-secondary students with disabilities identified self-determination (e.g., problem solving, learning about oneself, goal setting, self-management) as important to success. Yet activities that promote self-determination are often not included in transition planning, and when they are, secondary teachers report spending an average of only 6 hours a month on them (Getzel & Thoma, 2005).

HOW TO DECIDE ON GOALS

During the transition planning process, the student and his or her family must make clear their aspirations for after high school so that the transition team can translate those dreams into goals. This is the future orientation of the transition IEP; an essential element that cannot be overlooked. All too often, a student's transition IEP is conducted after the annual education goals of a student's IEP are decided.

Let's look at the following example:

Stanley is a young man with autism who has 1 more year of school left. Stanley's transition planning team felt that Stanley could benefit from a course of study that included English, history, music, computers, personal care skills, communication, and vocational training. These courses were meant to address his educational goals of obtaining a diploma, dressing neatly and shaving, responding to feedback from teachers without being aggressive, learning job interviewing skills, interacting appropriately with classmates, and developing computer skills. At the end of the IEP meeting, a teacher asked both Stanley and his parents what he would like to do after graduation. The outcome was unanimous: Stanley and his parents cited working, living in an apartment, having friends, being more financially independent, using the public bus, and having opportunities to play video games and have fun with others who have similar interests.

Unfortunately, Stanley's educational goals do not address employment, independent living, transportation, community participation, self-determination, or financial and social competence, nor do they move him closer to achieving his desired postsecondary outcomes. Stanley's recommended transition services included referral to vocational rehabilitation, service coordination, and placement on the Medicaid waiver list.

Today, 3 years after graduation, Stanley is still unemployed, sitting at home, and spending most of his time with his mother. He has learned to ride the public bus and travels to hang out at computer game stores.

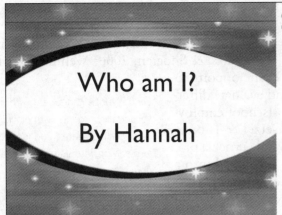

Who am I?

By Hannah

Strengths

- On time to work and have good attendance record
- Responsible at jobsite
- Interact well with co-workers
- Follow directions and observant to work when others are gone.

Goals for the Future

- Graduate from CHS
- Work as a Certified Nurses Aide
- Listen to parents, CHS staff, co-workers, Plainsview staff & friends
- I want to work at Broadmeadow serving pop & popcorn helping the residents get to their appointments.
- Go to college for nursing class.

Challenges (things I would like to improve)

- Be honest
- Take responsibility for my mistakes
- Safe boundaries when talking to friends
- Treating others with respect & accepting positive feedback from staff co-workers & friends

Why I choose to go to college to be a Certified Nurses Aide

- I want to help the nursing home residents get to their appointments & get their groceries. Then I want to work with nursing home residents part time. Also, I want to work with a kindergarten class to help them read better vocabulary comprehension & they would understand the harder vocabulary words when they get in the real world

Benefits of being a CNA

- Health insurance
- Paid vacations
- Days off for your children

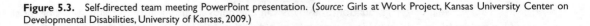

Figure 5.3. Self-directed team meeting PowerPoint presentation. (*Source:* Girls at Work Project, Kansas University Center on Developmental Disabilities, University of Kansas, 2009.)

Look to the Future

A very different scenario is encountered when the present level of performance, annual goals, course of study, and related services are developed with life after high school in mind (Wittig, 2009).

The IEP meeting starts by identifying what the student and family want for adulthood, which in turn defines the postsecondary goals or outcomes that drive this process. The educator shares the student's present level of performance as determined by a variety of formal and informal assessments (see Chapter 4 for more information on present level of performance). The discrepancies between where the student is currently and where he or she wants to be in adulthood are then broken down into broad steps that become annual IEP goals.

Each annual IEP goal is then broken down into specific objectives that, when combined, will help the student achieve the targeted goal. Completing every secondary goal each year will bring the student closer to achieving his or her overall postsecondary outcomes. This process is completed across all domains relevant to that student's predicted and current situation, including career and economic self-sufficiency (e.g., employment, vocational or technical training), postsecondary education and training (e.g., higher education, continuing/adult/career/technical education), and community integration and functional participation (e.g., residence, transportation and mobility, finances and income, self-determination, social competence, health and safety, recreation and leisure; Wehman & Wittig, 2009).

Take a Task Analysis Approach

Writing goals and objectives is similar to developing a task analysis (Snell, 1987; Wehman et al., 2007). For example, Gary works as a part-time office assistant in a large banking institution. His major duties include punching in, mailing bank statements, sorting mail, making departmental deliveries, vacuuming the vault, straightening the conference and break rooms, collecting the recycling, encoding documents, and wiping windows and mirrors. Each task has been broken down into steps that, when completed, result in the accomplishment of one work task and the need to move on to the next. Gary varies in his initial ability to perform each task and reaches skill acquisition at different times across tasks. His level of performance and mastery dictates how, when, and for how long he receives instruction as well as what modifications or supports are needed.

Just as completing each step leads to completing a work task and successfully performing his job, achieving each transition IEP objective leads to accomplishing an annual goal and successfully achieving postsecondary goals and outcomes. Conceptualizing goals and objectives in this way demonstrates the importance of connecting each component in the transition process to the ultimate outcome. Because everything relates back to postschool outcomes, the importance of writing functional, useful, and outcome-oriented goals in the transition IEP cannot be overstated (Wehman, 2009).

HOW TO GET STARTED

Although starting the transition process early is certainly desirable, it is never too late to get started on transition planning. Sophomores, juniors, seniors, and students in an 18-to-21 program should not be ruled out because they are older than the mandated age of 16. Start by considering where these students currently are, identify where they want to be as adults, determine the steps to get there, establish annual goals and objectives, and revisit the plan regularly to evaluate progress and make modifications as needed.

For example, Sally would like a full-time job working as a hair stylist or nail technician when she leaves school. She has no formal training and practices on family and friends. The steps to accomplish this goal include the following:

1. Explore different careers in the hair and nail fields.
2. Visit community colleges and technical schools to find out admission requirements and disability support services.
3. Visit hair and nail salons and learn more about the job market.
4. Talk with friends who are working as stylists and technicians.
5. Develop a portfolio of completed nails and hairstyles and personal testimonials.
6. Participate in a community-based work experience at a hair or nail salon.
7. Investigate alternative employment options, such as apprenticeships, resource ownership, self-employment, or carved and created jobs.
8. Complete the referral process for adult services.
9. Obtain paid employment in a hair or nail salon.
10. Apply to postsecondary classes or programs or pursue alternative employment options.

If Sally were in 9th or 10th grade it would seem likely that she could complete all of these steps while still in school. If she were a junior then perhaps she would omit Steps 1, 3, 5, and 6. If she were a senior, then Steps 2, 7, 8, and 10 would seem to have the most priority. If she were in an 18-to-21 program, emphasis on Steps 6, 7, 8, 9, and 10 might be most helpful.

Remember that transition IEP planning is an individualized process that is driven by the postschool goals of the student and family, the student's present level of performance, and the amount of time before graduation. Therefore, two students guided by the same adult outcome may vary in the specific blueprint they follow to achieve it.

WHAT TO INCLUDE IN THE TRANSITION INDIVIDUALIZED EDUCATION PROGRAM

Although the format of the transition IEP may vary across states and local school districts, the component parts of the document have many mandated similarities, such as transition assessment, measurable postsecondary goals, course of study, transition services, present levels of educational performance, and Summary of Performance (see Chapter 4 for more information on Summary of Performance). The time frame for completing each goal and objective and the person responsible for each goal is specified. Informal communication among team members and formal transition planning meetings provide opportunities to monitor progress and make adjustments as needed.

The transition IEP is the tool for helping students with disabilities achieve improved outcomes as indicated by satisfactory performance on the above transition measures.

EXAMPLES OF SUCCESSFUL POSTSCHOOL OUTCOMES

The strength of implementing a good transition IEP cannot be overemphasized. Consider the following case studies and the impact that the transition IEP has on helping each student achieve successful postschool outcomes.

 ## Amy

Amy is an 18-year-old who wants to graduate from school, get a job, live on her own, and drive her own car. Amy also has a cognitive disability. Her transition coordinator started early to help Amy achieve her life goals. During her sophomore year, Amy worked in the school-based enterprise learning how to run a business, interact with customers, handle finances, and develop a work ethic. The next year she began working at a variety of community-based work experiences arranged by the school. Amy decided she wanted to work in senior day care, so a specific work experience was arranged for her at a senior center during her last year in high school, which soon turned into permanent paid employment. Amy was able to move into her own apartment with a roommate using the money she was making at her job. Issues arose including transportation and the need for health insurance. Carpooling was arranged with co-workers and the Medicaid buy-in program was utilized for health care. Amy started taking a driver's education course with support from vocational rehabilitation. After 2 years Amy was able to pass her course, and vocational rehabilitation bought her a car.

 ## Matthew

Matthew, who has a cognitive disability, is 20 years old, lives in a small town, and is getting ready to leave school. By participating in community-based school–work experiences he found his passion—washing windows. Matthew's postschool goal was to obtain self-employment as a window washer. During the school year he received additional training on washing windows and conducted a needs assessment of his potential customers by delivering a brief survey he had designed. Vocational rehabilitation provided start-up funds to purchase equipment, advertising, signs, and a logo jacket. Matthew's paraprofessional assisted him during school with starting his own business, including putting together an appointment calendar, implementing a billing system, and using a receipt book. Matthew's clientele is expanding as word spreads about the excellent job he does.

 ## Heather

Heather, a young woman with cerebral palsy, is graduating at the age of 18 from a small, rural school. Her transition coordinator organized her transition team, which includes Heather, her mom, a service coordinator, a rehabilitation counselor, and teachers. Heather completed office tasks during her school-based work experience and participated in the school's student-run vending machine business. She liked the area of technology but was not sure what kind of job she wanted. Heather's teacher helped her explore different careers through online web sites and community visits. Her transition coordinator had heard about someone who had a business refurbishing scratched DVDs and investigated such a possibility for Heather.

She found out that one of the two video stores in town had a refurbishing machine, but the other did not. Heather's rehabilitation counselor purchased the equipment, and Heather is conducting an informal survey of potential customers regarding their disk repair needs. Her transition coordinator found a pawn shop in which Heather could set up her refurbishing machine, an arrangement known as a *business within a business*. The pawn shop readily agreed, believing that their sales of used games and disks would be boosted by the convenience of Heather's business right in their store. Heather's business plan outlines a plan for growth and expansion, including advertised drop boxes around town and eventually a mail-order component.

HOW TO OBTAIN SUPPORT FROM COMMUNITY AGENCIES AND RESOURCES

Transition is a collaborative process that requires schools and community agencies to work together to accomplish student goals (Rusch, 2008; Wehman, 2006b). It is too large of a process for any one agency to do alone. What is critical is that one agency assumes responsibility for bringing these entities together. Because education is an entitlement, but most adult services are based on eligibility, it makes sense that the school system be that coordinating link. Educators cannot operate in isolation without knowledge of and good working relationships with adult and community agencies. Often a school district will enter into a formal interagency agreement with certain adult service agencies to specify the roles of each. It is amazing what can be accomplished in a community when relationships among direct services professionals are developed, regardless of whether a formal agreement is in place.

Data from the Transition Service Integration Model indicated successful transition outcomes for 293 youth with disabilities who exited school at age 21. The majority (89%) experienced a seamless continuation of support, and more than half (60%) obtained competitive employment averaging 14 hours a week (Certo et al., 2008).

Use Locally Driven Services

Like school districts, many adult service agencies, such as vocational rehabilitation, are locally driven. This helps explain why one transition counselor will accept referrals for students at age 16, whereas another will not even talk with students until the second semester of their senior year of school. In addition, the capacity and quality of adult services can vary across locales and agencies. Whereas some community agencies are responsive, proactive, and innovative, others struggle with less than adequate service capacity, poor-quality services, or lack of funding. Many of these systemic issues are bigger than the school and need to be addressed on a local, state, or national level. Making and documenting referrals, bringing issues to the attention of school and agency administrators, and sharing possibilities with families will provide momentum for increased advocacy and systems change.

Stay Focused and Be Creative

Student transition IEP plans cannot be jeopardized because something that is needed for successful transition is not available in their present communities. If one applies the future-oriented, outcome-driven transition process described here and extensively documented in the literature, then student-directed goals remain the same, but the steps that teams take to achieve them might be different. This is the time to be creative, think beyond the typical, and change the way you do things.

For example, one rural community had no rehabilitation counselor because of hiring freezes. No one would be able to attend the transition meeting for an upcoming senior, and it might have been months before the traveling counselor would be in the area. The special educator met with the vocational rehabilitation secretary, found out what vocational rehabilitation could do for the student, and conveyed that information in the transition meeting. In addition, an arrangement was worked out that the paperwork could be completed, so the secretary sent it to central office to begin processing. In this way, when the itinerant rehabilitation counselor visited the area, an individualized plan for employment could be developed and service delivery initiated.

Was this the ideal situation for this student? Certainly not. But making these modifications ensured that critical services were not interrupted for this young lady, who wanted to attend cosmetology school and needed vocational rehabilitation support in order to do so.

Have a Strategy for Accomplishing Goals

One helpful strategy is to look at a goal and determine what it would take to accomplish it. If one of the steps is lacking a responsible agency or person, then explore within the planning team what other options might be available. Perhaps the educational curriculum can be modified, or another agency can provide the service, or a natural support can be used.

Next, break down the support and funding needs and brainstorm who can assist with each one. If one support need has five options and another has only one, then it would be most productive to use the one option for the support need that has it alone as its only option and choose among the four options for the other support need. Similar to a chess game, resources can be moved around and blended in different combinations to ensure a need is met (Morris, 2006).

For example, a rehabilitation counselor offered a student interested in working as a teaching assistant in a preschool job coach support, transportation assistance, environmental modifications for wheelchair accessibility, or a computer and educational software for negotiating a resource ownership situation with an employer (Griffin, Brooks-Lane, Hammis, & Crandell, 2006). The benefits specialist suggested the use of Social Security work incentives to cover transportation costs, and the service coordinator stated that he could purchase a computer for the student. Because no other funding options were identified for job coach support, environmental modifications, and educational software, vocational rehabilitation purchased these while the benefits specialist and service coordinator arranged the other resource options. This successful outcome was accomplished by creatively using the resources identified by the team. The key is not to write goals just to match the resources available. Rather, as one transition coordinator described it, "You just figure it out; you just do it."

Girls at Work offers young women with disabilities a self-directed, computerized curriculum built on recommended practice strategies for self-determination, supported and customized employment, and gender awareness. This curriculum guides the students through an eight-step, goal-oriented, problem-solving process to achieve an intended outcome of employment or postsecondary education (Wehmeyer et al., 2009).

Build Community Capacity

It is important to continue to build community capacity and not lose sight of the larger student population and upcoming transition-age students. One idea is to take the lead and visit community agencies that should be on board. Figuring out what their challenges are and what would help them to participate can be effective.

Another suggestion is to promote transition successes when the team comes together and makes it work. Developing a newsletter article for the school and adult agencies, posting a story on each organization's web site, or having a student and his or her family come and talk at an interagency meeting can be useful strategies.

Some communities conduct shared in-service training with school and adult service personnel. This provides participants with not only knowledge of recommended practices but also opportunities for networking and strategizing about approaches to transition.

Finally, data collection and evaluation are essential for improved transition services and outcomes. Referrals should always be made, even if services are not available. Without accurate data it is extremely difficult to encourage systems to expand capacity and accommodate students, particularly if the need for services is not evident. Sharing data, including postschool outcomes, support needs, student and family satisfaction, stakeholder feedback, service delivery gaps, and effective implementation strategies is essential for enabling evidence-based decision making that enhances local transition practices.

CONCLUSION

The transition IEP outlines the specific actions to take to help a student achieve his or her vision of a successful adult life. It is driven by the postschool goals identified by the student and his or her family, the student's present level of performance, and the amount of time before graduation.

It is important that transition teams set high expectations for students and emphasize employment as a postschool goal. Teams can determine suitable areas of employment by identifying students' personal passions and helping them explore jobs and careers. Once an employment is established it is important to be creative and flexible when planning for supports. Throughout the process, involve students as active partners in helping plan their own successful futures.

FOR FURTHER INFORMATION

Aligning Community Resources

National Center on Secondary Education and Transition (http://www.ncset.org/topics/resources/default.asp?topic=0)

Includes information on how state agencies and local communities can align resources to serve individuals with disabilities.

Writing a Transition IEP

Colorado Department of Education (http://www.cde.state.co.us/cdesped/TK.asp)

Includes information on writing a transition IEP and access to the transition planning toolkit.

National Dissemination Center for Children with Disabilities (http://www.nichcy.org/EducateChildren/transition_adulthood/Pages/iep.aspx)

Includes information to include in a student's IEP as part of transition planning.

6

Implementing the Transition Individualized Education Program

Ryan is 21 years old and graduated from the local special education program last year. He has a diagnosis of severe intellectual disability with an IQ score of 37 and a secondary diagnosis of mild cerebral palsy and visual impairment. He has a long history of getting his own way by acting out when he becomes upset. On occasion this behavior has been directed at teachers when they have attempted to intervene. Typically, his aggressive behavior is limited to temper tantrums.

Ryan lives at home with his parents, and they hope that he will be able to work soon. Until recently his parents thought that their son's only option was a sheltered workshop or an adult activity center. Ryan assists his family with household chores such as cleaning, laundry, and lawn work. He participates in a men's club with his father and other retired men from the community.

After graduating from high school, Ryan was referred to the vocational rehabilitation (VR) program, which arranged for him to receive a vocational evaluation. This testing indicated that he had a short attention span and performed poorly on routine, manipulative, and sorting tasks but was able to follow simple directions when they were specific and when prior demonstration had occurred. However, Ryan became uncooperative and noncompliant after working on a task for several minutes.

What will Ryan and his family do now that his education is completed? Who will help him get a job or more training? What hope can he have for his future? These are the questions thousands of students with disabilities and their families consider as they move closer to completing secondary-level education (Wehman, 2006b). The opportunities and challenges that await these young people in the adult community are unclear and depend heavily on the local economy and job opportunities, residential and transportation services, and community awareness and support for people with disabilities. For example, a student with severe cerebral palsy in one city may have tremendous opportunities for special travel accommodations and work opportunities, yet only 75 miles away, in a town with less money or less interest in helping people with disabilities, virtually no extra help may be available.

It should not and does not have to be this way, however. When the best practices in transition have been followed, students and their families should leave the familiar educational environment, in which they are legally entitled to a coordinated education plan, and smoothly enter the multilayered adult service system. To help make sure this happens, students and their families will need training, education, and experience to understand and take advantage of the opportunities offered through accessing and working with adult services. This, too, will help ensure that these individuals avoid potential pitfalls that arise from being unaware or unprepared.

The high school educator is a key resource person for making sure that students identify and use needed services and supports in their community. For example, he or she facilitates the involvement of the adult community service providers in planning and implementing a student's transition IEP. That is what this chapter is about.

It begins by taking a look at the interagency team, including some specific guidelines associated with implementing the transition IEP. This is followed by a look at interagency collaboration. Excerpts from interviews with various representatives from adult services who may be involved in the student's transition are included, particularly in the area of work, including the adult developmental disabilities agency, vocational rehabilitation, and employment service providers. The interviews provide insight in how to meet the needs of students with disabilities and how to make transition from school to adult services a positive experience. Next is a more in-depth look at the role of the school and community-based work experiences and their relationship with vocational rehabilitation. The chapter concludes with some questions for the interagency team to consider that will help ensure the successful implementation of a student's IEP.

THE INTERAGENCY PLANNING TEAM

An interagency transition planning team involves a number of key stakeholders who share responsibility for planning and implementing transition. Each member of the team can contribute to the process and oversees certain specific activities in implementation. As mentioned in other chapters, the members of the transition planning team will vary from school to school and, more important, will depend on the vision that the student and his or her parents have for a long-term transition IEP. Table 6.1 gives a brief overview of some of the primary responsibilities of each of the major participants in the transition planning process.

The team's major responsibility is to develop, implement, and monitor the transition IEP. For example, examination and interpretation of various assessments by team members can guide plan development and change, if necessary. The plan should identify not only the target adult outcomes in the areas of postsecondary education, training, employment, or community living that the student and his or her family desire at the time of graduation but also the steps and supports necessary to achieve and maintain these outcomes and who is responsible for each step.

Implementing the transition IEP involves working with the student and his or her family to create a vision of that student's future, developing goals and objectives, and setting a time line for achieving these objectives. The Individuals with Disabilities Education Improvement Act (IDEA) of 2004 (PL 108-446) requires that transition IEPs contain a time line for completing each goal and identify who is responsible for helping to implement these goals. The time line should be discussed by the transition team, with due consideration given to the time that will be required to meet some of the more challenging goals in the plan. See Table 6.2 for some dos and don'ts of the transition IEP implementation process as noted by Wehman and Wittig (2009).

As always the team must listen very carefully to the student and his or her family to understand what it is they want, where it is they want to go, and how they prioritize their goals. No transition IEP can be totally comprehensive because there rarely are enough resources or time to implement every necessary goal. Therefore, the team will have to help the student and family with the somewhat painful decision of deciding which areas to focus on most extensively in the early stages of the transition period. The team, too, must

Table 6.1. Responsibilities of individualized education program (IEP) team participants in the transition process

Team member	Responsibilities
Student	Leads and/or participates in the IEP meeting
	Understands and discusses possible educational goals
	Communicates with the teacher about wants and needs
Parents	Attends transition planning meetings
	Focuses the team's planning on the student and family's needs
	Provides input to the team on the student and family's needs
	Provides informal home and community skill training if possible
	Provides information to the team on sexual, medical, social, financial, or guardianship issues
Vocational rehabilitation counselor	Serves as a consultant to the transition planning team throughout the student's secondary school years
	Coordinates the student's vocational training job placement or supported employment placement
	Provides oversight and direct assistance into the eligibility process for vocational rehabilitation, including initial evaluations as well as job placement
Secondary special educator	Targets the student for transition planning and coordinates data management
	Organizes and attends individual transition planning meetings
	Identifies key referral needs and ensures that referrals are made to appropriate adult service agencies
	Coordinates the development and implementation of transition plans
	Ensures that student and parent choice and participation are maximized
Vocational educator	Attends transition planning meetings if the student requires vocational training or placement
	Consults with the transition team on local employment trends and specific skills required for jobs
	Helps identify and analyze community-based vocational training sites
	Provides instruction at community-based vocational training sites as necessary
	Provides a leadership role and job placement for students during their final years of school
Service coordinator from adult services agencies	Shares responsibility for assessing the student's needs as necessary
	Conducts home visits as needed
	Attends transition planning meetings if the student is in the final years of school or is at high risk of dropping out
	Provides follow-along services once the student has been placed in a supported living or a supported employment arrangement

remember that students and families will need information, guidance, and support from both the school and community service providers.

Naturally, what parents and students will need to know will vary from one to the next. However, one commonality tends to be that all parents begin to develop concerns as they come closer to the reality of their sons and daughters leaving the school system. For parents these issues generally relate to their loved one's well-being. For example, parents may ask, "Where will he live?" "How will she earn money?" "Will he have friends?" And, of course, "What will happen to her when I am no longer able to care for her?"

Educators at the high school level must help families and students connect with adult services before the students exit school. Some of the potential concerns that may be faced are illustrated in the replies from families to the following questions: "In your opinion, what

Table 6.2.   Dos and don'ts of transition IEP implementation

Dos

1. Do provide formal transition planning for students when they are 14 years of age. Do provide transition planning for those students who are at high risk of dropping out of school.

2. Do involve all school staff as appropriate in the transition IEP. The person who is responsible for organizing the IEP meeting should determine which staff from key disciplines should participate. The main factor will be their level of contact with the student and whether they understand what that student's goals and outcomes should be.

3. Do involve the student in the transition meeting. Structure the meeting in such a way that the student has an opportunity to take an active role in the planning process. Parents and/or other family members should also be directly involved in such a way that they do not feel overwhelmed by a large number of intimidating staff members.

4. Do make sure that each of the goals in the transition IEP is stated in such a way that it specifies a meaningful desired outcome, such as attendance at a local community college or participation in a local recreation program. A good goal involves a measurable outcome; a poor goal involves a process activity, such as getting on a waiting list.

5. Do establish a checklist that notes the services that the student will need to be matched with in the local community, such as mental health, Social Security, or employment services.

6. Do make sure that a lead person is identified as being responsible for providing oversight on each of the goals in the transition IEP. This person does not necessarily have to implement the goals but must be accountable to the student, the family, and the rest of the team. The person designated must have the authority to be able to cut across bureaucratic lines and different disciplines.

7. Do arrange for increased involvement by selected adult service agencies as the student nears graduation or exits school. This is a key time. It may also be the time when the greatest breakdown occurs, leaving the student with no place to turn once the special education entitlement has ended.

Don'ts

1. Don't involve large numbers of adult service programs that are not going to be able to help the student because they do not provide a service that the student needs.

2. Don't involve adult service programs too early in the transition planning process. The rest of the team as well as the adult service agency will view this as poor planning, because the time between completion of school and exit is too great.

3. Don't hold a transition meeting in such a way that the parents, family, or student feel that they are being patronized, or that the IEP has already been developed and that they are merely being told what has to be completed.

4. Don't give up easily at gaining input from the student and his or her parents. Instead, work at finding original and creative ways to gain the confidence of the family. Help the student and family design a future-oriented vision of where they want to be in the next 5 to 7 years.

5. Don't simply craft paper interagency agreements that have no specific outcomes or resources allocated to the goals. The lead person on the transition IEP team must take responsibility for ensuring that interagency participation is genuine and that there is true integrity in what agencies say they will do.

6. Don't stop communicating with parents just because the transition IEP is signed and the meeting has been completed. Be sure to have an ongoing time line for completing various goals, and make sure the student or family has taken partial responsibility for completing those goals.

7. Don't fail to follow up after the student leaves school. Follow up within the first 6 to 12 months after the student has exited school to determine how effective the transition plan has been at helping the student attain his or her goals.

information is needed by families to help ensure that their sons and daughters make a successful transition from school to adult services?" And "What concerns do you have for your son or daughter as he or she makes the transition from school to adult life?"

- "I believe the family needs to know what services are available, exactly what they can or cannot offer the young adult, and who is to be contacted to obtain services."

- "We want to know what is available in the job market—what we can expect when our child is no longer in school. Will there be someone to take over where schools left off, or will our child be forced to stay at home being nonproductive? Suppose she is placed in a situation where he is not happy? Will she go to the bottom of the list again? Are there enough personnel in the adult service system to take over this task, or is the person with a disability put on the back burner until something or someone becomes available to assist?"

- "We want our son to live as independently as possible in the least restrictive setting and to work in the community, live in a group home or apartment, and have opportunities for recreational activities and social outings for continual social growth. We have fears and concerns: not enough resources available, not enough finances to fund programs for our family members, our son being ridiculed or not accepted for who he is by others without disabilities, and opportunities not being offered to him because of lack of understanding and fear on the part of employers and co-workers."

The parents' responses speak volumes about the need for information about resources, staffing, and service opportunities. The poignant responses also show hope that promises will be fulfilled, fear of rejection, guarded optimism about opportunities for meaningful work and growth, and concerns about their adult child being misunderstood and isolated. For teenagers, preparing for and entering the adult community can be puzzling. For students with disabilities and their families, who must deal not only with the normal complexities of adult life but also the additional complexities of an unfamiliar service and support system, the preparation and transition process can be most challenging. For this reason, the school must play a leading role in fostering transition for these students.

Questions for Consideration

The interagency planning team also works to plan, develop, and implement the student's transition IEP. Some of the questions the teams consider when implementing the plan follow.

- Does formal transition planning begin for students when they reach the age of 16?
- Are the appropriate school and adult service personnel involved?
- Has a transition planning meeting been held? Has a transition IEP been written to include who is supposed to do what and on what time line?
- Does the transition plan cover the appropriate target areas, such as employment, post-secondary education, independent living services, financial and income needs, recreation and leisure needs, medical and therapeutic needs, social and recreational needs, transportation needs, and advocacy and legal needs?
- Does the plan reflect a true vision of the potential of the student, or does it merely offer only what the service delivery system provides?
- Is the plan updated annually (at a minimum)?
- Are exit meetings held to finalize plans for the transition from school to employment?

The answers to these and other student-specific questions will give the team the direction needed to provide quality services and make any modifications. The result should be sound plan implementation including the smooth transition of the student from school to adult services.

Families with youth with disabilities have a number of challenges including balancing expectations, available time and energy, understanding and gaining access to resources and services, and understanding role of transition specialist (Chambers, Hughes, & Carter, 2004; Cooney, 2002; Grigal & Neubert, 2004).

INTERAGENCY COLLABORATION

The role of the teacher overseeing transition services is much easier and more effective when there are targeted agencies working together to help the student move closer to his or her goals. Although there are a number of possible services, this section focuses on three partners that may be involved with facilitating or providing employment services and supports to individuals with disabilities. This includes the state developmental disabilities agencies, state vocational rehabilitation services, and community employment service providers. Notably, the services available through these entities are most effective if the school program proactively incorporates transition planning into middle school and secondary-level activities. The following interviews with key players offer insight into how services may be collaborated and implemented.

State Developmental Disabilities Agencies

State mental health and developmental disability agencies are located in each state. Many programs serve only people with intellectual and psychiatric disabilities. Also, unlike public schools, these programs have waiting lists and eligibility requirements. If indicated, the school may help facilitate the family of a young adolescent with a disability with signing up for service coordination assistance from local mental health/mental retardation services programs as early as possible. For youth with intellectual and developmental disabilities, these agencies offer case management, housing and employment services, and funding for eligible individuals. Job coaching and supported employment services may be provided or contracted from community employment service providers for eligible individuals.

An excerpt from an interview with a program manager yields some insights into possible ways to coordinate with them for employment services.

Interviewer: How can the school system coordinate with developmental disabilities agencies and why is this important?

Program Director: First, the school staff should become familiar with services and who to contact. Then, generally we recommend that the designated personnel initially contact the provider when the student's IEP includes community employment as a long-range goal. As a member of the student's transition team, we can help design a transition plan and help determine case management needs and ongoing funding resources. It is advisable for students and their families or advocates to apply for VR and other adult services early on.

There are often waiting lists for these services, although fortunately, some states have made transitioning youth a funding priority (Stancliffe & Lakin, 2005). Therefore transition specialists need to be aware of services in their local communities.

Interviewer: What advice do you have for school personnel who are leading transition?

Program Director: Schools and other team members play an important role in helping young adults with disabilities prepare for their futures, including work. It is very important to remember that these students' typically developing peers and classmates will be their future employers, co-workers, and neighbors. Fully integrating students with disabilities into the school and educating others on the abilities of those with disabilities should help reduce future barriers to employment and community integration. In addition, transition specialists need to be aware of the circumstances in their local communities so that they can help youth identify and obtain these services accordingly. For example, it is very important to not only know how we work but also how we work with the state VR agency and employment service providers as well as our eligibility requirements for services. Keep in mind, too, that we are a valuable resource for referral to other services.

Interviewer: Why should service coordinators within the local developmental disabilities agencies attend IEP meetings in early stages of transition planning?

Program Director: They should attend because they have a wealth of information to share. For example, service coordinators have very specific knowledge that can greatly benefit older students, but it can also benefit younger students by helping them understand the opportunities available in the community. Service coordinators can also provide examples about how others have succeeded. Illustrations on what is possible not only helps the student and parents envision a positive future but can also assist the team in developing a meaningful plan.

State Vocational Rehabilitation Services

A primary resource for transition employment support is the state VR agency. Federal regulations favor the active participation for VR in planning for youth in transition. A few years before leaving school, the state VR counselor can participate in IEP planning meetings and can also be a party to interagency cooperative transition agreements so that services are delivered as efficiently as possible.

Therefore, long-range planning should also take place. Various activities and associated time frames (prior to the student exiting school) to both initiate adult services and vocational rehabilitation's involvement and to coordinate or receive direct services if indicated should be addressed. For example, many experts recommend referring youth to services available through VR as early as their secondary school years so there is plenty of time for services to be arranged. Furthermore, early referral leads to stronger partnerships and better service delivery to youth. The range of service that can be provided to youth is considerable, yet these are not entitlement services. Therefore, eligibility requirements have to be met for services, and funding resources will vary. Thus, the teacher must become familiar with their states practices.

The VR counselor helps students plan for and secure appropriate employment. For students with more significant support needs, VR counseling ideally occurs prior to their leaving school. It may also require a referral for supported employment services in order for these students to obtain and maintain work in the

Special education and VR programs are required by law to cooperatively plan for the transition of students with disabilities into the work environment (Certo et al., 2008). Facilitating a student's transition from a school program to the workplace requires providing school instruction, planning for the transition process, and placing that student into meaningful community-integrated employment. The interagency planning team also works to plan, develop, and implement the student's transition IEP.

community. The VR counselor not only helps students access supported employment services but also remains in contact with students and supports them as they adjust to work and community living. Some students pursue postsecondary training or education in preparation for employment; the counselor can assist these students in planning and securing the postsecondary activities that will lead to future employment. Finally, some students will seek employment directly on exiting their school program. The counselor can help ensure that these students receive timely, well-planned job development and job placement assistance to bridge the gap between school and work.

The counselor must take a leadership role in individualizing the employment service plan and must time the implementation of this plan to the student's school program and postsecondary interests. The following dialogue describes the role of a VR counselor who serves transition-age students. Note that policies and procedures will vary from state to state.

Interviewer: Tell me about your role as a member of the transition team.

VR Counselor: In first meeting with the student, family, and school staff, I emphasize two features: the vocational goal and the means to obtain that goal. At this point, the school and family can assist the student by providing volunteer experience, externships, or in-school training programs. This allows the student to experience many types of work environments as well as determine his or her interests, skills, and abilities and potential support needs. It makes choosing a goal during the senior year much more realistic and accurate. It also helps identify which employment support services may be needed, such as supported employment. I also make sure that the family and client have a good understanding of local adult services and the role these services can play in transition.

I typically become involved with clients during a student's last couple years of school, and then meet regularly with the student during the last year of school. This is not to say that vocational planning should wait until then. Exploration and training as early as ages 14 to 16 is very helpful and essential for some students, like those with significant support needs.

VR counselors can provide vocational counseling and guidance and vocational evaluation to students. They can also assist a student with making decisions about what he or she needs to do in order to achieve a specific vocational goal and recommend supports and areas that need to be worked on to enhance employment opportunities. As the student moves closer to leaving school, formal plans can be made by writing an individualized plan for employment, and that plan may be implemented, perhaps through a referral for job development services.

The rehabilitation counselor should be a vital member of the transition team, leading the team in the area of employment but also lending expertise, resources, and ideas to all areas that will affect the student's employability. Referrals made to specific service providers can provide the VR counselor with a good core group of adult service providers with which to coordinate services and lend support.

Interviewer: Many adolescents and young adults with disabilities have limited vocational training and employment experience. How can VR help these individuals?

VR Counselor: The VR counselor can start with a vocational evaluation. For example, a series of vocational situational assessments at real job sites offers valuable information. You can observe a student's skills and behaviors while he or she is performing work tasks. This helps you form a more accurate opinion about the student's interests, abilities, and potential support needs. Participation in community-based vocational educational programs that include opportunities to explore the world of work through situational assessment and on-the-job training can enhance the student's vocational guidance.

Interviewer: What sets the stage for an effective working relationship between VR and the school system?

VR Counselor: The VR counselor must know the policies and procedures of his or her organization, including the roles and responsibilities of key stakeholders. There must be open communication and a relaxed rapport among parties to give the student and family the feeling of having a united team, as well as a willingness to exchange information freely and quickly to expedite cases, meetings, and reports. However, most of all, there must be a sense of sharing responsibility for the future of the student. The parties must share background information, opinions, ideas, and resource knowledge and lend support to final plans. The VR counselor can be the bridge between the school program and the adult community for the student with a disability. It is important for school staff to be aware of VR resources and their potential role in assisting the exiting student with a disability.

Interviewer: Does the vocational rehabilitation counselor's role in the transition process vary according to local needs and resources?

VR Counselor: In a few instances rehabilitation counselors are school based and are employed by a school district or a cooperative of districts; however, most counselors are employed by state VR agencies and may have limited time and resources to devote to coordinating transition services. Whether a counselor is based in a school or a state agency, his or her activities may include career and psychosocial counseling; consultation with special education and vocational education teachers; and coordination of school, family, and community efforts at career planning and implementation.

Community Employment Service Organizations

These agencies assist people with disabilities in obtaining and maintaining employment. The following excerpt from an interview with a program manager provides information on what they may be able to bring to the table.

Interviewer: What services are typically offered by an ESO?

Program Manager: Specific services vary but could include vocational assessments, benefits planning and counseling, job placement assistance, and supported employment. Some providers may also offer life skills training.

Interviewer: How are you funded?

Program Manager: Many programs obtain funding through contractual agreements, for example, with the vocational rehabilitation services. Some work cooperatively through contracts with school systems to offer work experience programs and/or employment services like job coaching or supported employment.

Interviewer: When do employment support organizations get involved with transition?

Program Manager: Our involvement often relies on the availability of funding from a resource like VR or the school. Sometimes, we have been involved with serving those students who have more significant support needs by providing situational assessments and/or supported employment prior to or during the last year or two before exiting school. However, it was not always this way. Over the years we have formed a strong partnership with the schools and VR. Together we are committed to enhancing transition to work for youth with disabilities. Right now, we are working in partnership to develop community-based vocational programs in various business settings. There is also a move toward supporting students in postsecondary educational settings. We are working now to find ways to establish contracts to offer this type of support service to students. The bottom line is that we are always working together as a team to identify service gaps and find ways to make sure that our students make a smooth transition from the school to adult life and services. This means continually evaluating what we are doing right and finding new ways to solve any problems that surface along the way. It also means staying abreast of best practices. This allows us to enhance service delivery.

Interviewer: What are One-Stop Career Centers?

Program Manager: One-Stop Career Centers are increasingly becoming available across the country. These organizations can assist in a variety of areas, including with the job search, job accommodations, adaptive housing, mobility training, and skills training to promote self-awareness and self-esteem for the person with a disability. It is important for secondary-level educators working with students with disabilities to learn about and interact directly with specific adult service resources in their individual communities.

Table 6.3 offers more examples of how One-Stop Career Centers can help in implementing the transition IEP. The remainder of this chapter will take a closer look at the role of the school and its relationship with vocational rehabilitation.

The School

Schools require a number of administrative procedures to implement effective transition planning. It is helpful first to designate the teacher who is responsible for the IEP as the transition service coordinator for the student. This teacher will then develop an individualized transition plan in cooperation with the developmental disabilities service coordinator, the VR counselor, and any other people whom the student or family wishes to invite to transition-oriented IEP meetings. This assists in establishing clear communication among all people involved in long-range planning for the student. The IDEA legislation states

Table 6.3. Examples of how One-Stop Career Centers can help in implementing the transition IEP.

Building Awareness About Employment, Careers, and Available Services Among Students with Disabilities

Students visit the One-Stop Career Center to use the resource area to develop awareness of job and career possibilities and to learn about services that are available.

Making Opportunities Available for Career Exploration

Career club curricula are developed within school programs and aligned with standards of learning. Collaborative outreach takes place with the Parent Resource Center (PRC) to engage parents more actively in their children/students's transition planning. Career club activities are coordinated with One-Stop Career Center resources and services.

Mentoring programs are established with local businesses through the One-Stops and school programs.

Internship opportunities with local businesses are developed for youth students with disabilities from the public schools and programs are developed with local businesses.

Staff are trained to target the community and labor market as resources for enhancing career exploration.

Supporting Actual Engagement by Participants in Career Development Through Employment

Support services focus on job outcomes and career development and are individualized and continuous.

Customized employment resource staff at One-Stops provide individualized representation and negotiation with employers at the work place, when needed.

From Targett, P., Young, C., Revell, G., Williams, S., & Wehman, P. (2007). Customized employment in the One-Stop Career Centers. *TEACHING Exceptional Children, 40*(2)8; reprinted by permission.

that when transition services are not being delivered and/or objectives are not being met in a timely manner, the school system is responsible for reconvening the transition committee.

Many students with disabilities and their families experience a sense of isolation from the community. A primary example of this isolation is the limited participation of these students in work and work-related activities. By encouraging and supporting middle school and high school students with disabilities to obtain identification cards, develop and maintain résumés, and seek out work opportunities, the school program can expand student involvement in the community, knowledge of work requirements, and awareness of individual interests. These activities provide a firm base of information for the transition committee to use in helping individual students to plan for postsecondary interests and service needs.

The following interview with a special education teacher of students with intellectual disabilities lends insight into this important perspective.

Interviewer: What is community-based instruction, and why is it important?

Teacher: The greater one's independence in basic skills of daily living, the less one will have to depend on others for support. Therefore, it is important to teach skills where they will be used. With greater independence comes more community participation and choices. Community-based instruction is instruction that takes place within the community itself. Community skills, such as those having to do with travel, grocery shopping, and eating out, are used in the community. Community-based vocational education takes place in real workplaces. A well-developed curriculum provides students with an opportunity to use new skills and apply them across multiple settings, thereby enhancing skill acquisition.

Interviewer: Are work experiences especially critical to students with limited career options?

Teacher: Yes, students should be engaged in some type of work experience by age 15. As students get older, the focus shifts to paid employment. VR involvement is individualized to students' needs. Work experiences, including paid employment, offer opportunities for students to learn about themselves and the world of work. Students learn soft skills to succeed in the workplace and other skills. They also gain insight into their vocational likes and dislikes and the potential accommodations or workplace supports they will need.

Work also has a positive impact on family members. Often, this is when they really begin to see what is possible for their child in the future.

It is also important to remember that this is not done in isolation. The success of community-based instruction hinges on the team working together for the common good of the student.

Table 6.4 lists the steps for designing and implementing a community-based vocational instruction program.

Table 6.4.   Designing and implementing a community-based vocational instructional program

Step	Activities
1. Conduct a job market analysis to identify potential jobs in the community that would be appropriate for students with severe disabilities.	Survey the telephone yellow pages. Read the classified section of the newspaper. Contact local business organizations (e.g., chamber of commerce). Survey school graduates to determine jobs held by individuals with disabilities in the community.
2. Identify businesses with the targeted jobs.	Establish a school policy for contacting businesses. Identify individual(s) responsible for contacting businesses. Determine school insurance coverage and liability issues. Develop a list of employers to approach. Schedule a time to write letters, telephone, and visit employers. Create a file for each business contacted.
3. Contact personnel directors or employers.	*By letter and/or telephone* a. Briefly describe the school's community-based program. b. Identify jobs that may be appropriate for training. c. Schedule a time to visit and explain the program further. *In person* a. Describe the purpose of community-based instruction. b. Discuss employer, teacher, and student responsibilities on the job site. c. Discuss the school's insurance and liability policies. d. Target tasks and time periods for training. e. Schedule a visit to observe the identified tasks to develop job duty and task analyses. f. Send a thank-you note.
4. Select and analyze appropriate jobs for community-based training.	Visit the job site location. Discuss the identified jobs with the site supervisor. Discuss the job site rules and regulations. Observe co-workers performing the job duties. Select the tasks best suited for students with severe disabilities. Develop a job duty schedule and task analysis for the activities selected. Identify times when the employer or department supervisor is available for training. Request at least 1- to 2-hour blocks of time for each site identified. Agree on a start date.

5. Schedule community-based training.	Identify students to receive vocational training.
	Hold IEP/ITP meetings for students.
	a. Identify student training needs.
	b. Discuss the purpose of community-based vocational training with transition team members.
	c. Write vocational goals and objectives.
	Match students to available sites.
	Have the student, parent(s), employer, and school representatives sign community-based training agreements.
	Develop a daily schedule.
	Develop a transportation schedule.
	Send a copy of all schedules to the school principal, special education supervisor, parents, and employers.
	Provide parents with information on individual insurance coverage for liability.
6. Design individual systematic instruction programs.	Modify job duty schedules and task analyses based on student characteristics.
	Select a data collection procedure.
	Take a baseline of student performance on all tasks to be taught.
	Select an instructional procedure.
	Select a reinforcer.
	Implement the training program.
	Take probe data on student performance.
	Routinely review student data and modify the program format as needed.
	Review student goals and objectives for training and update as needed.

Key: IEP/ITP, individualized education program/individualized transition plan.

COOPERATIVE RELATIONSHIPS

The Rehabilitation Act Amendments of 1998 and the Transition Process

The Rehabilitation Act Amendments of 1998 (PL 105-220) emphasize the provision of support and services through the rehabilitation system for high school students with disabilities who are exiting or preparing to exit school programs. The Rehabilitation Act Amendments of 1992 (PL 102-569) contain a definition of transition services that matches what is contained in IDEA:

1. A coordinated set of activities for a student, designed within an outcome-oriented process, that promotes movement from school to postschool activities, including postsecondary education, vocational training, integrated employment (including supported employment), continuing and adult education, adult services, independent living, or community participation.

2. The coordinated set of activities shall be based upon the individual student's needs, taking into account the student's preferences and interests, and shall include instruction, community experiences, the development of employment and other postschool adult living objectives, and, when appropriate, acquisition of daily living skills and functional vocational evaluation. (§300.18)

The first part of this definition focuses on services that the student receives after exiting the school program. These services reflect a representative sample of the wide array of postschool activities that might be used by students with a disability who are entering the adult community. At times these services are used in sequence, such as postsecondary education followed by employment. But services might also be used simultaneously, such as supported employment along with other adult services and community living supports. The second part of this definition of transition services focuses on activities that may occur during the school program to support preparation and planning for transition. This section emphasizes relating the school program to the community and incorporating postschool employment and daily living objectives into classroom activities and planning.

This definition is a balanced statement of how the transition process is embedded in the Rehabilitation Act Amendments. It is similar to the IDEA definition of the school's transition responsibilities. Why is this important to students such as Ryan, the student discussed at the beginning of this chapter? Parents and professionals alike can draw on the resources provided by The Rehabilitation Act to facilitate the transition of Ryan and students like him from school to adulthood.

Ryan needs transition planning and VR services in his community. He needs support at all levels for getting a job, getting training on the job, and maintaining the job. Table 6.5 lists some of Ryan's employability issues and ways they might be resolved. This table provides guidelines for how rehabilitation counselors and local community rehabilitation programs can work together.

Components of meaningful school- and community-based work experiences include high-quality work experiences, careful planning to match work experiences with each youth's interests and assets, linkages between work experience and academic content or school curriculum, and individual supports and accommodations (American Youth Policy Forum & Center for Workforce Development, 2000; Benz, Yovanoff, & Doren et al., 1997; Bremer & Madzar, 1995; Goldberger, Keough, & Almeida, 2001; Haimson & Bellotti, 2001; Luecking & Fabian, 2000; Mooney & Scholl, 2004; Scholl & Mooney, 2005).

The Vocational Rehabilitation Counselor and the School

The goal of the cooperative relationship between the VR program and the educational system is to prevent any gap in services as students with disabilities make the transition from school to their postsecondary activities. The number of people with disabilities served at any one time by a VR counselor varies, however, and it is not unusual for an individual counselor to be responsible for assisting 100 to 200 people at various stages of the VR process. Even those VR counselors who spend the majority of their time working with young people who have disabilities usually carry large caseloads. VR counselors cannot possibly attend every IEP meeting for every student with a disability age 14 and older and still effectively respond to the multiple and diverse needs of the full range of people for whom they coordinate services. It cannot be emphasized enough that services must be planned much earlier than the year the student will leave school.

Table 6.5. Ryan's work needs

Employability issue	Intervention
Getting oriented to the job site	Implement route training within work area.
Learning to ride a bus	Develop instructional program.
Learning specific job	Teach easiest tasks first.
Refusing to work	Devise a paycheck reinforcement schedule.
Working fast enough	Build up speed little by little using a reward system.
Getting along with co-workers	Identify interested co-workers.

CONCLUSION

This chapter has focused on some ways to enhance implementation of the student's transition IEP. Different roles of some of the professionals involved in helping to implement the transition IEP were provided. It is important to use adult service professionals in the IEP transition process and to understand and take advantage of the expertise that educators, caseworkers, and VR counselors can provide. And of course, it is important for the student and his or her family to be the driving force behind implementing the IEP transition plan.

FOR FURTHER INFORMATION

Improving Practices

Regional Resource Center Program (http://www.rrfcnetwork.org.)

Provides services including consultation, information services, specially designed technical assistance, training, and product development to all states as well as the Pacific jurisdictions, the Virgin Islands, and Puerto Rico. Services offered by the RRC Program.

National Standards and Quality Indicators for Secondary Education and Transition

Transition Solutions (http://www.transitionsolutions.org/)

A strategic alliance of top researchers, educators, and technical assistance providers in the areas of transition systems change, education reform, postsecondary education, workforce preparation, and team and leadership development.

One-Stop Career Centers and Available Services

America's Service Locator/Career One Stop (http://www.servicelocator.org)

Provides wealth of information by state on career opportunities, salaries and benefits, education and training, and résumé advice, among other things.

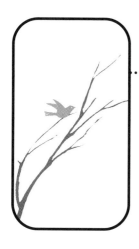

7

Employment

Community-Based Choices

Pamela Sherron Targett and Paul Wehman

Excitement is in the air as Ms. Franklin's students put on their coats and jackets and prepare to leave the classroom. Today is the first day that the students will participate in the school's community-based vocational education program. Over the years, Ms. Franklin and her colleagues have worked hard to incorporate work experiences into every student's educational program. However, this has proved challenging at times, especially for some of the students with more significant support needs, because of limited resources and time constraints. Now, finally, after months of planning, a new, more comprehensive program has been developed to facilitate work experiences for students in transition. During program development, the team was very careful to incorporate into the design recommended practices such as person-centered planning, strong individual support during the work experiences, family involvement, and objective evaluation of the student's performance throughout the process.

The work experiences will take place within a variety of community businesses. The goal is to give each student an opportunity to learn about work. Not only does each student get exposure to a variety of employment settings and vocational skills across occupations but also those people involved with the student's transition to work (e.g., the transition coordinator, the vocational rehabilitation counselor, job coaches, family members) have the opportunity to learn more about the student's vocational abilities, interests, preferences, and potential support needs. Although this information will prove beneficial to all students, it is particularly useful to those students who have more significant support needs and require assistance with obtaining and maintaining work in their community.

The newly developed work experience program offers opportunities to learn about work in a variety of businesses in the retail (clothing store), financial (bank), and health (hospital) fields as well as in the government (local and state). In addition, students who have particular aptitudes, talents, or interests in other areas will have the opportunity to participate in vocational exploration, assessment, and training in other businesses that are more specifically related to their particular desires. For instance, if a student has a passion for animals, he or she may participate in a work experience at a veterinarian's office, a pet store, or an animal grooming service; if a student has a passion for cars, he or she might spend time learning more about work at an automobile dealership, a garage, or a rental car establishment.

Over the past months, Ms. Franklin and other members of the team have met with human resources representatives and other officials within the various businesses to discuss the purpose of the work experiences, expected outcomes, and other conditions, including site supervision. In addition, legal aspects of the work experiences have been examined, such as compliance with the Fair Labor Standards Act (FLSA) of 1938 (PL 75-718) and the Americans with Disabilities Act (ADA) of 1990 (PL 101-336).

Whenever there was a commitment from a business to participate, the following steps were initiated, with some variation by workplace. First the team was introduced to department managers. This involved learning more about the various positions within the business, workplace policies and procedures, and existing workplace supports. In addition, instructional materials, including a process for student evaluation and feedback, were developed. Through these and other activities, an array of typical tasks within various departments was identified for students to sample. For example, in state government the following tasks were identified: office work (e.g., entering data, filing, shredding documents), grounds work (e.g., mowing, watering, weeding flower beds), building maintenance (e.g., painting, blowing debris off sidewalks, cleaning elevators), and parking division (e.g., refilling ticket dispensers, washing the vehicles used to police the lots). After developing the program, the team devised a plan for supporting each student's experience.

All students, regardless of the severity of their disability, should look forward to growing up and leading an adult life. This includes having an opportunity to pursue happiness, live in the community, and work to earn money to enhance the quality of their life. Yet there is no doubt that this is easier said than done. How can employment become a reality for students with disabilities—particularly those with the most significant support needs? Just like anyone else, a student with a disability has two work options: work for someone else or be self-employed. Individualized planning specific to each student's needs must take place to realize either option. Based on information uncovered during this planning process, students will choose and access various education and transition services.

Some students may learn about work by participating in the school's community-based vocational education program and from there seek employment. Others may access postsecondary education options by choosing one of two pathways. The first pathway is to take courses guided by career goals and interests in various postsecondary settings (e.g., community college, university, adult education programs). This path, which typically includes a work-based learning component (e.g., an internship, service-learning), gives a student an opportunity to experience college and other adult learning options. All of this is geared toward meeting the student's personal and vocational goals.

Some students may pursue the more traditional pathway in postsecondary education by pursuing a particular course of study (e.g., degree, certification) that is aligned with their future vocational desires. Note that no matter what approach the student takes, the ultimate goal is for him or her to become employed.

So how does a student with a disability, particularly one with significant support needs, make employment a reality? This chapter discusses ways to assist students with disabilities to obtain competitive employment. We begin by taking a look at some approaches to vocational training in community businesses, including employer-led initiatives. We also review emerging practices in which students participate in activities or courses in postsecondary education settings that do not

The knowledge base about postsecondary education often focuses on students with learning disabilities, including those with sensory and physical impairments, who compose the largest percentage of college students with disabilities (National Longitudinal Transition Study–2, 2006). Much less is known about students with intellectual disabilities because these students have not typically been supported in the area of postsecondary education. The existing research provides descriptions of students and program outcomes (Grigal, Neubert, & Moon, 2001; Hart & Grigal, 2008; Neubert, Moon, & Grigal, 2004). These and other studies show the potential that postsecondary education programs have to increase access to integrated work and social activities as well as to improve collaboration among local education agencies and adult service providers.

focus on earning an undergraduate degree. Then we review vocational support models, including supported employment, which assist students with more significant disabilities with obtaining and maintaining work in the community. This is followed by a look at ways to support students with disabilities who choose to pursue a course of study through higher education. The chapter concludes with some recommendations for how to move forward with employment for all. A driving force behind employment for all is individualization of services. Thus, the information presented here is not prescriptive in nature but instead is descriptive of the range of possibilities that exist. Although there is great variability in the approaches, one major commonality is that what happens must be driven by the student.

VOCATIONAL EDUCATION, CAREER, AND TRAINING MODELS

Students with disabilities have several options for continuing their education beyond age 18, when their peers without disabilities usually graduate. For example, by deferring graduation or receiving a special education diploma or certificate, a student with a disability can continue to participate in vocational education and training programs. This could include participating in the school's community-based vocational education training program, including employer-led initiatives or, in the case of dual enrollment, attending a postsecondary education and training program at a college or university. The ultimate goal of these programs, such as the one described in the example that opened this chapter, is for students to become employed prior to leaving the school system.

The models described here simply illustrate what is possible and by no means represent an exhaustive list of all of a student's possibilities. More important is that it is not necessary to have a structured program in place to begin to incorporate work experiences into each student's educational program. Furthermore, students may desire and/or need additional experiences that are outside the realm of what an established program has to offer. It is important to ensure that each student's transition individualized education program (IEP) is personalized and that his or her needs are being met. Additional work experiences will need to be developed for one student at a time.

Community-Based Vocational Education

Many school districts partner with area businesses to offer community-based vocational education programs for students with more significant support needs. Students covered under the Individuals with Disabilities Education Improvement Act (IDEA) of 2004 (PL 108-446) can continue to participate in such programs until they reach age 22 (or age 26 in Michigan). This work experience gives students an opportunity to self-assess and to learn more about their personal vocational strengths, preferences, and potential support needs as they receive training and education on specific tasks and work-related skills.

Obtaining meaningful work experiences during high school is an important predictor of favorable postschool outcomes (Baer et al., 2003; Benz et al., 2000). A study of 104 transitioning youth with severe disabilities indicated that variables associated with a paid job upon leaving were 1) duration of community-based training that included on-the-job training and 2) age-appropriate physical integration with peers without disabilities (White & Weiner, 2004). Summer work experiences can be advantageous, because unlike work experiences offered during the year they do not compete with access to the general curriculum, study time, or extracurricular activities (Singh, Chang, & Dika, 2007).

Community-based vocational education programs must adhere to standards set by the FLSA. At some point, each student should begin to pursue employment rather than spend their time in school involved in only exploratory or unpaid work experiences. Individualized vocational support services should be provided to each student who is taking steps to enter the work force.

Transition Services Integration Model

The transition services integration model combines school and postschool service system resources to provide services to students with significant disabilities who are enrolled in school until age 21. Public schools contract with agencies that receive funding from vocational rehabilitation and developmental disabilities agencies to provide community-based services in the students' final year of school. This setup often ensures that the same personnel will support students, therefore providing for a more seamless transition from school to work and community living. Many of the students who obtain services under this model are not candidates for jobs being advertised in the community because of a lack of qualifications or requisite skills. Thus, time is taken to develop a specific job opportunity for each student.

The postschool employment rate for students who participated in the transition services integration model was more than 65%, compared with 15% for youth who did not participate. In addition, for more than 5 years postschool, employment outcomes were better than the national average for students with intellectual disabilities (Certo & Luecking, 2006).

Visionary Business Practices

The talent pool of people with disabilities is often not fully understood or valued by corporations. However, through heightened awareness as a result of training and education and through ongoing experiences, every day more and more organizations are finding new ways to include individuals with disabilities in the work force. Here we take a look at two organizations that are dedicated to creating a culture of inclusion and that understand the importance of tapping into this valuable human capital.

Walgreens

Walgreens set out to hire individuals with disabilities into at least one third of the 600 jobs at two distribution plants in 2006. During an interview, Senior Vice President of Distribution and Logistics Randy Lewis was asked about how the idea for the initiative came about (Oregon Business Leadership Network, 2006). He stated that the decision was based on awareness. As a parent of a son with autism, he has seen over the years his own son and other children with disabilities deal with and overcome challenges. This led to seeing each child as an individual and feeling a growing concern about what would happen when the students left school.

Today, Walgreens continues to hire individuals with disabilities and works with schools to establish community-based vocational education programs. For example, eight schools in Topeka, Kansas, have partnered with area Walgreens stores. The students are accompanied by job coaches and receive high school credit for the time they spend there learning about work. Over the past 2 years, more than 40 students have been through the program, which also includes social skills training. Some students have moved on to become Walgreens employees or to work elsewhere in the community. The company web site provides information on how to apply for jobs and tips on ways that organizations that are seeking to assist individuals with disabilities with employment can establish a relationship with store management.

Cincinnati Children's Hospital Project SEARCH

Cincinnati Children's Hospital Project SEARCH offers employment training and education opportunities in a hospital setting for individuals with significant disabilities. Sometimes students move on to become paid employees of Cincinnati Children's Hospital. Because of its success, Project SEARCH is now being replicated in more than 140 health care or business settings across the United States. Daily activities for students usually include classroom instruction on topics related to employment and independent living skills as well as rotation through various work areas to experience various job tasks. Once rotations are completed, job opportunities are developed, both at the site and in the community. Once hired, a student may receive job site support as needed, such as job coaching and other workplace supports.

Walgreens, Cincinnati Children's Hospital, and many other notable businesses have played a major role in assisting students with disabilities with assimilating into the community and work force through participation in vocational training and education programs. Each represents a model of community involvement in local education and helps further the business case for hiring individuals with disabilities. Most important, some students in these programs move on to become valued long-term employees.

Postsecondary Education Models

In addition to offering community-based vocational education programs, some local school systems partner with 2- and 4-year public and private colleges or universities to offer dual enrollment options to students with disabilities. In other instances a student with a disability may pursue postsecondary education after leaving the school system. Indicator 14 (required under IDEA) requires data on the percentage of students who have been through their IEPs, who are no longer in secondary school (e.g., have graduated or aged out), and who were competitively employed or enrolled in some type of postsecondary school or both within 1 year of leaving high school (20 USC 1416[a][3][B]). Thus, more and more school systems are looking at dual enrollment options. Dual enrollment is available to students who are age 18 and older and who are still receiving services from their school system under IDEA. Of the existing dual enrollment programs, 74% support students with disabilities other than intellectual disabilities, 33% support students with intellectual disabilities, and some support both (Hart, Grigal, Sax, Martinez, & Will, 2006).

Students with intellectual disabilities who receive transition services in postsecondary settings may take college classes (for credit or audit) or participate in adult or continuing education classes (Neubert et al., 2004). While there, most students are also involved in integrated community employment or in training with a goal of obtaining paid work. Students also participate in a variety of campus experiences with similar-age peers without disabilities, such as student organizations, sports activities, and cultural events.

Supports and services vary widely within postsecondary education options. For example, in the least restrictive, most inclusive option, students participate in social activities and academic classes with students without disabilities. In addition, life skills training for students with disabilities takes place along with employment experiences either on or off campus. Other programs offer a separate model in which students participate in classes and activities with other students with disabilities. The three main postsecondary education models were described by Hart et al. (2006) and are listed in order of prevalence in Table 7.1.

These programs are often funded in part by the school system through IDEA or local school district funds, and if coursework relates to employment, state vocational rehabilitation funds may be accessed or a tuition waiver may be available to the student. State developmental disabilities services may provide some funds, too. Other funding comes from the family or scholarships. In some instances, a student may be able to use a Social Security work incentive like a Plan for Achieving Self Support (PATH). A PATH allows a student to save money while working to use later for postsecondary education.

Transition services in postsecondary settings have the potential to increase students' access to integrated employment, education, and social activities as well as to improve interagency collaboration between local education agencies and adult service providers (Hart, Mele-McCarthy, Pasternack, Zimbrich, & Parker, 2004; Neubert et al., 2004; Zafft, Hart, & Zimbrich, 2004). Programs offer opportunities for students to expand their independence, self-advocacy skills, employment options, and aspects of their social and community integration during their final years of mandated public schooling (Grigal et al., 2001; Hall, Kleinert, & Kearns, 2000; Hart et al., 2004).

In our opinion, the focus within this new frontier of postsecondary education needs to remain on how to individualize instruction, services, and supports to promote a totally inclusive experience for each student rather than developing programs for students with disabilities. This educational experience would support the student's future work goals. In this scenario, a student would have an opportunity to participate in general college courses (with or without credit) and continuing education with individualized educational supports (Grigal et al., 2001).

In summary, community-based vocational education programs and postsecondary education options can promote the employment of students with disabilities. Although these

Table 7.1. Postsecondary education models, in order of prevalence

- *Mixed/hybrid model:* Students participate in social activities and/or academic classes with students without disabilities for audit or credit and also participate in classes with other students with disabilities (sometimes referred to as *life skills* or *transition* classes). This model typically provides students with employment experience on or off campus.

- *Substantially separate model:* Students participate only in classes with other students with disabilities (sometimes referred to as a *life skills* or *transition* program). Students may have the opportunity to participate in generic social activities on campus and may be offered employment experience, often through a rotation of pre-established employment slots on or off campus.

- *Inclusive individual support model:* Students receive individualized services (e.g., educational coach, tutor, technology, natural supports) in college courses, certificate programs, and/or degree programs for audit or credit. The individual student's vision and career goals drive services. There is no program base on campus. The focus is on establishing a student-identified career goal that directs the course of study and employment experiences (e.g., internships, apprenticeships, work-based learning). Using a collaborative approach, an interagency team comprised of representatives from adult service agencies, generic community services, and the college's disability support office identifies a flexible range of services and shares costs.

Source: Hart, Zimbrich, and Parker (2005).

experiences are helpful, it is important not to lose sight of the ultimate outcome: employment. This is especially true for students with more significant disabilities. When recommended practices are followed, these students receive the necessary support services to move into paid employment prior to aging out of school (Wehman, 2006b). Failing to do so may relegate these students to being placed on a long waiting list for vocational support services; being enrolled in a day program or workshop; or sitting at home, essentially uninvolved with the community.

VOCATIONAL SUPPORT SERVICE MODELS

Two vocational support options, supported and customized employment, have been used to successfully assist individuals with more significant disabilities with employment, both prior to and after leaving school. The major goal of vocational education and training options is to assist students in becoming employed in the community prior to leaving school. However, many students will not become employed without guidance or assistance. The main point to consider is how much support a particular student needs to obtain and maintain employment.

Before taking a more in-depth look at some vocational support models, we feel it is important to briefly review the segregated employment options that still exist in many communities. Although such options are not recommended, they are included here to raise awareness about what they are and why we all should expect more.

Day Programs and Sheltered Workshops

Thousands of adult activity centers serve individuals with disabilities in the United States. It is not unusual to find anywhere from 50 to several hundred individuals with disabilities congregating at a particular center to learn skills that are geared toward helping them succeed in "the real world." Operations usually take place from 9 a.m. to 3 p.m. on weekdays. The programs may be sponsored by a variety of community organizations, including disability-specific agencies or churches. Some may offer prevocational educational and training and recreational activities, and most offer transportation to and from the facility.

These adult work training programs are often geared toward teaching "job readiness" skills. The premise behind the approach is that the person with the disability should be able to prove that he or she is "employable" or "work ready." Even when these organizations offer a continuum of services, whereby some attendees may eventually "graduate" to receive assistance and support with locating a job in the community (such as supported employment), most lean toward segregated employment. In order to make sure that students have access to recommended practices, the transition

In 2005, senators publicly questioned the value of day programs, and most agree they should be phased out so funds can be used to assist individuals with more productive and dignified pursuits (Murphy, Rogan, Handley, Kincaid, & Royce Davis, 2002; Wehman, Revell & Brooke, 2003). A wealth of data from more than 20 cost-effectiveness and cost-efficiency studies completed since the early 1980s indicate that dollars for supported employment is a better taxpayer investment than dollars for sheltered workshops (Cimera, 2000, 2008; Cimera & Rusch, 1999; Kregel, Wehman, Revell, Hill, & Cimera, 2000).

team needs to know about the options for supporting students in real work for real pay in the community.

Some communities may have well-developed and effective services that assist students with more significant support needs to achieve real work, such as supported employment. Others do not. Rather than accepting the status quo, communities with poor and/or limited options should 1) help develop the skills of existing service providers to implement effective employment services; and/or 2) introduce new providers who can offer effective individualized services, such as those offered in a supported employment approach.

Competitive Employment Models

When it comes to *competitive employment,* or real work for real pay, students with disabilities have a number of options. These include working for someone else or becoming self-employed. No matter which option a student pursues, it may be necessary to use supports to reduce barriers associated with the student's ability to obtain and or maintain employment.

The type, level, and intensity of support needed will depend on the student (Wehman, 2006b). For example, the need for support will be influenced by the student's past experiences, including what worked or did not work; his or her learning style and instructional needs; his or her personal abilities, such as communication, physical, and cognitive skills; and family support. In addition, unless the student is self-employed, supports will also be driven by the employer's policies, practices, procedures, experience with a diverse work force, attitudes, beliefs, and expectations.

How the student and employer are supported will be greatly influenced by the knowledge, skills, and attitudes of various professionals. Those charged with helping students with disabilities obtain and maintain employment need to be well trained and well educated. Knowledge, skills, and competencies in transition planning are essential components of preparation programs for special and general educators. Professionals will need to possess these if real work for real pay is to become a reality for students with disabilities, and particularly for those with significant support needs.

Supported Employment

For decades, supported employment options have enabled individuals with significant support needs to become employed in the community. According to the *Federal Register* (2001), the definition of *supported employment* is as follows.

> (1) Supported employment means–(i) Competitive employment in an integrated setting with ongoing support services for individuals with the most severe disabilities–(A) For whom competitive employment has not traditionally occurred or for whom competitive employment has been interrupted or intermittent as a result of a severe disability; and (B) Who, because of the nature and severity of their disabilities, need intensive supported employment services from the designated State unit and extended services after transition in order to perform this work; or (ii) Transitional employment for individuals with the most severe disabilities due to mental illness. (34 CFR 363.6 [c], [2], [iv]).

In the 1970s and 1980s, group models emerged as an alternative to workshops. In these models, individuals with disabilities worked in business in small groups (e.g., enclaves, mobile work crews) under the supervision of an adult service provider. This approach was designed to serve individuals with the most significant disabilities, those viewed as unemployable. Then, in the late 1980s and early 1990s, advances in the field led to a better approach, in which one individual is served at a time. This is usually referred to as the *individual approach* to supported employment.

Through the years, supported employment has primarily been used to assist individuals with developmental disabilities with employment (Wehman, 2006a, b). Based upon the success of the approach in serving these individuals, the model was later modified and refined to serve other populations, such as individuals with mental illness (Bond et al., 2001), physical disabilities (Inge, Strobel, Wehman, Todd, & Targett, 2000; Inge, Wehman, Kregel, & Targett, 1996; Wehman, 2006b), and traumatic brain injury (Wehman, Targett, West, & Kregel, 2005).

Although no longer in vogue, the group models served an important purpose by challenging the field to look for better and more dignified ways to support individuals with significant support needs in employment, one person at a time. By the end of the 1990s, use of the individual approach was in full force, and individuals with significant disabilities had another choice. Facility-based programs or group models were no longer the only choice.

In the individual approach, a professional vocational rehabilitation specialist (often referred to as a *job coach* or *employment specialist*) provides an array of supports to assist a person with a significant disability with obtaining and maintaining competitive employment in the community. The initial component of the service involves assisting the job seeker with 1) identifying his or her abilities and how these may relate to work, and 2) specifying vocational interests and preferences. Next, job development services geared toward helping the person secure work are offered. Sometimes existing positions within a business are pursued and, at other times, employers may be approached about creating a specific position for the job seeker. Typically, the employment specialist first meets with an employer to learn more about a business's operations and potential labor needs. Then, when viable opportunities begin to emerge, a meeting may be set up between the employer and the job seeker. At this point the typical pre-employment process begins, which involves completing an application and participating in an interview, all of which is supported by the employment specialist. The level of involvement will vary from business to business and is dependent on the skill level of the job seeker. If a job is found or developed that is a suitable match for the job seeker and the employer is agreeable, employment is secured.

Then the employment specialist's role shifts to one of facilitating and providing an array of on- and off-the-job supports to help ensure that the new hire becomes successful at work. One of the most common supports for individuals with significant cognitive disabilities is on-the-job skills training, because it often takes these individuals longer to learn a job than it does a person hired off the street. If a job has been created specifically for the job seeker, on-the-job training time is reduced.

Whatever the case, the employment specialist provides training until the new hire is able to perform the agreed-on work tasks to the employer's performance standards and expectations. Sometimes, while the new hire is still learning the job duties, the employment specialist will ensure that the work will be completed, which serves as a guarantee to the employer that the job will be done.

An employment specialist may provide or facilitate an array of other types of workplace supports, such as arranging for and putting into place assistive technology; designing compensatory memory strategies; facilitating communications with job site personnel and relationships with co-workers; and, if needed, teaching the person to use technology or strategies or other skills. The employment specialist may be on site for weeks or months; the length of time depends upon a number of factors, including the new hire's abilities, the nature of the work to be done in relation to the worker's abilities, employer expectations, support from significant others or caregivers, and the skills of the specialist.

Eventually, the specialist fades from the new hire's employment site, such that he or she is no longer there throughout the workday. Sometimes, services can be faded to a point where the specialist is "checking" on how things are going a couple of times a month. During this follow-along phase, the specialist has an eye on the employee's performance and is prepared to offer additional support services as needed. Additional support may involve more skills training on how to perform certain job duties or a change in functions. Sometimes, off-the-job support is needed to assist the individual with solving problems outside of work that, if left unattended, would likely lead to job termination (e.g., getting to work on time and wearing clean clothing). The following case study illustrates supported employment in action.

 **George**

George is a 21-year-old man with autism. He speaks in complete sentences and often initiates conversations; however, he only talks about a few topics, such as football statistics, old coins, and birds. He has difficulty understanding the nuances associated with language and communication. Sometimes he asks personal questions, and he frequently interrupts others while they are talking.

He often wants to hug others and invade their personal space by standing too close or sitting down where someone else is about to be seated. He has difficulty sitting still and staying on task. He has great reading skills. In addition, he is physically fit but has a tendency to sweat profusely.

Over the past couple of years, George participated in community-based vocational training in a number of community businesses. There, along with some other students, he explored various types of jobs by trying out tasks associated with each. As a result, the teacher was able to assess some of his vocational abilities, preferences, and potential support needs.

Based on this and other functional assessment information, George was referred for supported employment services. A job coach spent some time getting to know George by reading existing information, observing him during his community-based vocational training, spending time with him in other settings, and interviewing those who know him best. Armed with this information, the job coach was able to work with a local business to create a job for him at a warehouse that recycled paper products. However, this did not last very long. George was terminated after a month because of slow work speed and some behaviors.

Next, a position was secured at a retail store that sold a variety of merchandise, such as clothing, electronics, food, and more. The management agreed to hire George part time 3 days a week and on weekends as a processor in the back of the store. There he would help unpack and tag items that would later make their way to the sales floor.

The job coach began to train George on the job, but soon it became apparent that this work may not have been a good match for him. For instance, he refused to stay in the back of the store. Instead, he kept running from the back of the store out to the main floor. One time, he sat on the floor and refused to get up when asked.

Fortunately, the employer was willing to let George try working in some other departments. Next, he was assigned to the food section of the store. There he was instructed on how to examine packages in the dairy and frozen foods aisles for expiration dates. Expired products were placed into a shopping cart and later dumped in to a trash compactor.

It was soon evident that this was a much better match for George for several reasons. For example, when performing the work George made use of his excellent reading skills, including his ability to read numbers. This position also allowed him to move around from place to place to inspect products. In addition, the work took place on the retail floor. George's running behaviors stopped once he was allowed to stay out on the floor. Apparently, for some reason, work in the back was not agreeable to him. The job coach suspected that the sounds associated with the conveyor belt, the lighting, or the heat may have been bothersome. Finally, George stayed cooler in this area because he was working with refrigerated and/or frozen products. This seemed to make him feel more comfortable.

After locating and negotiating this better job match, once again, the job coach began to provide one-to-one on-the-job skills training. Over time, George learned how to do the job, and after a couple of months the coach began to fade his support from the job site.

Today, the job coach remains in touch with George and the employer and is prepared to offer additional on-the-job support if needed. For example, recently George was paired with another worker to perform similar work in the bakery area. The job coach returned to the job site and provided some additional support, including tips for the co-worker on how to train George on a new skill. George has been employed for close to a year and was recently named employee of the month.

Supported employment requires individualized services that are tailored to the situation on hand. The employment specialist uses practical ways to get to know the job seeker, and then meets with businesses to develop and negotiate possible job options. Once the individual is hired, the specialist provides or facilitates an array of workplace supports and offers long-term follow-up throughout the employee's work tenure. This employment specialist's scope of work involves defining and conceptualizing problems, thinking about solutions, and using a general and flexible approach to implement solutions.

Customized Employment

As part of its commitment to improving the employment of people with disabilities, the Office of Disability Employment Policy within the U.S. Department of Labor established grant initiatives to build the capacity of their One-Stop Career Centers to serve all people. From this research the concept of customized employment emerged. *Customized employment* is "the voluntary negotiation of a personalized employment relationship between a specific individual and an employer that fulfills the business needs of the employer" (n.d., http://www.dol.gov/odep/pubs/custom/indicators.htm)

The *Federal Register* (2002) defines it as follows:

> Customized employment means individualizing the employment relationship between employees and employers in ways that meet the needs of both. It is based

on an individualized determination of strengths, needs and interests of the person with a disability and it is also designed to meet the specific needs of the employer. It may include employment developed through job carving, self-employment, or entrepreneurial initiatives or other job development or restructuring strategies that result in job responsibilities being customized and individually negotiated to fit the needs of individuals with disability. Customized employment assumes the provision of reasonable accommodations and supports necessary for the individual to perform the functions of a job that is individually negotiated and developed.

Funding for customized employment comes from individual accounts that provide funding for One-Stop Career Center services. Other sources of funds may include state vocational rehabilitation programs or state mental health or developmental agencies. Often funding is "blended" or "braided" from a variety of resources (Brooks-Lane, Hutcheson, & Revell, 2005).

Sometimes, a personal representative is hired to assist an individual with negotiating a job as well as identifying and putting into place various workplace supports (e.g., job coaching). Customized employment services have also been geared toward assisting individuals with business start-ups. Much of what experts have learned to date about self-employment for individuals with more significant support needs came from this initiative. Various supports are orchestrated as needed to assist individuals with disabilities who choose to pursue this option.

According to The National Report on Employment Services and Outcomes *(Butterworth, Smith, Cohen-Hall, Migliore, & Winsor, 2008), despite advances in federal policy and the leadership of some high-performing states, widespread expansion of integrated employment has not occurred. State systems continue to invest in sheltered employment and nonwork services. Expansion of community-based nonwork services has competed with integrated employment, despite evidence that the former are poorly defined and do not consistently achieve their stated goals of community membership (Sulewski, Butterworth, & Gilmore, 2006).*

Self-Employment

Self-employment is a rehabilitative option under the Rehabilitation Act of 1973 (PL 93-112) and the Workforce Investment Act of 1998 (PL 105-220). Today, self-employment and entrepreneurship are part of a nationwide strategy to help people with disabilities make the transition from unemployment, underemployment, or entitlement-based programs to gainful employment and self-sufficiency. Some of the advantages associated with self-employment are the following:

• Chosen work can be tailored to highlight personal talents, interests, and abilities.
• Barriers to employment may be reduced or eliminated.
• There are many available work incentives, such as the Plan to Achieve Self-Support.
• Depending on the nature of the business, self-employment may offer the opportunity to work from home or to telework.

Assistance may be available to assist individuals with purchasing equipment and/or assistive technology and accessing supports related to daily business operations. The Plan to Achieve Self-Support through the Social Security Administration may also help fund operating costs (Griffin & Hammis, 2003).

Starting a new business begins by matching a person's dreams and talents to an economic activity. Initially, time is spent doing person-centered planning and getting to know the individual. Questions are asked and observations are made to get lots of ideas related to the person's talents and how they may lead to self-employment. The person's ideal conditions of employment, strengths, interests, support, and relationships are also investigated.

After an idea is formulated, a business plan is written up and a feasibility study is initiated. Depending on how this goes, a new business may be formed. New business start-ups are as varied as the individuals who start them and can range from photographer to puppet party master. Operations may take place in the person's home or in the community. Some individuals even set up shop operating a business within a business. For example, one young lady set up a retail operation in a coffee shop; there she sells magazines and newspapers to the patrons.

Professionals involved with assisting individuals with disabilities with pursuing self-employment will need training and experience in this area. For example, they will need to understand business planning, know about community resources, and know how to coordinate financial resources and other assistance programs. (Information from grant-funded projects such as START-UP USA can be a good resource; see For Further Information.)

PRACTICES SUPPORTING HIGHER EDUCATION

Today an increasing number of students with disabilities are attending college. For more than a decade, the National Longitudinal Transitional Study–2 has conducted research on the transition of students with disabilities across the country. Research conducted by Wagner, Cameto, and Newman (http://www.nlts2.org) has found that more students are identifying college, in particular 2-year colleges, as a potential goal regardless of their disability. This good news supports research findings that a college education increases the chances for people with disabilities to obtain and maintain employment. Being employed enables these individuals to earn a higher annual income, which helps create a pathway to lifelong independence and a better quality of life (Fairweather & Shaver, 1991).

Students will need to choose an appropriate higher education setting to meet their needs and interests, determine the entrance requirements of the chosen program, apply for admission, and obtain any needed accommodations. The degree of support required by a student will vary depending upon his or her abilities. Table 7.2 lists some things for the student and team to consider related to preparing for, choosing, and staying in college.

Eligible students who enroll in community college, vocational-technical school, or 4-year college are protected by Section 504 of the Rehabilitation Act and the ADA, which prohibit discrimination on the basis of a disability. Colleges and universities must ensure that their educational programs, extracurricular activities, buildings, and housing are accessible to students with disabilities. However, unlike high schools, postsecondary schools are only required to provide reasonable academic adjustments, including accommodations and modifications.

Researchers surveyed perceptions among students with disabilities who attended a precollege transition program between 1999 and 2006. Participants valued information on self-advocacy, rights under the ADA, their own disabilities, and other participants' disabilities. It is interesting that career counseling was rated as least important (Rothman, Maldonado, & Rothman, 2008).

On every campus there is an office (often called the Disabilities Support Services Office) that determines what kinds of help students will need in terms of accommodations.

Table 7.2. Things for students to consider when going to college

Preparing	Choosing	Staying
Learn new terms specific to college (e.g., *add, drop, withdrawal*).	Research the school (e.g., size, housing options).	Register with the Disabilities Support Services Office as a student with a disability in order to get accommodations.
Learn about the role of the disability services office and your rights.	Investigate costs and financial aid options.	Give professors your accommodation letter.
Learn about your abilities.	Review the written policy on course substitution.	Develop a calendar that includes structuring time to study.
Explore potential accommodations and support needs.	Explore disability services and other supports available to all students (e.g., tutoring, writing or math lab).	Take a balanced course load.
Take the required coursework.		Stay in touch with your academic advisor.
		Take advantage of any extracurricular activities and supports offered.

Table 7.3 briefly outlines some of the responsibilities of this office and of students who are seeking accommodations.

As noted, students must inform the school that they have a disability and need assistance. Schools usually require documentation prepared by an appropriate professional, such as a physician or psychologist. Then accommodations are approved on the basis of students' disability and individual needs. Although every accommodation must be individualized to the student and situation at hand, some common college accommodations that can be provided for students with disabilities include

- Recordings of class lectures
- Notetakers
- Audio books or other readings
- Enlarged text
- Extended time on tests or assignments
- Alternative testing procedures
- Limited distraction room for testing
- Permitted use of a calculator

A less well-known accommodation for students with disabilities is priority registration. This ensures that students can create a schedule that will assist them in meeting the demands of their coursework. For example, students may want to spread classes that have a great deal of reading out throughout the week so that they do not all fall on the same day.

Table 7.3. Responsibilities of the disabilities support services office and of the student

Disability support services (DSS) office	Student
Inform the student of documentation requirements (varies widely).	Register with DSS and provide required documentation.
Determine eligibility and, if a student is eligible, provide a letter or memo to the student outlining accommodations.	Meet with the DSS coordinator or director to review and discuss your needs.
Assist faculty members with disability-specific issues as needed.	Provide a letter or memo on your needs to instructors.
	Ensure that accommodations are provided.
	Take concerns or grievances to DSS; if unsatisfied, file a complaint with the U.S. Office for Civil Rights.

Or students can arrange their schedules so that classes meet on certain days of the week or so that they have time in between classes to study.

Postsecondary schools are not required to lower the essential requirements of a class. In addition, they do not have to provide personal attendants, readers for personal use or study, or other devices or services of a personal nature, such as tutoring and typing. This case study illustrates how one student pursued postsecondary education.

 **Christine**

Christine is an 18-year-old student with a spinal cord injury and an undiagnosed mild traumatic brain injury. Although she appears to be a quick study, sometimes she does not retain small details unless she refers to some type of compensatory memory aid, such as her BlackBerry or a daily reminder. After some prolonged career guidance and counseling with both her school and vocational rehabilitation counselors, Christine has decided to pursue her dream of becoming an instructional support technician. In this capacity she hopes to one day oversee the development of online programs, courses, and services, including implementation of public relations and marketing in this area.

Over the past year she participated in a paid internship in which she worked with the coordinator of web systems at a local university. There she learned about managing web systems requests and coordinating and providing technical services.

Prior to starting the work experience, Christine was guided on how to perform a self-assessment of the internship site and her workstation so that she could identify and request any accommodations that she may need. Then, using the self-advocacy skills she had been taught over the years, she made a presentation to the school's human resources office a few days before the internship started. She disclosed her disability and requested specific accommodations to ease her access to the workstation and materials. Accommodations were made, and her internship proved to be a valuable experience.

Earlier this year, Christine put in applications at four colleges and was accepted at two. Now she needs to find out which accommodations colleges will authorize for her. She knows she must initiate this process herself. This is something she learned about over the past few years when studying how her rights will change when she leaves the public school system to pursue higher education.

After committing to the college of her choice, Christine registered as a student with a disability through the school's DSS, sent in the required documentation, and specifically asked for an accessible building and classroom. She asked for proper hookups for her laptop in the classroom and asked to be seated in the front of the class within range to record her instructor's lessons. She also requested additional time to take tests and has received permission to take tests using a computer or a scribe to record her answers. Finally, she requested a personal reader for study group.

The disability services coordinator reviewed the documentation and considered the requests. In the summer, Christine received a letter from DSS stating that her request is under final review. The letter goes on to say that all requests have been granted except for the reader for the study group. The school does not have to provide a reader for study; however, if the professor requires participation in the study group, this decision may be reconsidered. Christine is ready to pack her bags and head for school in the fall.

Upon graduating or otherwise ending their studies, some students may require vocational support services to assist them with obtaining and maintaining employment. For example, a student with a history of severe mental illness or severe physical disability may need more help to obtain employment than students with less severe disabilities and may benefit from some of the supports described in the sections on supported and customized employment.

NEXT STEPS

The National Longitudinal Transition Study–2 revealed that employment outcomes are improving for students with disabilities as they make the transition from school to adulthood (Wagner, Newman, Cameto, & Levine, 2005). However, much remains to be done. The framework and methodologies to continue to make improvements exist; some have even been around for decades, but for whatever reason remain unacknowledged.

So how does the field move ahead, particularly in light of the fact that legislation is in place and recommended practices do indeed exist? The following suggestions offer a place to start.

First, be aware of and use strategies that work. Turn to evidence-based practices such as those presented throughout this book. Avoid referring students to organizations that lack the leadership and fortitude to provide individualized services and supports. Be aware of organizations that promote a continuum of services to get students prepared to work or further their education. Look for organizations that have a clear mission statement that espouses the values associated with recommended practices. Know what makes providers competent, and hold them to high expectations. If students choose to pursue higher education, be familiar with their rights and the supports available to them in these settings.

Second, look for ways to advocate for legislation and policy changes to support recommended practices and ensure that students receive the required transition services consistent with IDEA's statutory and regulatory provisions. Encourage others to do the same.

Third, believe. If those charged with overseeing employment efforts (especially for those with significant support needs) do not believe that all students with disabilities can work in the community, then it is not likely that students will succeed. Instead, adult day care and employment within workshop settings and business-based enclaves will continue. Similarly, if these individuals do not believe that students with disabilities can go on to postsecondary education opportunities, these students will not. Encourage the pursuit of education. Share success stories.

Adopting higher expectations for students with disabilities ultimately needs to happen on all levels: individual, family, professional, employer, government, and societal. This means that students and their families must be empowered. They must have input, make choices, and take responsibility for employment outcomes. Transition teams, families, and students need to take the steps necessary to make work a reality. For some students, this means going to work prior to exiting school; for others, it involves pursuing higher education before pursuing a career.

CONCLUSION

Educators play a major role in ensuring that students with disabilities, particularly those with the most severe disabilities, go to work in their communities in real jobs. To this end, educators should adhere to recommended practices such as preparing students for employment using a rigorous curriculum that emphasizes work experiences in real business settings. Such efforts should culminate in a student becoming employed prior to exiting the school system through vocational support models such as supported or customized employment, if appropriate.

Educators should also ensure that students and their families make connections with postschool and adult services providers years before leaving the public school system. Too often students encounter long waiting lists for adult employment services or, in some instances, wait years before connecting with postschool employment services (if they connect at all). Students should exit school with services already lined up.

Educators also play an important role in preparing students for postsecondary education. Recommended practices suggest that these students connect with support services they may need, such as campus disability and/or state vocational rehabilitation services, before graduating from school. Assistance from educators may also come in the form of coordinating and accessing such services. As with other adult services, connections with postsecondary support services and disability education offices should be made well before students exit school.

FOR FURTHER INFORMATION

Developing Work Experiences

Luecking, R.G. (2009). *The way to work: How to facilitate work experiences for youth in transition.* Baltimore: Paul H. Brookes Publishing Co.

To help with every step of facilitating meaningful employment, readers will get examples of model programs, stories that illustrate what works and doesn't work, more than a dozen photocopiable tools and forms, and end-of-chapter "Learning Labs" with reflection questions and thought-provoking activities.

Postsecondary Education

Grigal, M., & Hart, D. (2010). *Think college! Postsecondary education options for students with intellectual disabilities.* Baltimore: Paul H. Brookes Publishing Co.

Uncovers the big picture of today's postsecondary options and reveals how to support students with disabilities before, during, and after a successful transition to college.

Supported Employment

Virginia Commonwealth University Rehabilitation Research and Training Center on Workplace Supports and Job Retention (http://www.worksupport.com)
Contains a wealth of information about supported employment.

8

Strategies for Funding and Resources Needed for Transition Individualized Education Programs

W. Grant Revell, Jr. and Paul Wehman

Sondra is 22 years old and has a significant intellectual disability. She has had very limited community and work experience while in school, and she does not have a specific area of identified vocational interest as she nears the completion of her secondary program. Sondra is eligible for services funded through the Home- and Community-Based Services (HCBS) Medicaid Waiver program. Without these services, Sondra is at risk for placement in an institutional setting. Sondra's transition plan emphasizes the need for her to have an extended period of community exploration and experience, including observing job sites and trying out new jobs. The state developmental disabilities program and the local community services board will arrange for her to live in a supported living situation and will coordinate a program of community exploration designed to give her an opportunity to "discover" (Griffin, Hammis, Geary, & Sullivan, 2008) her vocational interests and abilities.

Noah is 19 years old and has received special education services because of an emotional disability. He has periodic episodes of severe depression. Working with Noah and his family on his transition plan, his transition team has noted a number of needed support services if he is to live and work successfully in the community. Noah needs continued mental health treatment services and assistance with managing his medication. He needs job placement assistance and ongoing support and encouragement once he is employed. He will also need supported living assistance if he is to reach his goal of living independently. Noah's transition team is seeking assistance in these areas from the state mental health program and its community treatment program. The community mental health program has an integrated treatment and employment program for which Noah is eligible. His transition plan includes assistance from the state vocational rehabilitation (VR) program and his local mental health community services program in supported living and an integrated mental health treatment and employment program.

These are two examples of how state developmental disabilities/mental health agencies and community boards can assist in providing employment and related resources for eligible transitioning youth with disabilities. But there are many ways to plan for and implement the funding that is essential to make the transition individualized education program (IEP) a reality.

Effective transition from school to employment in the adult community for youth with disabilities requires knowledge of the resources available through an array of state and community agencies and organizations. As students with disabilities, their families, and their transition teams explore and plan for employment after high school, they need to develop an understanding of these services and the challenges of obtaining them. This chapter focuses on the importance of becoming well informed and learning how to network with key community agencies and organizations.

Once they reach age 22 or complete their secondary-level program, youth with disabilities no longer have a legal right to the variety of services covered by the Individuals with Disabilities Education Improvement Act (IDEA) of 2004 (PL 108-446). For the most part, services in the adult system are not based on entitlement. Instead, most postsecondary employment and related service agencies have their own individual eligibility requirements that students must meet to be accepted into an individual program. Different laws and policies govern each of these programs. Families of individuals with disabilities may find that identifying, accessing, and paying for needed adult services involves working through a complex public and private service system.

COMMUNITY TRAINING AND EMPLOYMENT SUPPORT PROGRAMS

Youth with disabilities who are making the transition from school to the community potentially have access to a variety of community training, employment, and support programs (Certo et al., 2008). These programs offer an array of service coordination assistance, employment services, and funding possibilities. However, these programs operate under a wide assortment of federal, state, and local laws, regulations, policies, and service arrangements. The key to a successful transition outcome is becoming involved with these programs early on in the planning process and blending resources.

Blending Resources

The following is a set of key steps for blending resources into individualized transition plans:

- Become fully educated about the resources and services in your community that provide community training, employment, and support programs specific to youth in transition.
- Identify the primary community agencies that are critical to the success of each student's transition plan.
- Identify the primary service coordination resource among these community agencies. Different agencies might take on this role for different youth in transition depending on the nature of their disability, their core service needs, and/or local eligibility requirements. Early transition planning can help to establish these key relationships with community

No one specific program or agency serves all individuals with disabilities in the adult service system. Transitioning youth with disabilities and their families have the potential to receive services and support from a variety of public and private programs. The exact mix of programs will vary depending upon the needs of the student and his or her transition goals, the nature of the disability, the economic resources of the community, and the eligibility requirements of the program (Wittenburg et al., 2002).

agencies and the primary- and secondary-level participation needed by each to support a successful employment outcome.

Community Organizations

Community organizations that are important transition resources include federally funded state VR programs, community rehabilitation service providers, One-Stop Career Centers, state agencies and community services boards that serve groups with specific disabilities, and Work Incentives Planning and Assistance (WIPA) projects.

It is important to involve these community agencies early in the transition process so that the student, his or her family, and the entire transition team can learn about and become familiar with the resources they offer (Wehman, 2006b). Without continued involvement, planning, and collaboration with key community agencies, the potential for a successful transition from secondary education to the community and employment will be greatly diminished. Consider the case study of John. How might he be able to use state and community resources in his school transition program to help implement his transition IEP and achieve his employment goal?

 **John**

John is 20 and in the final months of his secondary-level education program. As a component of his IEP, he has participated in a series of work experience activities arranged by his school consistent with his employment goal of working for a business that provides care, exercise, and boarding for small domestic animals. Although John has demonstrated an ability to work effectively with many animals, he is particularly interested in grooming dogs. Because John is receiving Supplemental Security Income (SSI), it is important that he and his family fully understand the potential impact of wages through employment on his disability benefits. This information will be obtained from a WIPA representative.

The transition team has identified a number of supports that will be needed for John to achieve his desired employment outcome. John has an intellectual disability and learns most effectively in one-to-one training situations. Therefore, he will need access to an employment specialist who can provide training at the workplace. This service is available through a supported employment resource provided by a community rehabilitation program (CRP). Funding for this service is potentially available through the state VR program. The employment supports John will need also include assistance in job development consistent with his employment goal, potential negotiation with an employer for a position that matches John's abilities and interests, and the purchase of equipment John might need to perform his job duties as a dog groomer. The supported employment program will assist with the job development and job negotiation. VR is a potential resource for equipment purchases. Given that VR services are time limited and the expectation is that John will need ongoing job training, funding for extended supported employment services will be sought from the State Developmental Disabilities program using funds through the HCBS Medicaid Waiver.

For John to be successful in his transition from work experience to employment, he will first need access to information on employment and his Social Security benefits. He will also need access to funding that will pay for job development, job training, and ongoing assistance for him to remain employed over time and to funding to purchase certain equipment needed for him to perform his desired job as dog groomer. A skilled employment specialist could use John's ownership of equipment as a resource in negotiating a position for him with a prospective employer. This approach to employer negotiation is called *resource ownership* (Brooks-Lane et al., 2005). Thus, John's transition IEP includes participation from four key adult service resources: 1) WIPA, 2) VR, 3) a CRP, and 4) a developmental disabilities services program using funds through the HCBS Medicaid Waiver.

It is important to understand that transition planning frequently involves blending resources from a variety of adult service programs into a coordinated plan of service. This blend of service resources can vary considerably from person to person based on individual employment goals and support needs.

TRANSITION RESOURCES IN THE ADULT SERVICE SYSTEM

A number of resources in the adult service system can be used individually or blended together in a transition plan. It is most helpful if students, their families, and the transition team understand the basic role and function of each agency in the areas of service planning and coordination, service provision, and funding. This section provides an overview of key community organizations and programs that frequently provide funding and services to transitioning youth with disabilities. Examples of how these resources can assist in transition are also provided.

State Vocational Rehabilitation Services

The Rehabilitation Act of 1973 (PL 93-112), as amended in 1998 (PL 105-220), provides states with federal grants to operate comprehensive VR programs for individuals with disabilities. VR is a cooperative program between state and federal governments that exists in all 50 states, the District of Columbia, and U.S. territories. It should be a core resource that students with disabilities can refer to throughout the transition process. VR provides an array of services and supports that focus specifically on achieving an employment outcome. Some of these include

- Assessment for determining eligibility for VR services
- Vocational counseling, guidance, and referral services
- Vocational and other training, including on-the-job training
- Personal assistant services, including training in managing and directing a personal assistant

VR agencies will usually arrange with other community providers to acquire services such as rehabilitation technology and supported employment. The ability of VR agencies to reach out into the community for individualized services is one of their key strengths. VR agencies are well positioned to serve as service coordination hubs for employment-oriented community services for eligible youth with disabilities making the transition from secondary-level programs (Wehman, 2006a).

- Rehabilitation technology services
- Job placement services and supported employment services

Eligibility Determination and Plan Development

Before a person can access any VR services, he or she must complete an application that is then reviewed and approved (or denied) by a VR counselor. Eligibility for VR services is based on 1) the presence of a disability that is an impediment to employment and 2) the expectation that the provision of VR services will result in the individual achieving an employment outcome.

Once eligibility for VR is determined, the VR counselor develops an individualized plan for employment (IPE). The IPE identifies both the employment goal chosen by the student and the services needed to achieve that goal. The IPE is developed in close cooperation with the student, the student's family, and the transition team. It can serve as a road map for transition into employment after the completion of high school.

Role in Transition

Rehabilitation counselors can be a helpful resource for teachers, students, and families in planning and implementing the transition plan. Counselors coordinate services and often have extensive connections with community agencies and employers. Service coordination through VR continues until case closure. Case closure can occur after a person is employed a minimum of 90 days in a job consistent with the employment objective established in the IPE. Case closure can also occur if the individual is not making progress toward achieving an employment outcome.

Access to Funding

VR counselors have access to funds that can be used to purchase services from authorized vendors. If a service (e.g., postsecondary education and training, supported employment, transportation, tools and uniforms) supports the employment goal established in the IPE, VR funds can be used to purchase it. VR counselors are also usually very familiar with other funding sources that can be used to complement VR funding.

As a student with a disability nears completion of his or her secondary education program, the rehabilitation counselor can become actively involved to ensure that an IPE is in place as the student prepares to exit the school program. IPEs are frequently completed during the final year of a student's secondary program to ensure that VR services are in place by the time the student completes the program.

Following are examples of how two students with disabilities used VR services in their transition planning.

Mary is 19 years old and has been receiving special education services within her secondary program because of a moderate intellectual disability. She is participating in a work-study program through the school and has gained work experience in a variety of areas. She has demonstrated interests and abilities in working in an office setting doing clerical work such as assembling documents, filing, delivering mail, and making copies. Mary learns best when given consistent one-to-one training with repeated practice opportunities. To achieve her transition goal of becoming employed in an office setting, Mary will need assistance with job placement to identify a setting that matches her abilities and interests, an extended initial period of on-site training in the expectations and routines of her job, and an ongoing, periodic follow-up contact to monitor her stability in the job. The state VR counselor serving Mary's school and transition program receives her application for services and finds that she is eligible for VR services. The counselor develops an IPE with Mary that identifies resources in her community for the needed job development and job site training services. These services will be purchased through VR case service funds. The counselor also identifies an additional resource that will pay for the ongoing periodic follow-up services that will continue after VR case closure once Mary demonstrates that she is stable in her job performance.

Marcus is 21 years old. He has multiple mobility, dexterity, and communication impairments resulting from cerebral palsy. He has demonstrated interests and abilities in web site design and is interested in working in marketing using his computer and web site design skills. Marcus applies for and is found eligible for VR services. His IPE includes a 1-year period of training in a postsecondary web site design program, personal assistant services, transportation services, and purchases of required computer hardware and software for use in his training. Once his training is completed, Marcus will receive job placement assistance and continued personal assistant services. VR funding will pay for his training, transportation, and equipment and will arrange for job placement assistance once he completes his training. The VR counselor also identified an alternative source of funding outside of VR funds for Marcus's personal assistant services.

In the case of both Mary and Marcus, VR provides the key resources in the transition plan that enable them to achieve their employment goals. VR is indeed a critical transition resource.

Community Rehabilitation Programs/Employment Service Organizations

CRPs are usually not-for-profit or for-profit private agencies that assist people with disabilities in obtaining and maintaining competitive employment. Specific services offered by providers vary. Many CRPs offer career counseling, assessments, job placement, and supported employment services designed to assist individuals with disabilities to live and work in the community. Because many CRPs obtain much of their funding through contractual arrangements, accessing their services can require a funding authorization from an agency such as VR.

Role in Transition

CRPs occasionally work cooperatively through contracts with secondary-level school systems to offer work experience programs while students are in school. For the most part, CRPs are linked closely to the adult service community and derive their primary funding from agencies such as VR. CRPs might be considered future potential resources during early transition planning and exploration for younger students. Before selecting a specific CRP, transition teams should use key quality indicators to assess the effectiveness of employment services provided to students with disabilities by all available CRPs (Brooke, Revell, & Wehman, 2009).

The employment support staff at CRPs are usually called *employment consultants* or *specialists, job coaches,* or something similar. As a component of an IPE, an employment consultant may cooperate with a referring VR counselor to seek out as-needed support services, such as benefits counseling assistance, child care options, mental health services, or other supports needed for an individual to be successful in employment.

Eligibility/Provision of Services

CRPs provide a variety of employment-related services, such as assistance with exploring potential job and career options and services related to job preparation, job development, and job placement. These services might include practice with job interviews, job-seeking skills classes, résumé preparation, guided job searches, and negotiations with employers. For example, an employer has a job with multiple job duties. Some of these duties match well to the abilities of the job applicant with a disability; others are a poor match. With the permission of the applicant, the employment consultant might work with the employer to negotiate a customized job carved out of the original job description that is a good match for the individual with a disability (Brooks-Lane et al., 2005). Once the job match is completed, the employment consultant can assist with training at the job site, help the worker adjust to the demands of the job, and provide ongoing support as needed to help the worker maintain the job or to assist with job change.

Robert is 21 years old and has received special education services while in school because of an autism spectrum disorder. He has difficulty mainly in the areas of socialization and communication, particularly in new and unfamiliar situations. He performs well with supervision and close guidance when he can remain active and interact with a limited number of people. With funding arranged through VR, an employment specialist from a local CRP is hired to provide job development and job placement services for Robert. A retirement community in Robert's neighborhood has a large in-house laundry facility, and a position in the laundry area matches well with Robert's abilities and interests. The employment specialist accompanies Robert for a job interview and arranges for a "working interview" in which he is given the opportunity to demonstrate his ability to do the required job tasks as an alternative to undergoing a predominantly verbal interview. Robert is hired. His employment plan will include the employment specialist spending an extended period of time with him at the job site learning the required job duties and assisting him in becoming comfortable in his work and in his social interactions with co-workers.

CRPs can be the primary source of employment and related training and support for a variety of transitioning youth with disabilities who can benefit from job placement, job site training, and ongoing support services.

State Developmental Disabilities/Mental Health Agencies and Local Community Services Boards

Transition-age youth with disabilities may be eligible for services administered through state developmental disabilities administrations, state mental health agencies, and/or local community services boards. For example, Maryland uses a state-administered developmental disabilities administration system (http://www.ddamaryland.org/services.htm) and Virginia uses a community services board system (http://www.dmhmrsas.virginia.gov/SVC-CSBs.asp).

Unlike state VR agencies, state developmental disabilities/mental health agencies and community services boards do not operate under a specific set of federal laws and may operate under a variety of names, including intellectual disabilities, mental health, developmental disabilities, and/or substance abuse services.

Role in Transition

When available, service coordinators within local community services programs are excellent resources for the transition planning team. In general, service coordinators serve as a coordination hub with very specific knowledge of services for students as well as for family members. Service coordinators can attend transition meetings, both to provide information and referral and also to help plan for specific transition support services, including employment and employment-related services. The knowledge that these service coordinators bring to the table is more likely to benefit older students (i.e., those closer to graduation), but including these individuals on the team can certainly still benefit younger students by making them aware of the opportunities available in their community.

Eligibility/Provision of Services

For both state-administered developmental disabilities administrations and locally administered community services boards, eligibility for services is based on the presence of a disability that meets specific guidelines. Yet eligibility criteria can vary considerably from state to state and community to community. Students with disabilities, their families, and school representatives need to learn early on about the eligibility requirements and service opportunities in their specific state and community. Parent groups, VR, CRPs, and other members of the adult service system network are great resources for this information.

Because there are times when even eligible individuals are placed on a waiting list because of lack of funding, making contact well in advance of the actual transition point could enable a student to work through the eligibility and waiting list steps in time for services to be available when they are actually needed (Braddock, Hemp, & Rizzolo, 2008).

Access to Funding

Service coordinators might also have access to a variety of funding resources to assist students in acquiring employment supports and related services. A primary funding source is the HCBS Medicaid Waiver (Braddock et al., 2008). The purpose of these waivers is to provide services for individuals who otherwise would need to live in an institutional setting because of the significant nature of their disability and resulting support needs. The HCBS Medicaid Waiver can provide eligible individuals with access to supports for community living and employment (West et al., 2002). The HCBS Medicaid Waiver might be a resource for some youth with disabilities who have more significant support needs. However, Medicaid Waiver applications are made at the state level, and the content of waiver programs varies considerably from state to state. Each waiver defines a specific target population and specifies the services that will be available (Braddock et al., 2008), so it is important for transition team members to understand the waiver program in their state and to determine how it might provide additional support.

State developmental disabilities/mental health agencies and local community service programs can be valuable transition resources in a variety of community living areas, including employment. As noted, the eligibility requirements and service capacities of these programs vary substantially from state to state and from community to community. Active networking between transition teams and community service representatives is critically important to learn about the specific services and resources available.

Jolyn is 21 years old and is making the transition from her secondary-level education program into adult services. She is eligible for services through the HCBS Medicaid Waiver program. The service coordinator with her local developmental disabilities program works with Jolyn's transition team to arrange for funding for a supported living apartment in her community as well as extended follow-along services for her supported employment program. Her initial supported employment services are being funded by VR.

One-Stop Career Centers

The Workforce Investment Act of 1998 (PL 105-220) created One-Stop Career Centers as key employment resources in the community. The core services of One-Stops are available to anyone in the community who needs help locating employment. These core services mainly involve access through self-directed job searches of available job openings in the community. Individuals who meet the eligibility criteria for more intensive service through the One-Stop can receive a variety of services that are more individualized, including access to vocational training and assistance with job placement (Targett et al., 2007).

Role in Transition

Youth and young adults with disabilities are targeted for services through One-Stop Career Centers. Therefore, One-Stops can play a significant role in delivering transition services to the student and helping the school team develop a plan for transition. For those One-Stop customers who move beyond the general core services, plan managers and/or disability program navigators can assist in planning employment-related services, including reaching out into the community to help identify and acquire other needed transition services. The One-Stop by design frequently serves as a home base for many community partners, such as VR and CRPs, who co-locate staff within the One-Stop setting.

One-Stops have job listings of available employment opportunities. Information from interest inventories can help guide a job search. One-Stop workstations are frequently equipped with accessibility kits that

One-Stop Career Centers offer job clubs from which an individual looking for employment can get support and information from peers and a group facilitator. Some One-Stops have more customized employment resources, such as staff who will represent the job interests of an individual with a disability to a potential employer and help negotiate a job opportunity (Targett et al., 2007).

accommodate a variety of disabilities, for example by enabling computerized job searches (Gervey, Gao, & Rizzo, 2004).

Additional employment services of potential value to youth in transition include paid and unpaid work experiences, occupational skills training, job placement, and follow-up services after hire to help with job retention and career development. Funding for employment services through a One-Stop is frequently through the One-Stop's direct links with community agencies that fund employment services, such as VR and community services boards.

Career awareness and exploration can involve use of the career exploration lab at the One-Stop, which might include various interest tests and links to web-based job information. Exploration can include planned visits to job sites to review different employment opportunities, meetings with employer representatives, and summer job programs. As transition-age youth with disabilities move toward completion of their school program, exploration can progress to more extended internships or part-time employment built into the school program and transition plan. One-Stops are an evolving community resource. Students with disabilities, their families, and their transition teams need to become thoroughly familiar with the resources and services available from the One-Stop in their community early on in the transition process.

Access to Funding

One-Stop Career Centers can be a primary source of career awareness, career exploration, training, and employment support. Accessing the One-Stop can be helpful for a variety of transitioning youth with disabilities. One-Stops are very dependent on partner agencies such as VR for funding services beyond those directly provided by the One-Stop. However, One-Stops also have funding through individual training accounts for eligible individuals. These accounts are frequently used to purchase vocational training services in support of employment goals.

The following is an example of how a One-Stop Career Center can assist in providing employment and related resources for eligible transitioning youth with disabilities.

Curtis is 17 years old and is receiving special education services because of a severe learning disability. He has participated in a variety of in-school career awareness and career exploration activities. His local One-Stop Career Center offers a Summer Youth Work Experience Program in which he can work in a paid position for 30 hours a week for 8 weeks. The One-Stop also has a work-study program during the regular school year for which Curtis is eligible. His IEP and transition plan includes his participation in the summer youth program and the work-study program as he completes his secondary program. His plan also includes application to the local vocational rehabilitation agency to assist his transition from school to the adult community.

Social Security Administration

Vital to the transition process for all students with disabilities is important consideration of Social Security benefits from the Social Security Administration (SSA). School-to-work transition has become a growing emphasis for the Social Security Administration (Virginia Commonwealth University, 2008). Many youth with disabilities either receive or are eligible to receive Social Security disability benefits such as SSI or Title II Childhood Disability Benefits. Knowing how employment might affect eligibility for these benefits is critical to students with disabilities and their families. Therefore, it makes sense for representatives from SSA or professionals with expertise in SSA benefits and employment supports to be active partners in the transition process.

Social Security benefits are a valuable resource for eligible students as they make the transition from school to adult life. Yet far too many teams fail to consider the impact of Social Security benefits on students during the formal transition planning process. Although there may be many reasons why SSA representatives are not part of the transition process, not having them on the team represents a lost opportunity to educate students with disabilities and their families at a pivotal time when they can actually apply this information. Moreover, failure to focus on Social Security benefits during transition can cause real harm when students and family members are not aware of the effects of earnings on their eligibility for cash benefits and medical insurance.

Role in Transition

Despite the many advantages of reviewing Social Security benefits as a major component of a successful transition from school to work, this is not consistently done as a major part of the transition planning process. Most school personnel do not consider the family's financial considerations to be within the scope of their responsibility. Once transition planning moves away from academic programs and into the area of financial security, teachers may become very uncomfortable. Also, school personnel themselves may not be familiar with Social Security benefits and work incentives. Without intensive training, school personnel may simply feel unprepared to address this complex issue with students and family members. Finally, schools may have limited budgets and resources. Many schools simply do not have the money or the personnel to adequately address this area when confronted with a multitude of important transition issues.

Eligibility/Provision of Services

Within the SSA, there are two major programs for individuals with disabilities: 1) the SSI program and 2) Title II Benefits including Childhood Disability Benefits and Social Security Disability Insurance. Each program has specific guidelines for participation for all U.S. citizens. The intent of the SSI program is to provide financial support and medical benefits to low-income individuals who have few resources. Qualified individuals must be 65 years of age or older, be blind, or have a disability. Table 8.1 provides an overview of the SSI program eligibility requirements (Brooke & McDonough, 2009). Title II is a disability insurance program for former workers who have paid into the Social Security system or for dependents of a retired or deceased worker, or a worker with a disability (including children under the age of 18 and children with a disability over the age of 18 if their disability was acquired prior to the age of 22).

Both the SSI and Title II programs have their own application forms based on a unique set of eligibility criteria; however, both programs share the same disability application. The disability portion of the application process is initiated through the local SSA office, but the actual decision regarding the determination of a disability is made by the

Table 8.1.   SSI program eligibility

Social Security Income Program Eligibility	
Eligibility Rule #1	Applicant must be a US Citizen, or meet special requirements for non-citizens under the law.
Eligibility Rule #2	Applicant must have a disability that seriously limits him/her from activities that other students are engaged in. If the individual is 18 years of age or older, a disability must limit ability to do work, at least at the time of application for SSI.
Eligibility Rule #3	Applicant must have a limited amount of income and possess few resources. Resources are defined as money or other possessions which can not exceed $2,000 at the time of application or $3,000 if married and live with spouse.
Eligibility Rule #4	Once the applicant is found eligible for SSI go to the Disability Determination Office to file for Medicaid because of automatic eligibility.

From Social Security and Work Incentives, by V. Brooke & J. McDonough, 2009, *Transition IEPs: A Curriculum Guide for Teachers*, 3rd Ed. (p. 130), P. Wehman & K.M. Wittig (Eds.) 2009, Austin, TX: PRO-ED. Copyright 2009 by PRO-ED, Inc. Reprinted with permission.

state's Disability Determination Services office. For youth applying for SSI, the definition of *disability* that is used is that

> The child has very little income and resources (including the income and resources of family members in the same household) and is not engaging in substantial gainful work activity. Also, the child must have a physical or mental condition(s) that very seriously limits his or her activities; and the condition(s) must have lasted, or be expected to last, at least 1 year or result in death. (Social Security Administration, 2010a)

For an individual who applies for Title II as a disabled worker, disabled widow, or for a childhood disability benefit; and for an adult applying for SSI, the definition of *disability* that is used is

> The inability to engage in any substantial gainful activity by reason of any medically determinable physical or mental impairment which can be expected to result in death or which has lasted or can be expected to last a continuous period of not less than 12 months. (SSA, 2010b)

There are several differences between SSI and Title II. One difference is that eligibility for SSI is based on whether an individual needs the additional income in order to pay for food and rent. Title II is a benefit that people pay into like other insurance programs. This difference is apparent in the eligibility process for each program. SSA considers all of the income a person has (e.g., wages, other public benefits, bank accounts) when determining eligibility for SSI but only looks at wages to determine Title II eligibility.

Another difference between the two programs is how the amount of the benefits is determined. For SSI, SSA uses a specific calculation that takes into consideration any unearned income (e.g., Title II) an individual receives, his or her earnings from a job (if the person has one), and applicable work incentives. Once all of the numbers are calculated, the SSI amount is determined. The amount of someone's SSI check can vary from month to month based on these factors. The most an individual could receive in SSI per month in 2010 was $674 (http://www.ssa.gov/OACT/COLA/SSI.html).

In contrast, the amount of an individual's Title II check will not vary from month to month. However, the amount does vary from person to person. One individual may receive a Title II check of $1,000, whereas another will only receive $200. This represents the difference in how long a person has paid into the system and how many credits he or she had when he or she became disabled, by SSA standards.

A final difference between the two programs is how they are affected by work. When an individual receives SSI only and also works, the amount of the SSI will decrease as the paycheck increases. If the person decreases his or her number of work hours (and, therefore, the paycheck amount), then that individual's SSI will increase. Individuals who receive Title II receive either the full Title II benefit check or no check at all. This depends on where they are in their benefits cycle as well as how much they are earning. There is no gradual increase or decrease as their paycheck fluctuates. Table 8.2 describes the major work

Table 8.2. SSI and Title II employment supports: Work incentives and exclusions

Program and type of work incentive/ exclusion	Description of work incentive	SSA web resources
SSI 1619(a)	Special SSI payments received by individuals when working over the substantial gainful activity level	http://www.socialsecurity.gov/redbook/eng/ssisupports.htm#5
SSI 1619(b)	Protects individuals' Medicaid coverage when their earnings are high enough to result in the loss of their SSI payment	http://www.socialsecurity.gov/redbook/eng/ssi-only-employment-supports.htm#8
SSI Blind Work Expense	Expenses necessary for work that individuals with blindness incur	http://www.ssa.gov/ssi/spotlights/spot-blind-work.htm http://www.ssa.gov/redbook/eng/blindrules.htm#3
SSI Plan to Achieve Self-Support	Allows individuals to set aside income and/or resources to reach a vocational goal, resulting in greater financial success	http://www.ssa.gov/pubs/11017.html http://www.socialsecurity.gov/redbook/eng/ssi-only-employment-supports.htm#3 http://www.ssa.gov/ssi/spotlights/spot-plans-self-support.htm
SSI student earned income exclusion	Allows people under the age of 22 who are regularly attending school to exclude up to $1,550 of monthly earnings and up to $6,240 of yearly earnings	http://www.socialsecurity.gov/redbook/eng/ssi-only-employment-supports.htm#2 http://www.ssa.gov/ssi/spotlights/spot-student-earned-income.htm
SSI and Title II impairment-related work expense	Expenses necessary for work that people incur because of a disability and that are paid by the individuals themselves	http://www.socialsecurity.gov/redbook/eng/ssdi-and-ssi-employments-supports.htm#3 http://www.ssa.gov/ssi/spotlights/spot-work-expenses.htm
Title II extended period of eligibility	Period of 36 months immediately following the trial work period in which individuals will receive cash benefits for any month in which earnings fall below the substantial gainful activity level	http://www.socialsecurity.gov/redbook/eng/ssdi-only-employment-supports.htm#2
Title II trial work period	Period of at least 9 months in which individuals can try out work (at any earnings level) without losing their cash benefit	http://www.socialsecurity.gov/redbook/eng/ssdi-only-employment-supports.htm#1
Title II unsuccessful work attempt	Earnings that ended or fell below the substantial gainful activity level after 6 months or less because of disability or the loss of necessary supports needed to work	http://www.socialsecurity.gov/redbook/2010/glossary.htm

From Social Security and Work Incentives, by V. Brooke & J. McDonough, 2009, *Transition IEPs: A Curriculum Guide for Teachers, 3rd Ed.* (pp. 133-134), P. Wehman & K.M. Wittig (Eds.) 2009, Austin, TX: PRO-ED. Copyright 2009 by PRO-ED, Inc. Adapted with permission.
Key: SSI, Supplemental Security Income; SSDI, Social Security Disability Insurance; SSA, Social Security Administration.

incentives associated with both the SSI and the Title II programs and lists web resources to consult for additional information.

Each of the work incentives and exclusions listed in Table 8.2 has its own set of guidelines. Unfortunately, for many years the SSA work incentives have been grossly underutilized.

- *1619(a)*. This is a special provision established by the Employment Opportunity for Disabled Americans Act of 1986 (PL 99-643). When SSI recipients work, the amount of their SSI is dependent on their income and earnings. Provision 1619(a) enables individuals who continue to be disabled to receive special SSI cash benefits in place of their regular SSI payments when their earnings exceed the substantial gainful activity level. There are no observable differences in SSI payments to individuals who are in 1619(a) status.

- *1619(b)*. This provision was also established by Public Law 99-643. This status allows SSI recipients to keep their Medicaid eligibility when their earnings become too high to receive an SSI cash payment. Individuals are eligible for 1619(b) up until they reach their state's threshold amount. These amounts may vary from state to state as a result of variations in the cost of medical services.

Gaining a full understanding of these employment supports prior to engaging in work can enable transition-age youth and their families to make informed decisions and to make a smoother transition into employment and independence.

CONCLUSION: PULLING THE RESOURCES TOGETHER

For youth with disabilities, their families, and the educators supporting them, moving from the secondary-level education system to the adult services community is truly a mix of opportunities and challenges. The opportunities come from the array of services and resources that are potentially available. VR offers a national network of state agencies and community services that are specifically designed to assist individuals with disabilities to achieve and maintain employment outcomes. CRPs can offer more prescriptive localized services that match to local cultures and economies. Community services boards and agencies can mix a variety of community living supports such as service coordination and supported living with access to funding for employment through, for example, a prescriptive HCBS Medicaid Waiver program. One-Stop Career Centers offer a variety of resources and services that directly support transition to community living and employment. Timely and effective WIPA can provide families with a confident understanding of the relationship between employment and receipt of disability benefits.

The challenge faced by youth with disabilities and local school systems is that these many resources vary considerably at the state and local levels. Some do not exist in certain communities or have limited funding and long waiting lists. Eligibility requirements vary from state to state and program to program. Being well informed about resources at the community and state levels *and* learning how to network effectively is key to representatives of the school system and the adult service system working together to plan and implement a successful, effective transition program for youth with disabilities. For example, the transition team can reach out to key community resources both formally (e.g., with an invitation for them to join the transition team) and more informally (e.g., as sources of general information and referrals for families). The key to successful transition is for a youth with disabilities and his or her family to be well informed early on in the transition process about which community resources are of value and then networking effectively with those resources throughout the transition process.

The adult service system is complex, but understanding it is essential for effective transition planning. While in school, students receive services and supports as mandated by federal and state laws. After they graduate from school or turn 22 years of age, they may be eligible for services from adult service agencies, but because these services are usually not an entitlement, there is no guarantee that they will receive them. Consequently, it is essential that educators, parents, and students understand the adult service system years before they will need to access it.

FOR FURTHER INFORMATION

Accessing Community-Based Services

Ticket to Work Service Provider Directory (https://secure.ssa.gov/apps10/oesp/providers.nsf/bystate)

This is an online directory of protection and advocacy centers, Workplace Incentives Planning and Assistance providers, and rehabilitation providers in each state.

Benefits Offered by HCBS Medicaid Waivers

Clearinghouse for Home- and Community-Based Services (http://www.hcbs.org/)

This comprehensive web site details many services offered by state, topic, and specific product type or source.

Vocational Rehabilitation Services and States' Offices

U.S. Department of Education (http://www2.ed.gov/about/contacts/state/index.html)

This site, called ED.gov, includes state offices of education including information on contacts for disability-related issues.

References

Agran, M., Cain, H.M., & Cavin, J.D. (2002). Enhancing the involvement of rehabilitation counselors in the transition process. *Career Development for Exceptional Individuals, 25,* 123–137.

Agran, M., & Hughes, C. (2008). Students' opinions regarding their individualized education program involvement. *Career Development for Exceptional Individuals, 31,* 69–76.

Alwell, M., & Cobb, B. (2009). Functional life skills curricular interventions for youth with disabilities. *Career Development for Exceptional Individuals, 32,* 82–93.

American Youth Policy Forum & Center for Workforce Development. (2000, June). Looking forward: School-to-work principles and strategies for sustainability. Washington, DC: Author.

Americans with Disabilities Act of 1990, PL 101-336, 42 U.S.C. §§ 12101 *et seq.*

Armstrong, T. (2007). The curriculum superhighway. *Educational Leadership, 64*(8), 16–20.

Baer, R.M., Flexer, R.W., Beck, S., Amstutz, N., Hoffman, L., Brothers, J., et al. (2003). A collaborative follow-up study on transition service utilization and post-school outcomes. *Career Development for Exceptional Individuals, 26,* 7–25.

Bambara, L.M., Wilson, B.A., & McKenzie, M. (2007). Post school and adult issues. *Transition and Quality of Life, 18,* 371–389.

Bassett, D.S., & Kochhar-Bryant, C.A. (2006). Strategies for aligning standards-based education and transition. *Focus on Exceptional Children, 39*(2), 1–19.

Bateman, B.D., & Linden, M. (1997). *Better IEPs: How to develop legally correct and educationally useful programs.* Longmont, CO: Sopris West.

Beach Center on Disability. (n.d.). *Quality indicators of exemplary transition programs.* Retrieved April 20, 2010, from http://www.fcsn.org/pti/topics/transition/tools/handouts/quality_indicators.pdf

Benz, M.R., Lindstrom, L., & Halpern, A.S. (1995). Mobilizing local communities to improve transition services. *Career Development for Exceptional Individuals, 18,* 21–32.

Benz, M.R., Lindstrom, L., & Yovanoff, P. (2000). Improving graduation and employment outcomes of students with disabilities: Predictive factors and student perspectives. *Exceptional Children, 66,* 509–529.

Benz, M.R., Yovanoff, P., & Doren, B. (1997). School-to-work components that predict postschool success for students with and without disabilities. *Exceptional Children, 63,* 151–165.

Black, R., & Langone, J. (1997). Social awareness and transition to employment for adolescents with mental retardation. *Remedial and Special Education, 18,* 214–222.

Boeltzig, H., Gilmore, D., & Butterworth, J. (2006, July). *The national survey of community rehabilitation providers, FY 2004-2005: Employment outcomes of people with developmental disabilities in integrated employment.* Boston: University of Massachusetts Boston, Institute for Community Inclusion.

Bond, G.R., Becker, D.R., Drake, R.E., Rapp, C.A., Meisler, N., Lehman, A.F., et al. (2001). Implementing supported employment as an evidence-based practice. *Psychiatric Services, 52*(3), 313–322.

Bouck, E.C. (2009). No Child Left Behind, the Individuals with Disabilities Education Act and functional curricula: A conflict of interest? *Education and Training in Developmental Disabilities, 44,* 3–13.

Braddock, D., Hemp, R., & Rizzolo, M.C. (2004). State of the states in developmental disabilities: 2004. *Mental Retardation, 42,* 356–370.

Braddock, D., Hemp, P., & Rizzolo, M. (2008). *The state of the states in developmental disabilities* (7th ed.). Washington, DC: American Association on Intellectual and Developmental Disabilities.

Braddock, D., Rizzolo, M., & Hemp, R. (2004). Most employment services growth in developmental disabilities during 1988–2002 was in segregated settings. *Mental Retardation, 42,* 317–320.

Brady, M.P., Rosenberg, H., & Frain, M.P. (2008). A self-evaluation instrument for work performance and support needs. *Career Development for Exceptional Individuals, 31,* 175–185.

Bremer, C.D., & Madzar, S. (1995). Encouraging employer involvement in youth apprenticeship and other work-based learning experiences for high school students. *Journal of Vocational and Technical Education, 12*(1), 15–26.

Brooke, V., Green, J.H., Revell, W.G., & Wehman, P. (2006). Transition planning in the community: Using all of the resources. In P. Wehman, *Life beyond the classroom: Transition strategies for young people with disabilities* (4th ed., pp. 97–129). Baltimore: Paul H. Brookes Publishing Co.

Brooke, V., & McDonough, J. (2009). Social security and work incentives. In P. Wehman & K.M. Wittig (Eds.), *Transition IEPs: A curriculum guide for teachers and transition practitioners* (3rd ed., pp. 129–139). Austin, TX: PRO-ED.

Brooke, V., Revell, G., & Wehman, P. (2009). Quality indicators for competitive employment outcomes: What special education teachers need to know in transition planning. *TEACHING Exceptional Children, 41*(4), 58–66.

Brooks-Lane, N., Hutcheson, S., & Revell, G. (2005). Supporting consumer-directed employment outcomes. *Journal of Vocational Rehabilitation, 23,* 123–134.

Brown, L., Long, E., Udvari-Solner, A., Davis, L., VanDeventer, P., Ahlgren, C., et al. (1989). The home school: Why students with severe intellectual disabilities must attend the schools of their brothers, sisters, friends, and neighbors. *Journal of The Association for Persons with Severe Handicaps, 14*(4), 1–7.

Butterworth, J., Smith, F.A., Cohen-Hall, A., Migliore, A., & Winsor, J.E. (2008). *StateData: The National Report on Employment Services and Outcomes.* Boston: University of Massachusetts Boston, Institute for Community Inclusion.

Camarena, P.M., & Sarigiani, P.A. (2009). Postsecondary education aspirations of high-functioning adolescents with autism spectrum disorders and their parents. *Focus on Autism and Other Developmental Disabilities, 24,* 115–128.

Cameto, R. (2005). *The transition planning process.* Minneapolis: University of Minnesota, National Center on Secondary Education and Transition.

Cameto, R., Newman, L., & Wagner, M. (2006, June). *The National Longitudinal Transition Study-2 (NLTS2) project update: Self-perceptions of youth with disabilities.* Washington, DC: Institute of Education Sciences.

Carter, E.W., & Hughes, C. (2006). Including high school students with severe disabilities in general education classes: Perspectives of general and special educators, paraprofessionals, and administrators. *Research and Practice for Persons with Severe Disabilities, 31,* 174–185.

Carter, E.W., & Lunsford, L.B. (2005). Meaningful work: Improving employment outcomes for transition-age youth with emotional and behavioral disorders. *Preventing School Failure, 49*(2), 63–69.

Carter, E.W., Owens, L., Trainor, A.A., Sun, Y., & Swedeen, B. (2009). Self-determination skills and opportunities of adolescents with severe intellectual and developmental disabilities. *American Journal on Intellectual and Developmental Disabilities, 114*(3), 179–192.

Carter, E.W., Trainor, A.A., Sun, Y., & Owens, L. (2009). Assessing the transition-related strengths and needs of adolescents with high-incidence disabilities. *Exceptional Children, 76,* 74–94.

Casner-Lotto, J., & Barrington, L. (2006). *Are they really ready to work? Employers' perspectives on the basic knowledge and applied skills of new entrants to the 21st century workforce.* Retrieved June 28, 2010, from http://www.21stcenturyskills.org.documents/FINAL_REPORT_PDF9-29-06.pdf

Center for Applied Special Technology. (2009). *Universal design for learning.* Retrieved August 31, 2009, from http://www.cast.org/

Certo, N., & Luecking, R. (2006). Service integration and school to work transition: Customized employment as an outcome for youth with significant disabilities. *Journal of Applied Rehabilitation Counseling, 37,* 29–35.

Certo, N., Luecking, R., Murphy, S., Brown, L., Courey, S., & Belanger, D. (2008). Seamless transition and long-term support for individuals with severe intellectual disabilities. *Research and Practice for Persons with Severe Disabilities, 33*(3), 85–95.

Chambers, C.R., Hughes, C., & Carter, E.W. (2004). Parent and sibling perspectives on the transition to adulthood. *Education and Training in Developmental Disabilities, 39*(2), 79–94.

Cimera, R.E. (2000). Improving the cost efficiency of supported employment programs. *Journal of Disability Policy Studies, 11,* 145–151.

Cimera, R.E. (2008). The cost-trends of supported versus sheltered employment. *Journal of Vocational Rehabilitation, 28,* 15–20.

Cimera, R.E., & Rusch, F.R. (1999). Empirical evidence on the long-term effectiveness of supported employment: A literature review. In L.M. Glidden (Ed.), *International research on mental retardation* (Vol. 22, pp. 175–226). San Diego: Academic Press.

Clark, G.M., & Patton, J.R. (2006). *Transition Planning Inventory–Updated Version: Administration and resource guide.* Austin, TX: PRO-ED.

Cobb, R.B., & Alwell, M. (2009). Transition planning/coordinating interventions for youth with disabilities: A systematic review. *Career Development for Exceptional Individuals, 32,* 70–81.

Colleg-Klingenberg, L.L. (1998). The reality of best practices in transition: A case study. *Exceptional Children, 65,* 67–78.

Colley, D.A., & Jamison, D. (1998). Postschool results for youth with disabilities: Key indicators and policy implications. *Career Development for Exceptional Individuals, 21,* 145–160.

Conley, R.W. (2003). Supported employment in Maryland: Success and issues. *Mental Retardation, 41*(4), 237–249.

Cooney, B.F. (2002). Exploring perspectives on transition of youth with disabilities: Voices of young adults, parents, and professionals. *Mental Retardation, 40,* 425–435.

Crane, K., & Mooney, M. (2005). *Essential tools: Community resource mapping.* Retrieved September 12, 2009, from http://www.ncset.org/publications/essentialtools/mapping/default.asp

Datillo, J., & Hoge, G. (1999). Effects of a leisure education program on youth with mental retardation. *Education and Training in Mental Retardation and Developmental Disabilities, 34,* 20–34.

deFur, S.H. (2005). Transition from school to adulthood. In P. Wehman, P.J. McLaughlin, & T. Wehman (Eds.), *Intellectual and developmental disabilities: Toward full community inclusion* (3rd ed., pp. 123–148). Austin, TX: PRO-ED.

deFur, S., & Korinek, L. (2008). The evolution toward lifelong learning as a critical transition outcome for the 21st century. *Exceptionality, 16,* 178–191.

deFur, S.H., & Taymans, J.M. (1995). Competencies needed for transition specialists in vocational rehabilitation, vocational education, and special education. *Exceptional Children, 62,* 38–51.

Eckes, S.E., & Ochoa, T.A. (2005). Students with disabilities: Transitioning from high school to higher education. *American Secondary Education, 33*(3), 6–20.

Eisenman, L.T. (2007). Social networks and careers of young adults with intellectual disabilities. *Intellectual and Developmental Disabilities, 45*(3), 199–208.

Eisenman, L.T., Tanverdi, A., Perrington, C., & Geiman, A. (2009). Secondary and postsecondary community activities of youth with significant intellectual disabilities. *Education and Training in Developmental Disabilities, 44,* 168–176.

Elliott, S.N., & Roach, A.T. (2007). Alternate assessments of students with significant cognitive disabilities: Alternate approaches, common technical challenges. *Applied Measurement in Education, 20,* 301–333.

Employment Opportunity for Disabled Americans Act of 1986, PL 99-643, 42 U.S.C. §§ 1382 *et seq.*

Epstein, M.H., Rudolph, S., & Epstein, A.A. (2000). Using strength-based assessment in transition planning. *TEACHING Exceptional Children, 32*(6), 50–54.

Etscheidt, S. (2006). Issues in transition planning. *Career Development for Exceptional Individuals, 29,* 28–47.

Fair Labor Standards Act of 1938. PL 106-151, 29 U.S.C. §§ 201, *et seq.*

Fairweather, J., & Shaver, D. (1991). Making the transition to postsecondary education and training. *Exceptional Children, 57,* 264–270.

Federal Register (2001, January). State Vocational Rehabilitation Services Program: Final rule. Retrieved May 16, 2010, from http://www2.ed.gov/legislation/FedRegister/finrule/2001-1/011701a.html

Federal Register. (2002, June). *67*(123), pp. 43149–43154.

Fowler, C.H., Konrad, M., Walker, A.R., Test, D.W., & Wood, W.M. (2007). Self-determination interventions' effects on the academic performance of students with developmental disabilities. *Education and Training in Developmental Disabilities, 42,* 270–285.

Frank, A.R., & Sitlington, P.L. (2000). Young adults with mental disabilities: Does transition planning make a difference? *Education and Training in Developmental Disabilities, 35,* 119–134.

Garner, D., Bartholomew, C. & Thoma, C.A. (2007, March). *Mission possible: Successful transition to postsecondary education.* Presentation at the Division of Career Development and Transition (DCDT) Transition Forum, Norfolk, VA.

Garner, D.B. (2008). Postsecondary education success: Stories of three students with learning disabilities. *TEACHING Exceptional Children Plus, 4*(4). Retrieved August 27, 2009, from http://escholarship.bc.edu/education/tecplus/vol4/iss4/art4

Geenen, S., Powers, L., & Lopez-Vasquez, A. (2001). Multicultural aspects of parent involvement in transition planning. *Exceptional Children, 67,* 265–282.

Gervey, R., Gao, N., & Rizzo, D. (2004). Gloucester county one-stop project: Baseline level of access and satisfaction of one-stop customers with disabilities. *Journal of Vocational Rehabilitation, 21,* 103–115.

Getzel, E.E., & Thoma, C.A. (2005). "Self-determination is what it's all about": What post-secondary students with disabilities tell us are important considerations for success. *Education and Training in Developmental Disabilities, 40,* 234–242.

Getzel, E.E., & Wehman, P. (Eds.). (2005). *Going to college: Expanding opportunities for people with disabilities.* Baltimore: Paul H. Brookes Publishing Co.

Goldberger, S., Keough, R., & Almeida, C. (2001). Benchmarks for success in high school education: Putting data to work in school-to-careers education reform. Providence, RI: The Education Alliance, Brown University.

Greene, G., & Kochhar-Bryant, C.A. (2003). *Pathways to successful transition for youth with disabilities.* Upper Saddle River, NJ: Prentice Hall.

Griffin, C., Brooks-Lane, N., Hammis, D.G., & Crandell, D. (2006). Self-employment: Owning the American dream. In P. Wehman, K.J. Inge, W.G. Revell, Jr., & V.A. Brooke (Eds.), *Real work for real pay: Inclusive employment for people with disabilities* (pp. 215–235). Baltimore: Paul H. Brookes Publishing Co.

Griffin, C., & Hammis, D. (2003). *Making self-employment work for people with disabilities.* Baltimore: Paul H. Brookes Publishing Co.

Griffin, C., Hammis, D., Geary, T., & Sullivan, M. (2008). Customized employment: Where we are; where we're headed. *Journal of Vocational Rehabilitation, 28,* 135–139.

Grigal, M., & Neubert, D.A. (2004). Parents' in-school values and post-school expectations for transition-aged youth with disabilities. *Career Development for Exceptional Individuals, 27,* 65–85.

Grigal, M., Neubert, D.A., & Moon, M.S. (2001). Public school programs for students with significant disabilities in postsecondary settings. *Education and Training in Developmental Disabilities, 36,* 244–254.

Gumpel, T.P., Tappe, P., & Araka, C. (2000). Comparison of social problem-solving abilities among adults with and without developmental disabilities. *Education and Training in Mental Retardation and Developmental Disabilities, 35,* 259–268.

Haimson J., & Belloti, J. (2001). *Schooling in the workplace: Increasing the scale and quality of work-based learning: Final report.* Princeton, NJ: Mathematica Policy Research, Inc.

Hall, A.C., Butterworth, J., Winsor, J., Gilmore, D., & Metzel, D. (2007). Pushing the employment agenda: Case study research of high performing states in integrated employment. *Intellectual and Developmental Disabilities, 45*(3), 182–198.

Hall, M., Kleinert, H.L., & Kearns, J.F. (2000). Going to college! Postsecondary programs for students with moderate and severe disabilities. *TEACHING Exceptional Children, 32*(3), 58–65.

Halpern, A.S. (1985). Transition: A look at the foundations. *Exceptional Children, 51,* 479–486.

Halpern, A.S. (1994). The transition of youth with disabilities to adult life: A position statement of the Division on Career Development and Transition, the Council for Exceptional Children. *Career Development for Exceptional Individuals, 17,* 115–124.

Halpern, A.S., Herr, C.M., Doren, B., & Wolf, N.K. (2000). Next S.T.E.P.: Student transition and educational planning. Austin, TX: PRO-ED.

Hart, D., & Grigal, M. (2008, March). New frontier: Post secondary education for youth with intellectual disabilities. In *Section 504 Compliance Handbook* (pp. 10–11). Tampa, FL: Thompson.

Hart, D., Grigal, M., Sax, C., Martinez, D., & Will, M. (2006). Postsecondary education options for students with intellectual disabilities. *Research to Practice, 45,* 1–4.

Hart, D., Mele-McCarthy, J., Pasternack, R.H., Zimbrich, K., & Parker, D.R. (2004). Community college: A pathway to success for youth with learning, cognitive, and intellectual disabilities in secondary settings. *Education and Training in Developmental Disabilities, 39,* 54–66.

Hart, D., Zimbrich, K., & Parker, D.R. (2005). Dual Enrollment as a Postsecondary Education Option for Students with Intellectual Disabilities. In E.E. Getzel & P. Wehman (Eds.) *Going to College: Expanding Opportunities for People with Disabilities* (pp. 256–257). Baltimore: Paul H. Brookes Publishing Co.

Hartman, M.A. (2009). Step by step: Creating a community-based transition program for students with intellectual disabilities. *TEACHING Exceptional Children, 41*(6), 6–11.

Hartwig, R., & Sitlington, P.L. (2008). Employer perspectives on high school diploma options for adolescents with disabilities. *Journal of Disability Policy Studies, 19,* 5–14.

Hasazi, S., Gordon, L. & Roe, C. (1985). Factors associated within the employment status of handicapped youth exiting high school from 1979–1983. *Exceptional Children, 51,* 455–469.

Hasazi, S., Johnson, D., Thurlow, M., Cobb, B., Trach, J., Stodden, B., et al. (2005). Transitions from home and school to the roles and supports of adulthood. In

K.C. Lakin & A. Turnbull (Eds.), *National goals & research for persons with intellectual & developmental disabilities* (pp. 65–92). Washington, DC: American Association on Mental Retardation and the Arc of the United States.

Hitchings, W.E., Retish, P., & Horvath, M. (2005). Academic preparation of adolescents with disabilities for postsecondary education. *Career Development for Exceptional Individuals, 28*(1), 26–35.

Hogansen, J.M., Powers, K., Geenen, S., Gil-Kashiwabara, E., & Powers, L. (2008). Transition goals and experiences of females with disabilities: Perceptions of youth, parents, and professionals. *Exceptional Children, 74*, 215–234.

Holburn, S. (2002). How science can evaluate and enhance person-center planning. *Research and Practice for Persons with Severe Disabilities, 27*(4), 250–260.

Hughes, C., & Carter, E.W. (2000). *The transition handbook: Strategies high school teachers use that work!* Baltimore: Paul H. Brookes Publishing Co.

Hughes, C., & Carter, E. (2001). Supporting the transition from school to work and adult life. In P. Wehman (Ed.), *Supported employment in business: Expanding the capacity of workers with disabilities* (pp. 239–250). St. Augustine, FL: Training Resource Network.

Individuals with Disabilities Education Act of 1990, PL 101-476, 20 U.S.C. §§ 1400 *et seq.*

Individuals with Disabilities Education Act Amendments of 1997, PL 105-17, 20 U.S.C. §§ 1400 *et seq.*

Individuals with Disabilities Education Improvement Act of 2004, PL 108-446, 20 U.S.C. §§ 1400 *et seq.*

Inge, K.J., Strobel, W., Wehman, P., Todd, J., & Targett, P. (2000). Vocational outcomes for persons with severe physical disabilities: Design and implementation of assistive technology and workplace supports. *NeuroRehabilitation, 14*, 1–13.

Inge, K., Wehman, P., Kregel, J., & Targett, P. (1996). Vocational rehabilitation for persons with spinal cord injuries and other severe physical disabilities. *American Rehabilitation, 22*(4), 2–12.

Izzo, M.V., & Kochhar-Bryant, C.A. (2006). Implementing the SOP for effective transition: Two case studies. *Career Development for Exceptional Individuals, 29*, 100–107.

Jefferson, G.L., & Putnam, R.F. (2002). Understanding transition services: A parent's guide to legal standards and effective practices. *Exceptional Parent Magazine, 32*, 70–77.

Johnson, D.R. (2005). Key provisions on transition: A comparison of IDEA 1997 and IDEA 2004. *Career Development for Exceptional Individuals, 28*, 60–63.

Johnson, D.R., Stodden, R.A., Emanuel, E.J., Luecking, R., & Mack, M. (2002). Current challenges facing sec-ondary education and transition services: What research tells us. *Exceptional Children, 68*, 519–531.

Johnson, D.R., Thurlow, M.L., & Stout, K.E. (2007). *Revisiting graduation requirements and diploma options for youth with disabilities: A national study* (Tech. Rep. No. 49). Minneapolis: University of Minnesota, National Center on Educational Outcomes. Retrieved August 4, 2009, from http://www.cehd.umn.edu/NCEO/OnlinePubs/Tech49/default.html

Kampfer, S.H., Hovarth, L.S., Kleinert, H.L., & Kearns, J.F. (2001). Teachers' perceptions of one state's alternate assessment: Implications for practice and preparation. *Exceptional Children, 67*, 361–374.

Karpur, A., Clark, H.B., Caproni, P., & Sterner, H. (2005). Transition to adult roles for students with emotional/behavioral disturbances: A follow-up study of student exiters from Steps-to-Success. *Career Development for Exceptional Individuals, 28*, 36–46.

Kennedy, C.H., & Fisher, D. (2001). *Inclusive middle schools.* Baltimore: Paul H. Brookes Publishing Co.

Khemka, I. (2000). Increasing independent decision-making skills of women and mental retardation in simulated interpersonal situations of abuse. *American Journal on Mental Retardation, 105*, 387–401.

Kochar-Bryant, C., Shaw, S., & Izzo, M. (2007). *Transition and IDEA 2004.* Upper Saddle River, NJ: Pearson Education.

Kohler, P.D., & Field, S. (2003). Transition-focused education: Foundation for the future. *Journal of Special Education, 37*(3), 174–183.

Konrad, M., & Test, D.W. (2004). Teaching middle school students with disabilities to use an IEP template. *Career Development for Exceptional Individuals, 27*, 101–124.

Kregel, J., Wehman, P., Revell, G., Hill, J., & Cimera, R. (2000). Supported employment benefit-cost analysis: Preliminary findings. *Journal of Vocational Rehabilitation, 14*, 153–161.

Levinson, E.M. (1993). *Transdisciplinary vocational assessments: Issues in school-based programs.* Brandon, VT: Clinical Psychology Publishing.

Luecking, R.G. (2009). Work-based learning and work experiences as indispensable educational tools. In R.G. Luecking, *The way to work: How to facilitate work experiences for youth in transition* (p. 9–25). Baltimore: Paul H. Brookes Publishing Co.

Luecking, R., & Fabian, E.S. (2000). Paid internships and employment success for youth in transition. *Career Development for Exceptional Individuals, 23*, 205–221.

Madaus, J.W., Bigaj, S., Chafouleas, S.M., & Simonsen, B.M. (2006). What key information can be included in a comprehensive summary of performance? *Career Development for Exceptional Individuals, 29,* 90–99.

Mank, D., Cioffi, A., & Yovanoff, P. (2003). Supported employment outcomes across a decade: Is there evidence of improvement in the quality of implementation? *Mental Retardation, 41,* 188–197.

Martin, J.E., & Marshall, L.H. (1995). Choicemaker: A comprehensive self-determination transition program. *Intervention in School and Clinic, 30,* 147–157

Martin, J.E., Mithaug, D.E., Cox, P., Peterson, L.Y., van Dycke, J.L., & Cash, M.E. (2003). Increasing self-determination: Teaching students to plan, work, evaluate, and adjust. *Exceptional Children, 69,* 431–447.

Martin, J.E., Mithaug, D.E., Oliphint, J.H., Husch, J.V., & Frazier, E.S. (2002). *Self-directed employment: A handbook for transition teachers and employment specialists.* Baltimore: Paul H. Brookes Publishing Co.

Martin, J.E., Van Dycke, J.L., Christensen, W.R., Greene, B.A., Gardner, J.E., & Lovett, D.L. (2006). Increasing student participation in IEP meetings: Establishing the self-directed IEP as an evidence-based practice. *Exceptional Children, 72,* 299–316.

Martin, J.E., Van Dycke, J.L., Greene, B.A., Gardner, J.E., Christensen, W.R., Woods, L.L., et al. (2006). Direct observation of teacher-directed IEP meetings: Establishing the need for student IEP meeting instruction. *Exceptional Children, 72,* 187–200.

Mason, C.Y., McGahee-Kovac, M., Johnson, L., & Stillerman, S. (2002). Implementing student-led IEPs: Student participation and student and teacher reactions. *Career Development for Exceptional Individuals, 25,* 171–192.

Mastropieri, M.A., & Scruggs, T.E. (2001). Promoting inclusion in secondary schools. *Learning Disability Quarterly, 24,* 265–274.

McColl, M.A., Davies, D., Carlson, P., Johnston, J., Harrick, L., Minnes, P., et al. (1999). Transition to independent living after ABI. *Brain Injury, 13*(5), 311–330.

McConnell, J., Johnson, J.W., Polychronis, S., & Risen, T. (2002). Effects of embedded instruction on students with moderate disabilities enrolled in general education classes. *Education and Training in Mental Retardation and Developmental Disabilities, 37,* 363–377.

McDonnell, J., & Hardman, M.L. (2010). *Successful transition programs: Pathways for students with intellectual and developmental disabilities.* Thousand Oaks, CA: Sage Publications.

McGuire, J., & McDonnell, J. (2008). Relationships between recreation and levels of self-determination for adolescents and young adults with disabilities. *Career Development for Exceptional Individuals, 31,* 154–163.

McMahan, R., & Baer, R. (2001). IDEA transition policy compliance and best practice: Perceptions of transition stakeholders. *Career Development for Exceptional Individuals, 24,* 169–184.

Merchant, D.J., & Gajar, A. (1997). A review of the literature on self-advocacy components in transition programs of students with learning disabilities. *Journal of Vocational Rehabilitation, 8,* 223–231.

Miller, L., & Newbill, C. (1998). *Section 504 in the classroom: How to design & implement accommodation plans.* Austin, TX: PRO-ED.

Miner, C.A., & Bates, P.E. (1997). The effect of person-centered planning activities on the IEP/transition planning process. *Education and Training in Mental Retardation and Developmental Disabilities, 32,* 105–112.

Mooney, M., & Scholl, L. (2004, Spring). Students with disabilities in Wisconsin youth apprenticeship programs: Supports and accommodations. *Career Development for Exceptional Individuals, 27*(1), 7–26.

Morningstar, M.E., Kleinhammer-Tramill, P.J., & Lattin, D.L. (1999). Using successful models of student-centered transition planning and services for adolescents with disabilities. *Focus on Exceptional Children, 31*(9), 2–20.

Morningstar, M.E., & Liss, J.M. (2008). A preliminary investigation of how states are responding to the transition assessment requirements under IDEA 2004. *Career Development for Exceptional Individuals, 31,* 48–55.

Morningstar, M.E., Turnbull, A.P., & Turnbull, H.R. (1995). What do students with disabilities tell us about the importance of family involvement in the transition from school to adult life? *Exceptional Children, 62,* 249–260.

Morris, M. (2006, June 28). *Employment for all: Start a revolution.* Retrieved April 20, 2010, from http://www.ndi-inc.org

Mount, B. (2000). *Person-centered planning: Finding directions for change using personal futures planning.* Amenia, NY: Capacity Works.

Napoli, A.R., & Wortman, P.M. (1998). Psychosocial factors related to retention and early departure of two-year community college students. *Research in Higher Education, 39,* 419–455.

National Longitudinal Transition Study 2. (2006). *NTLS2 data brief: Youth employment.* Retrieved April 2007, from http://www.ncset.org/publications/viewdesc.asp?id=1310

National Organization on Disability. (2004). *N.O.D./ Harris Survey of Americans with disabilities: Landmark survey finds pervasive disadvantages.* Washington, DC: Author. Available at http://www.at508.com/

National Secondary Transition Technical Assistance Center. (n.d.). What is Indicator 13? Retrieved April 20, 2010, from http://www.nsttac.org/indicator13/indicator13.aspx

Neubert, D.A. (2003). The role of assessment in the transition to adult life process for students with disabilities. *Exceptionality, 11,* 63–75.

Neubert, D.A., & Moon, M.S. (2000). How a transition profile helps students prepare for life in the community. *TEACHING Exceptional Children,* 20–25.

Neubert, D.A., Moon, M.S., & Grigal, M. (2004). Activities of students with significant disabilities receiving services in postsecondary settings. *Education and Training in Developmental Disabilities, 39,* 16–25.

Newman, L., Wagner, M., Cameto, R., & Knokey, A. (2009). *The post–high school outcomes of youth with disabilities up to 4 years after high school: A report from the National Longitudinal Transition Study-2 (NLTS2).* Arlington, VA: SRI International.

Niemac, B., Lavin, D., & Owen, L.A. (2009). *Establishing a national employment first agenda.* Rockville, MD: APSE.

No Child Left Behind Act of 2001, PL 107-110, 115 Stat. 1425, 20 U.S.C. §§ 6301 *et seq.*

Noonan, P.M., Morningstar, M.E., & Erickson, A.G. (2008). Improving interagency collaboration: Effective strategies used by high-performing local districts and communities. *Career Development for Exceptional Individuals, 31,* 132–143.

O'Brien, J. (2002). Person-centered planning as a contributing factor in organizational and social change. *Research and Practice for Persons with Severe Disabilities, 27*(4), 261–264.

Office of Disability Employment Policy. (2005, June). *Customized employment–Practical solutions for employment success.* Washington, DC: U.S. Department of Labor, Office of Disability Employment Policy, and the National Center on Workforce and Disability/Adult. Retrieved April 10, 2010, from http://www.dol.gov/odep/pubs/custom/index.htm

Office of Disability Employment Policy. (n.d.). *Customized employment: Principle and indicators.* Retrieved April 20, 2010, from http://www.dol.gov/odep/pubs/custom/indicators.htm

O'Reilly, M.F., Lancioni, G.E., & O'Kane, N. (2000). Using a problem solving approach to teach social skills to workers with brain injuries in supported employment settings. *Journal of Vocational Rehabilitation, 14,* 187–194.

Parent, W. (2009, June). *Turning passions into paychecks.* Presentation at the Association for Community Living, Boulder, CO.

Pearpoint, J., Forest, M., & O'Brien, J. (1996). MAPs, Circles of Friends, and PATH: Powerful tools to help build caring communities. In S. Stainback and W. Stainback (Eds.), *Inclusion: A guide for educators* (pp. 67–86). Baltimore: Paul H. Brookes Publishing Co.

Polychronis, S., & McDonnell, J. (2010). Developing IEPs/transition plans. In J. McDonnell & M.L. Hardman (Eds.), *Successful transition programs: Pathways for students with intellectual and developmental disabilities* (pp. 90–91). Thousand Oaks, CA: Sage Publications.

Powers, K.M., Gil-Kashiwabara, E., Greenen, S.J., Powers, L.E., Balandran, J., & Palmer, C. (2005). Mandates and effective transition planning practices reflected in IEPs. *Career Development for Exceptional Individuals, 28,* 47–59.

Rehabilitation Act of 1973, PL 93-112, 29 U.S.C. §§ 701 *et seq.*

Rehabilitation Act Amendments of 1992, PL 102-569, 29 U.S.C. §§ 701 *et seq.*

Rehabilitation Act Amendments of 1998, PL 105-220, 29 U.S.C. §§ 701 *et seq.*

Rothman, T., Maldonado, J.M., & Rothman, H. (2008). Building self-confidence and future career success through a pre-college transition program for individuals with disabilities. *Journal of Vocational Rehabilitation, 28,* 73–93.

Rusch, F.R. (2008). *Beyond high school: Preparing adolescents for tomorrow's challenges* (2nd ed.). Upper Saddle River, NJ: Prentice Hall.

Scanlon, D., & Mellard, D.F. (2002). Academic and participation profiles of school-age dropouts with and without disabilities. *Exceptional Children, 68,* 239–258.

Scherer, M.J., & Craddock, G. (2002). Matching person and technology (MPT) assessment process. *Technology and Disability, 14,* 125–131.

Schwartz, A.A., Holburn, S.C., & Jacobson, J.W. (2000). Defining person-centeredness: Results of two consensus methods. *Education and Training in Mental Retardation and Developmental Disabilities, 35*(3), 235–249.

Scholl, L., & Mooney, M. (Spring, 2005). Students with learning disabilities in work-based learning programs: Factors that influence success. *The Journal for Vocational Special Needs Education.*

Shaw, S. (2006). Legal and policy perspectives on transition assessment and documentation. *Career Development for Exceptional Individuals, 29,* 108–113.

Sinclair, M.F., Christenson, S.L., & Thurlow, M.L. (2005). Promoting school completion of urban secondary youth with emotional or behavioral disabilities. *Exceptional Children, 71,* 465–482.

Singh, K., Chang, M., & Dika, S. (2007). Effects of part-time work on school achievement during high school. *Journal of Educational Research, 101*(1), 12–23.

Sitlington, P.L., & Clark, G.M. (2007). The transition assessment process and IDEIA 2004. *Assessment for Effective Intervention, 32*(3), 133–142.

Sitlington, P.L., & Neubert, D.A. (2004). Preparing youths with emotional or behavioral disorders for transition to adult life: Can it be done within the standards-based reform movement? *Behavioral Disorders, 29*(3), 279–288.

Sitlington, P.L., Neubert, D.A., Begun, W.H., Lombard, R.C., & Leconte, P.J. (2007). *Assess for success: Handbook on transition assessment.* Reston, VA: Council for Exceptional Children, Division of Career Development and Transition.

Skinner, M.E., & Lindstrom, B. (2003). Bridging the gap between high school and college: Strategies for the successful transition of students with learning disabilities. *Preventing School Failure, 47*(3), 132–137.

Smith, P. (2007). Have we made any progress? Including students with intellectual disabilities in regular education classrooms. *Intellectual and Developmental Disabilities, 45*(5), 297–309.

Snell, M.E. (1987). *Systematic instruction of persons with severe handicaps* (3rd ed.). Columbus, OH: Charles E. Merrill.

Social Security Administration. (2010a). *Social Security handbook: What is the definition of Supplemental Security Income (SSI) children's disability benefits?* Retrieved April 20, 2010, from http://www.socialsecurity.gov/OP_Home/handbook/handbook.05/handbook-0517.html

Social Security Administration. (2010b). *2010 Red Book: Overview of our disability benefits.* Retrieved April 20, 2010, from http://www.socialsecurity.gov/redbook/2010/overview-disability.htm#5

Stancliffe, R.J., & Lakin, K.C. (Eds). (2005). *Costs and outcomes of community services for people with intellectual disabilities.* Baltimore: Paul H. Brookes Publishing Co.

Storey, K. (2002). Strategies for increasing interactions in supported employment settings: An updated review. *Journal of Vocational Rehabilitation, 17,* 231–237.

Sulewksi, J.S., Butterworth, J., & Gilmore, D.S. (2006). *Community-based non-work services: Findings from the National Survey of Day and Employment Programs for People with Developmental Disabilities* (Research to Practice Brief No. 42). Boston: University of Massachusetts Boston, Institute for Community Inclusion.

Sullivan, R.C. (2001). *Position paper on the national crisis in adult services for individuals with autism: A call to action.* Retrieved January 6, 2010, from http://www.autismservicescenter.org/articles_resources.html

Targett, P. (2006) Finding jobs for young people with disabilities. In Wehman, P. (Ed.), *Life beyond the classroom: Transition strategies for young people with disabilities.* Baltimore: Paul H. Brookes Publishing Co.

Targett, P., Young, C., Revell, G., Williams, S., & Wehman, P. (2007). Customized employment in the One Stop Career Centers. *TEACHING Exceptional Children, 40*(2), 6–11.

Test, D.W., Mason, C., Hughes, C., Konrad, M., Neale, M., & Wood, W. (2004). Student involvement in individualized education program meetings. *Exceptional Children, 70,* 391–412.

Thoma, C.A. (1999). Supporting student voice in transition planning. *TEACHING Exceptional Children, 31*(5), 4–9.

Thoma, C.A., Bartholomew, C.C., & Scott, L.A. (2009). *Universal design for transition: A roadmap for planning and instruction.* Baltimore: Paul H. Brookes Publishing Co.

Thoma, C.A., & Wehman, P. (2010). *Getting the most out of IEPs: An educator's guide to the student-directed approach.* Baltimore: Paul H. Brookes Publishing Co.

Thornburg, D. (2002). *The new basics: Education and the future of work in the telematic age.* Alexandria, VA: Association for Supervision and Curriculum Development.

Tillman, J.D., & Ford, L. (2001, April). *Analysis of transition services of individualized education programs for high school students with special needs.* Paper presented at the annual meeting of the National Association of School Psychologists, Washington, DC. Retrieved February 25, 2005, from http://www.eric.ed.gov/ERICDocs/data/ericdocs2sql/content_storage_01/0000019b/80/19/33/36.pdf

Trainor, A.A. (2008). Using cultural and social capital to improve postsecondary outcomes and expand transition models for youth with disabilities. *The Journal of Special Education, 42*(3), 148–162.

Turnbull, A., & Turnbull, R. (2009). *Whole lives: A curriculum for young people in transition from school to adulthood.* Lawrence: University of Kansas, Beach Center on Disability.

U.S. Department of Education. (2005). *Alternate achievement standards for students with the most significant cognitive disabilities: Non-regulatory guidance.* Washington, DC: U.S. Department of Education, Office of Elementary and Secondary Education.

U.S. Department of Education. (2007). *Modified academic achievement standards: Non-regulatory guidance.* Washington, DC: U.S. Department of Education, Office of Elementary and Secondary Education.

U.S. General Accounting Office. (2001). *Special minimum wage program: Characteristics of workers with disabilities, their employers, and labor's management, which needs to be improved.* Washington, DC: Author.

Villa, R.A., & Thousand, J.S. (1992). Restructuring public school systems: Strategies for organizational change and progress. In R.A. Villa, J.S. Thousand, W. Stainback, & S. Stainback (Eds.), *Restructuring for caring and effective education: An administrative guide to creating heterogeneous schools* (pp. 109–140). Baltimore: Paul H. Brookes Publishing Co.

Virginia Commonwealth University. (2008). *Age 18 check-up for youth transition demonstration project participants: A guide for students, parents, and professionals fact sheet.* Accessed at VCU Work Support web site on January 17, 2008, at http://www.worksupport.com/research/viewContent.cfm/597

Virginia Commonwealth University Rehabilitation Research and Training Center. (2001). *Academic and career plan.* Richmond: Virginia Commonwealth University.

Wagner, M. (1991). *Young people with disabilities: How are they doing?* Menlo Park, CA: SRI International.

Wagner, M., Newman, L., Cameto, R., Garza, N., & Levine, P. (2005). *After high school: A first look at the postschool experiences of youth with disabilities. A report from the National Longitudinal Transition Study-2 (NLTS2).* Menlo Park, CA: SRI International.

Wagner, M., Newman, L., Cameto, R., & Levine, P. (2005). *Changes over time in the early postschool outcomes of youth with disabilities: A report of findings from the National Longitudinal Transition Study (NLTS) and the National Longitudinal Transition Study-2 (NLTS2).* Menlo Park, CA: SRI International. Available at http://www.nlts2.org/reports/2005_06/nlts2_report_2005_06_complete.pdf

Wagner, M., Newman, L., Cameto, R., Levine, R., & Marder, C. (2007). *Perceptions and expectations of youth with disabilities: A special topic report of findings from the National Longitudinal Transition Study-2 (NLTS2).* Menlo Park, CA: SRI International.

Walther-Thomas, C., & Bryant, M. (1996). Planning for effective co-teaching. *Remedial and Special Education, 17,* 255–266.

Ward, M.J. (2006). Incorporating the summary of performance into transition planning. *Career Development for Exceptional Individuals, 29,* 67–69.

Wehman, P. (2001). *Life beyond the classroom: Transition strategies for young people with disabilities.* Baltimore: Paul H. Brookes Publishing Co.

Wehman, P. (2002). *Individual transition plans.* Austin, TX: PRO-ED.

Wehman, P. (2006a). Integrated employment: If not now, when? If not us, who? *Research and Practice for Persons with Severe Disabilities, 31*(2), 122–126.

Wehman, P. (2006b). *Life beyond the classroom: Transition strategies for young people with disabilities* (4th ed.). Baltimore: Paul H. Brookes Publishing Co.

Wehman, P., Inge, K.J., Revell, W.G., & Brooke, V.A. (Eds.). (2007). *Real work for real pay: Inclusive employment for people with disabilities.* Baltimore: Paul H. Brookes Publishing Co.

Wehman, P., Revell, G., & Brooke, V. (2003). Competitive employment: Has it become the first choice yet? *Journal of Disability Policy Studies, 14,* 163–173.

Wehman, P., Smith, M.D., & Schall, C. (2009). *Autism and the transition to adulthood: Success beyond the classroom.* Baltimore: Paul H. Brookes Publishing Co.

Wehman, P., Targett, P., West, M., & Kregel, J. (2005). Productive work and employment for persons with traumatic brain injury: What have we learned after 20 years? *Journal of Head Trauma Rehabilitation, 20*(2), 115–127.

Wehman, P., & Wittig, K.M. (Eds.). (2009). *Transition IEPs: A curriculum guide for teachers and transition practitioners* (3rd ed.). Austin, TX: PRO-ED.

Wehmeyer, M.L., Gragoudas, S., & Shogren, K. (2006). Self-determination, student involvement, and leadership development. In P. Wehman, *Life beyond the classroom: Transition strategies for young people with disabilities* (4th ed., pp. 41–70). Baltimore: Paul H. Brookes Publishing Co.

Wehmeyer, M., Lawrence, M., Kelchner, K., Palmer, S., Garner, N., & Soukup, J. (2004). *Whose future is it anyway? A student-directed transition planning process* (2nd ed.). Lawrence: University of Kansas, Beach Center on Disability.

Wehmeyer, M.L., & Palmer, S.B. (2003). Adult outcomes for students with cognitive disabilities three years after high school: The impact of self-determination. *Education and Training in Developmental Disabilities, 38,* 131–144.

Wehmeyer, M.L., Palmer, S.B., Agran, M., Mithaug, D.E., & Martin, J.E. (2000). Promoting causal agency: The self-determined model of instruction. *Exceptional Children, 66,* 439–453.

Wehmeyer, M.L., Parent, W., Lattimore, J., Obremski, S., & Poston, D. (in press). Promoting self-determination and self-directed employment planning for young women with disabilities. *Journal of Social Work in Disability & Rehabilitation, 8*(3–4), 117–131.

Wehmeyer, M.L., & Schwartz, M. (1997). Self-determination and positive adult outcomes: A follow-up study of youth with mental retardation or learning disabilities. *Exceptional Children, 63,* 245–255.

West, M., Hill, J., Revell, G., Smith, G., Kregel, J., & Campbell, L. (2002). Medicaid HCB waivers and supported employment: Pre- and post-Balanced Budget Act of 1997. *Mental Retardation, 40*(2), 142–147.

White, J., & Weiner, J.S. (2004). Influence of least restrictive environment and community based training on integrated employment outcomes for transitioning students with severe disabilities. *Journal of Vocational Rehabilitation, 21,* 149–156.

Whitney-Thomas, J., & Moloney, M. (2001). "Figuring out who I am and what I want": Relationships between adolescents' sense of self and their struggles. *Exceptional Children, 67,* 375–389.

Will, M. (1984). *OSERS programming for the transition of youth with disabilities: Bridges from school to working life.* Washington, DC: U.S. Department of Education, Office of Special Education and Rehabilitation Services.

Wittenburg, D., Golden, T., & Fishman, M. (2002). Transition options for youth with disabilities: An overview of the programs and polices that affect the transition from school. *Journal of Vocational Rehabilitation, 17,* 195–206.

Wittig, K.M. (2009). Setting transition IEP goals: How it all fits together. In P. Wehman & K.M. Wittig (Eds.), *Transition IEPs: A curriculum guide for teachers and transition specialists* (3rd ed., 29–56). Austin, TX: PRO-ED.

Wood, W.M., Karvonen, M., Test, D.W., Browder, D.M., & Algozzine, B. (2004). Promoting student self-determination skills in IEP planning. *TEACHING Exceptional Children, 36*(3), 8–16.

Workforce Investment Act of 1998, PL 105-220, 29 U.S.C. §§ 2801 *et seq.*

Yell, M.L., Ryan, J.B., Rozalski, M.E., & Katsiyannis, A. (2009). The U.S. Supreme Court and special education: 2005-2007. *TEACHING Exceptional Children, 41*(3), 68–75.

Zabala, D., Minnici, A., & McMurrer, J. (2008). *State high school exit exams: A move toward end-of-course exams.* Retrieved August 4, 2009, from the Center on Education Policy Web site: http://www.cep-dc.org/_data/n_0001/resources/live/HSEEPolicyMoveTowardEOCExamsJan2008.pdf

Zafft, C., Hart, D., & Zimbrich, K. (2004). College career connection: A study of youth with intellectual disabilities and the impact of postsecondary education. *Education and Training in Developmental Disabilities, 39,* 45–53.

Index

Page numbers followed by *t* indicate tables; those followed by *f* indicates figures.

Academic and Career Plan, 10*f*–11*f*
Academic performance
    access to general education curriculum and, 3, 52, 56
    portfolio-based assessment of, 24*t*
    real-world connections to, 43, 71, 72*t*–73*t*, 83
    self-determination and, 35–36
Access
    to accommodations and supports, 7–8
    to general education curriculum, 3, 52, 56
    at One-Stop workstations, 153–154
Accommodations
    assessment of, 9, 10*f*–11*f*, 26*t*
    case examples, 41, 43, 141–142
    employment and access to, 7–8
    for postsecondary education, 9, 10*f*–11*f*, 140–141, 140*t*
    see also Supports
Accountability, 5, 86
Achievement, *see* Academic performance
Activity centers, 133–134
ADA, *see* Americans with Disabilities Act of 1990
    (PL 101-336)
Administrative support for inclusion and transition, 31, 38
Adult activity centers, 133–134
Adult life domains in transition IEP, 77, 78*t*
Adult services agencies
    building community capacity and, 108
    community transition planning and, 33
    dos and don'ts for, 114*t*
    focus questions for involvement of, 32
    form for assessing use of, 44*f*–45*f*
    funding and resources from, 148–158, 156*t*
    see also Funding and resources in adult services system
    locally driven, 106
    mix of programs used from, 146–148
    obtaining support of, 106–108
    responsibilities of, 113*t*
    role and function of, 15*t*
    status of services, 138
    transition IEP and, 86, 87, 87*t*
    see also Community agencies; *specific state agencies*
Advocacy, 87*t*, 88
    see also Self-advocacy

Aggressive behavior, 82, 111, 124*t*
Alternative assessments, 50–51
Americans with Disabilities Act (ADA) of 1990 (PL 101-336)
    high school services and, 60*t*
    postsecondary education and, 139
    self-advocacy and, 6
    work experience and, 127
Apprenticeships, 12*t*
Asperger syndrome, 8
    see also Autism spectrum disorders
Assessment
    of accommodations, 9, 10*f*–11*f*, 26*t*
    of current levels of performance, 78–79, 80*f*, 83
    forms for, *see* Assessment forms; Forms
    of interests and preferences, 11*f*, 26*t*, 43
    legislation on, 4–5
    of needs for inclusion, 38
    overview of, 15*t*, 16
    person-centered planning and, 79, 91
    of student career goals, 42–43, 44*f*–45*f*, 46*f*, 47–48, 49*f*
    for student profile data, 26*t*
    of time to begin transition planning, 81–82
    transition IEP and, 75–76, 77
    types of, *see* Assessment types
Assessment and Diploma Options Form, 53*f*–55*f*
Assessment forms
    academic and career planning, 10*f*–11*f*
    Assessment and Diploma Options Form, 53*f*–55*f*
    Checklist of Steps in Designing a Functional Assessment,
        85*f*
    College Discussion Worksheet, 59*f*
    exiting student information, 44*f*–45*f*, 46*f*
    important questions for teachers to consider, 19*f*
    Self-Assessment Form, 100*f*
    Social Competencies Worksheet, 61*f*–63*f*, 65*f*–67*f*, 68*f*–70*f*
Assessment types
    alternative, 50–51
    functional, 84, 85*f*, 136–137
    high-stakes testing, 50–52, 53*f*–55*f*, 56
    portfolio-based, 24*t*
    standardized testing, 83–84, 85*f*, 86
    vocational, 1–2, 14, 47, 100*f*, 111, 118–119, 124*t*

Assistive technology, 56, 58
Attendance records, 31*t*
Auditory learners, 41, 43
Autism, 33, 101, 136–137
Autism spectrum disorders
    adult services and, 33
    case examples, 101, 136–137, 151
    postsecondary education and, 8

Barriers
    artificial limitations as, 97
    to inclusion, 37–38, 116–117
    to independent living, 12–13
    see also Challenges
Behavior problems, 36, 82, 111, 124*t*
Bill paying and transition activities, 72*t*
Blind Work Expense, 157*t*
Body language of team members, 88–89
Brainstorming for transition planning
    case examples, 27
    social competencies, 61*f*, 65*f*, 68*f*
Budget planning and transition activities, 72*t*
Business within a business, 105–106, 139
Businesses
    business within, 105–106, 139
    community integration and, 57
    community-based vocational education and, 122*t*, 129
    role and function of, 30*t*
    visionary practices of, 130–131
    see also specific types of business

Career(s)
    assessment of goals for, 42–43, 44*f*–45*f*, 46*f*, 47–48, 49*f*
    exploration of options for, 12*t*, 24*t*–25*t*, 47–48, 72*t*, 98, 99*f*, 100*f*, 154
    forms for, *see* Career forms; Employment forms
    goals for college and, 58
    models for, 129–133
    One-Stop Career Centers and, 30*t*, 87*t*, 120, 121*t*, 137–138, 153–154, 158
    self-determination and, 36*t*
    transition IEP and advancement of, 8–9, 10*f*–11*f*
    vocational assessment and, 14
    work experiences for, 42–43, 57, 127–128
    see also Employment; *specific careers*
Career and Vocational Transition Worksheet, 44*f*–45*f*
Career forms
    Career and Vocational Transition Worksheet, 44*f*–45*f*
    Employment Exploration Activity: What Did I Do? What Did I Learn?, 99*f*
    planning, 10*f*–11*f*
    Self-Assessment Form, 100*f*
Career maturity, 14
Case examples
    curriculum development, 41, 43, 48, 57–58, 65*f*–67*f*, 68*f*–70*f*
    employment, 1–2, 127–128, 136–137, 141–142
    funding and resources, 145, 147–148, 151, 154
    implementation of transition IEP, 111, 124*t*
    individual and community transition planning, 23, 24*t*–25*t*, 27, 33–34, 35, 75–76
    transition, 1–2

transition IEP, 75–76
    writing transition IEP, 95–96, 98, 101, 103, 105–106
Centers for independent living, 30*t*, 87*t*
Challenges
    of access to general education curriculum, 3, 52, 56
    artificial limitations as, 97
    of community-based programs, 31*t*
    of families, 115
    to resource use, 158–159
    see also Barriers
Checklist, Transition Planning, 20*f*
Checklist, What a Student Will Need Post-High School, 21*f*
Checklist for Supporting Transition Planning and Review, 18*f*
Checklist of Important Questions for a Teacher to Consider, 19*f*
Checklist of Steps for Including Parents in the Transition IEP Process, 90*f*
Checklist of Steps in Designing a Functional Assessment, 85*f*
Childhood Disability Benefits, 154–158, 156*t*, 157*t*
Circle of support, 75–76
Clerical work, 149–150
Cognitive disabilities, 24*t*, 105–106, 135
    see also Intellectual disabilities
Collaboration, *see* Interagency collaboration
College, *see* Postsecondary education
College Discussion Worksheet, 59*f*
Communication, 31*t*, 78*t*, 88–89
Community agencies
    blending resources and, 146
    case examples, 136–137
    community rehabilitation programs, 147–148, 150–151, 158
    community resource mapping and, 56–57
    community services boards, 30*t*, 145, 151–153, 158
    employment service organizations, 119–120, 121*t*, 150–151, 158
    funding and resources from, *see* Funding and community resources
    obtaining support of, 106–108
    One-Stop Career Centers, 30*t*, 87*t*, 120, 121*t*, 137–138, 153–154, 158
    policy compliance and, 7–8
    see also Adult services agencies; *specific state agencies*
Community college, 58, 77, 80
    see also Postsecondary education
Community employment service organizations (ESO)
    funding and resources from, 150–151, 158
    overview of, 119–120, 121*t*
Community integration, 57, 108
Community living
    building community capacity and, 108
    functional assessment for, 85*f*
    social competence and, 58, 60, 61*f*–63*f*, 64, 65*f*–67*f*, 68*f*–70*f*
    see also Independent living
Community participation
    building community capacity and, 108
    community-based instruction and, 121
    current level of performance examples, 80*f*
    as focus of transition, 78*t*
    goal example for, 78
Community rehabilitation programs (CRP)
    case examples, 147–148
    funding and resources in, 150–151, 158
    see also State vocational rehabilitation services

Community resource mapping (CRM), 56–57
Community services boards
    case examples, 145
    funding and resources from, 151–153, 158
    role and function of, 30t
Community transition planning
    case examples, 33–34, 35
    community resources for, 29–30, 30t
    see also Funding and community resources
    inclusion in schools and communities, 36–38
    interagency collaboration in, 29–33
    program development, 29, 31t
    self-determination and, 34–36, 36t
    supports, 33–34
    see also individual and community transition planning
Community-based instruction
    employment and, 97, 121
    overview of, 56–57, 121–122, 122t, 123t
    vocational education program, see Community-based
        vocational education program
Community-based vocational education program
    artificial limitations and, 97
    case examples, 25t, 127–128, 136–137
    designing and implementing, 121–122, 122t–123t
    models for, 129–133
    overview of, 57, 129–130
    vocational educators and, 15t, 113t
    work experiences in, 12t, 26–27
Companions and social competence, 9t
Competitive employment, 42, 134
    see also Employment
Computer science career, 57–58
Contracts, challenges of, 31t
Cooperative education experiences, 12t
Cooperative work, 12t
Core content, see General education curriculum
Counselors
    guidance counselors, 15t, 43, 51
    job coaches, 95–96, 135–137, 147–148
    vocational rehabilitation, see Vocational rehabilitation
        counselors
County human services agencies, 87t
    see also Adult services; Community agencies
Creativity in writing transition IEP, 106–107
CRM, see Community resource mapping
CRP, see Community rehabilitation programs
Current levels of performance, 78–79, 80f, 83
Curriculum development
    access to general education curriculum, 3, 52, 56
    career goal exploration for, 42–43, 44f–45f, 46f, 47–48, 49f
    case examples, 41, 43, 48, 57–58, 65f–67f, 68f–70f
    community-based instruction, 56–57
    forms for, see Curriculum development forms
    high-stakes testing and diploma decisions, 50–52, 53f–55f,
        56
    operationalizing skills, 64, 71, 72t–74t
    overview of, 41–42, 73
    postsecondary education and, 57–58, 59f, 60t
    social competence and, 58, 60, 61f–63f, 64, 65f–67f, 68f–70f
    ten precious minutes and, 49f, 71, 73
Curriculum development forms
    Assessment and Diploma Options Form, 53f–55f
    Career and Vocational Transition Worksheet, 44f–45f

College Discussion Worksheet, 59f
My Future, 49f
Postsecondary Education Transition Worksheet, 46f
Social Competencies Worksheet, 61f–63f, 65f–67f, 68f–70f
Customized employment, 137–138
    see also Employment

Dates for implementation in transition IEP, 79–80
Day care workers, 105
Day programs, 133–134
DDS, see Disabilities Support Services Office
Decision making by students, 6, 58, 59f
Depression case example, 145
Developmental disabilities/mental health agencies
    case examples, 145
    funding and resources from, 151–153, 158
    overview of, 116–117
    transition services integration model and, 130
    see also Adult services agencies; Community agencies;
        State vocational rehabilitation services
Diploma decisions, 50–52, 53f–55f, 56
Disabilities Support Services Office (DSS), 139, 140, 140t
Disability definition for eligibility, 156
Dos and don'ts of transition IEP implementation, 114t
Dual enrollment programs, 131–132

Earnings, see Wages
Ecological inventory of subenvironments, 85f
Educators
    challenges of, 31t
    forms for, 19f, 20f
    see also Forms
    on inclusive education, 38
    as key resources, 111–112
    roles and responsibilities of, 15t, 113t, 134, 142–143
    transition topics embedded by, 49f, 71, 73
Eligibility requirements
    challenges of, 146
    community rehabilitation programs, 151
    need to know, 117
    Social Security benefits, 155–156, 156t
    state developmental disabilities and community boards
        services, 152
    vocational rehabilitation services, 149
Emotional disorders, 82, 145
Employment
    assessment for, 1–2, 118–119
    case examples, 1–2, 127–128, 136–137, 141–142
    challenges of, 12–13
    community-based instruction and, 97, 121
    current level of performance examples, 80f
    exploration of, 98, 99f, 100f
    as focus of transition, 78t
    forms for, see Employment forms
    funding and resources for, 119–120, 133, 138, 146–148
    see also Funding and resources
    future steps on, 142
    Girls at Work program for, 107
    goal example, 77
    high school diploma types and, 52
    individualized plan for, 149–150

Employment—*continued*
  intellectual disabilities and, 8, 9*t*, 12, 130
  interagency collaboration and, 116
  legislation on, 4–5
  models for vocational education, career, training, 129–133
  One-Stop Career Centers and, 120, 121*t*
  as outcome intended, 98
  overview of, 128–129, 142–143
  parent involvement and, 89
  postsecondary education and, 139–142, 140*t*
  prevalence figures for, 97, 130
  self-determination and, 34–35, 36*t*, 101, 102*f*
  severe disabilities and, 27, 132–133
  significant support needs and, 120, 133–134, 135, 137–138
  social competence and, 8, 9*t*, 61*f*–63*f*, 64, 68*f*–70*f*
  Social Security benefits and, 148, 154–158, 157*t*
  student profile data questions for, 26*t*
  Summary of Performance and, 5
  supports and, 7–8, 9, 10*f*–11*f*, 12, 134
  task analysis approach to, 103
  technology and success in, 56
  transition IEP and, 8–9, 10*f*–11*f*
  types of, *see* Employment types
  vocational rehabilitation and, 117–118, 148
  vocational support service models for, 133–139
  work experiences for, *see* Employment and work experiences
  see also Career(s); *specific jobs*
Employment and work experiences
  case examples, 24*t*–25*t*, 33–34, 127–128
  community-based vocational activities, 57
  curriculum development and, 42–43, 57
  funding and resources for, 13
  impact on families, 122
  types of, 9, 12*t*
  in vocational education program, 12*t*, 26–27
  vocational rehabilitation counselors and, 118
Employment Exploration Activity: What Did I Do? What Did I Learn? 99*f*
Employment forms
  Employment Exploration Activity: What Did I Do? What Did I Learn? 99*f*
  planning, 10*f*–11*f*
  Self-Assessment Form, 100*f*
  skills summary, 43, 44*f*–45*f*, 46*f*
  Social Competencies Worksheet, 61*f*–63*f*, 68*f*–70*f*
  what students need, 21*f*
  see also Forms
Employment Opportunity for Disabled Americans Act of 1986 (PL 99-643), 157*t*, 158
Employment specialists (job coaches), 95–96, 135–137, 147–148
Employment types
  integrated, 13, 138
  paid, 12*t*, 13
  self-employment, 95–96, 138–139
  supported, 133, 134–137, 147–148
Empowerment and student involvement, 142
English and transition activities, 72*t*
ESO, *see* Community Employment Service Organizations
Evaluation of inclusion, 37–38
Exiting student assessment, 44*f*–45*f*, 46*f*

Expectations for students
  goals and, 23, 24*t*
  for graduation, 51–52, 53*f*–55*f*
  outcomes and, 142
  significant support needs and, 97, 142

Facilitators for meetings, 75–76
Fair Labor Standards Act (FLSA) of 1938 (PL 75-718), 12*t*, 127–128
Family involvement in transition planning
  concerns for student well-being and, 113–115
  dos and don'ts of, 114*t*
  expectations and empowerment, 142
  functional assessment and, 85*f*
  goals and, 97–98, 112–113
  importance of, 13, 15*t*, 86
  inclusion and, 37–38
  promoting, 88–89, 90*f*
  responsibilities in, 113*t*
  training families for, 31
  transition IEP and, 86
  work experiences, impact on, 122
  writing transition IEPs and, 97–98
FLSA, *see* Fair Labor Standards Act of 1938 (PL 75-718)
Follow-up after transition, 18*f*, 31, 136
Forms
  Academic and Career Plan, 10*f*–11*f*
  Assessment and Diploma Options Form, 53*f*–55*f*
  Career and Vocational Transition Worksheet, 44*f*–45*f*
  Checklist for Supporting Transition Planning and Review, 18*f*
  Checklist of Important Questions for a Teacher to Consider, 19*f*
  Checklist of Steps for Including Parents in the Transition IEP Process, 90*f*
  Checklist of Steps in Designing a Functional Assessment, 85*f*
  College Discussion Worksheet, 59*f*
  Employment Exploration Activity: What Did I Do? What Did I Learn?, 99*f*
  My Future, 49*f*
  Postsecondary Education Transition Worksheet, 46*f*
  Self-Assessment Form, 100*f*
  Social Competencies Worksheet, 61*f*–63*f*, 65*f*–67*f*, 68*f*–70*f*
  Transition Planning Checklist, 20*f*
  What a Student Will Need Post-High School Checklist, 21*f*
Friendships, 9*t*
Functional assessment, 84, 85*f*, 136–137
Functional curriculum, 52
Funding and community resources
  in adult services system, 148–158, 156*t*
  see also Funding and resources in adult services system
  blending resources, 146–148
  case examples, 145, 147–148, 151, 154
  Community Employment Service Organizations, 119–120
  for employment, 133, 138
  goal strategies and, 97–98, 107
  overview of, 29–30, 30*t*, 31, 145–147, 158–159
  for postsecondary education, 132
  supported employment versus sheltered workshops, 133
  for work experience, 13

writing transition IEP and, 106–108
  see also specific agencies and services systems
Funding and resources in adult services system
  case examples, 151, 154
  community rehabilitation programs/employment service
      organizations, 150–151, 158
  One-Stop Career Centers, 153–154, 158
  overview of, 158–159
  Social Security Administration, 148, 154–158, 156*t*, 157*t*
  state developmental disabilities/mental health agencies
      and community services boards, 151–153, 158
  state vocational rehabilitation services, 148–150, 158
Future orientation and outcomes, 101, 103

General education curriculum
  challenges of accessing, 3, 52, 56
  legislation on access to, 3
  transition activities linked to, 43, 71, 72*t*–73*t*, 83
General educators
  training and education of, 134
  vocational educators, 15*t*, 113*t*
  see also Educators
Generalization, 64, 121
Girls at Work, 107
Goals, National Transition, 2
Goals of planning, 25–26
Goals of students
  adult service agencies and, 87*t*
  annual review of transition IEP and, 96–97
  curriculum development and, 64, 71
  deciding on, 47, 49*f*, 101, 103
  dos and don'ts of, 114*t*
  examples of, 104
  expectations for students and, 23, 24*t*
  exploration of career, 42–43, 44*f*–45*f*, 46*f*, 47–48, 49*f*
  family involvement in, 97–98, 112–113
  functional assessment and, 85*f*
  growth and maturity and, 6
  legislation on, 4–5, 86, 112
  person-centered planning and, 91
  postsecondary education and, 9*t*, 58, 128–129
  quality outcomes lacking and, 7
  self-presentation of, 102*f*
  services/funding goals versus, 25*t*, 97–98
  strategies for accomplishing, 107
  task analysis approach to, 103
  in transition IEP, 77–78, 82
  vocational rehabilitation and, 118
Government work, 128–129
Graduation expectations, 51–52, 53*f*–55*f*
Groups models of supported employment, 135
Growth and goal setting, 6
Guidance counselors, 15*t*, 43, 51

HCBS, see Home- and Community-Based Services
      Medicaid Waiver Program
Health insurance, *see* Medicaid
High school
  adult services and, 149, 150, 153–154, 158–159
  community-based instruction during, 97
  diploma decisions, 50–52, 53*f*–55*f*, 56

dual enrollment programs, 131–132
  implementation of transition IEP by, 120–122, 122*t*–123*t*
  as key resource, 111–112
  postsecondary education compared with, 58, 60, 60*t*
  vocational rehabilitation and, 119, 124
  vocational support service models and, 133–139
Higher education, *see* Postsecondary education
High-stakes testing, 50–52, 53*f*–55*f*, 56
Home- and Community-Based Services (HCBS) Medicaid
      Waiver Program, 145, 147–148, 152–153
Home base sites, 31*t*
Hospital work, 41, 65*f*–67*f*, 68*f*–70*f*

IDEA, *see* Individuals with Disabilities Education Act
      (IDEA) of 1990 (PL 101–476)
IEP, *see* Transition individualized education program (IEP);
      Transition planning meetings; Transition planning
      teams
Impairment-related work expense, 157*t*
Implementation of transition individualized education
      program (IEP)
  case examples, 111, 124*t*
  cooperative relationships, 123–124, 124*t*
  dates in transition IEP, 79–80
  interagency collaboration, 115–123, 121*t*, 122*t*, 123*t*
  interagency planning team, 112–115, 113*t*, 114*t*
  overview of, 16, 111–112, 125
Inclusion
  administrative support for, 31, 38
  barriers to, 37–38, 116–117
  legislation on, 3
  overview of, 36–38
  in postsecondary education, 132*t*
Inclusive individual support model, 132*t*
Income, *see* Wages
Independent living
  barriers to, 12–13
  building community capacity and, 108
  case examples, 23
  centers for, 30*t*, 87*t*
  current level of performance examples, 80*f*
  as focus of transition, 78*t*
  forms for, 21*f*, 61*f*–63*f*, 65*f*–67*f*, 68*f*–70*f*
  functional assessment for, 85*f*
  goal example, 78
  legislation on, 4–5
  social competence and, 60, 61*f*–63*f*, 64, 65*f*–67*f*, 68*f*–70*f*
Independent living centers, 30*t*, 87*t*
Individual and community transition planning
  case examples, 23, 24*t*–25*t*, 27, 33–34, 35, 75–76
  community participation and collaboration, 28–33, 30*t*, 31*t*
  inclusion in schools and communities, 36–38
  individualized planning, 25–28, 26*t*, 28*t*
  overview of, 23–24, 24*t*–25*t*, 38
  self-determination and, 34–36, 36*t*
  transition IEP, *see* Transition individualized education
      program (IEP)
  transition supports, 33–34
Individual approach to supported employment, 134, 135
Individualized education program (IEP), *see* Transition
      individualized education program (IEP); Transition
      planning meetings; Transition planning teams

Individualized plan, 25–28, 26*t*, 28*t*
  see also Transition individualized education program (IEP)
Individualized plan for employment (IPE), 149–150
Individuals with Disabilities Education Act (IDEA) Amend-
    ments of 1997 (PL 105-17)
  functional curriculum and, 52
  on high-stakes testing, 50
  overview of, 3–5
Individuals with Disabilities Education Act (IDEA) of 1990
    (PL 101-476)
  adult services and, 33
  high school services and, 60*t*
  on outcome data, 131
  self-advocacy and, 6
  on services not delivered or objectives not met, 120–121
  on transition, 2–5
Individuals with Disabilities Education Improvement Act
    (IDEA) of 2004 (PL 108-446)
  age 22 and, 146
  on age-appropriate transition assessment, 83–84
  community-based vocational education and, 129
  on high-stakes testing, 50
  outcome variability and, 95–96
  overview of, 3–5
  on structure of transition individualized education
      process, 77–81
  on Summary of Performance, 43
  on transition goals, 86, 112
Informal assessments, 84
Information and advocacy service agencies, 87*t*
Informed decision making for postsecondary education, 58,
    59*f*
In-service training, 108
Instructional support technician career, 141–142
Integrated employment, 13, 138
  see also Employment
Integrated language arts and transition activities, 72*t*
Intellectual disabilities
  alternative assessments and, 50–51
  case examples, *see* Intellectual disabilities case examples
  community and social activities and, 37–38
  decision-making and, 6
  dual enrollment programs and, 131–132
  employment and, 8, 9*t*, 12, 130
  functional curriculum and, 52
  on-the-job skills training and, 135
  postsecondary education and, 128
  self-determination and, 34–35, 36, 36*t*
Intellectual disabilities case examples
  curriculum development, 41, 65*f*–67*f*, 68*f*–70*f*
  funding and resources, 145, 147–148, 149–150
  implementation of transition IEP, 111, 124*t*
  individual and community transition planning, 24*t*–25*t*
  transition, 1–2
Interagency agreements, 106
Interagency collaboration
  agreements and, 106
  building community capacity and, 108
  in community transition planning, 29–33
  dos and don'ts for, 114*t*
  in implementation of transition IEP, 114*t*, 115–123, 121*t*,
      122*t*, 123*t*
  for work experience, 13
Interests and preferences of students, 11*f*, 26*t*, 43

Internet for social networking, 8
Internships, 12*t*
Interviewing techniques, 72*t*, 151
IPE, *see* Individualized plan for employment

Job(s), *see* Career(s); Employment
Job carving, 151
Job clubs, 153–154
Job coaches, 95–96, 135–137, 147–148
Job experience program, 33–34
  see also Employment and work experiences
Job market analysis, 122*t*
Job match
  case examples, 1–2, 33–34, 136–137
  job carving and, 151
Job Observation and Behavior Scale: Opportunity for Self-
    Determination, 14
Job readiness skills, 133
Job search kits, 72*t*
Job shadowing, 12*t*

Language arts and transition activities, 72*t*
Laundry facility work, 151
Leadership by students
  leading IEP, 35, 35*t*, 86, 91, 101, 102*f*
  self-determination and, 35, 36*t*
Learning
  styles of, 41, 43, 47
  universal design for, 56
Learning disabilities
  case examples, 48, 57–58, 154
  postsecondary education and, 128
  self-determination and, 34–35, 36*t*
  strengths and needs ratings, 82
Learning styles, 41, 43, 47
Legislation
  on goals of students, 86, 112
  outcomes and, 3, 95–96, 131
  overview of, 2–5
  on self-determination, 6–7
  on service collaboration, 117
  on timing of transition planning, 81–82, 92
  see also specific laws
Leisure activities, 21*f*, 65*f*–67*f*
Life domains in transition IEP, 77, 78*t*
Life skills, *see* Social competence
Life skills program, 132*t*
  see also Postsecondary education
Local community services boards, 30*t*, 145, 151–153, 158
Long-range planning, 117
Lunch programs, 31*t*

Mathematics, 36, 72*t*
Maturity and goal setting, 6
Medicaid
  buy-in program, 105
  Home- and Community-Based Services (HCBS) Waiver
      Program, 145, 147–148, 152–153
  Supplemental Security Income (SSI) and, 156*t*
  wages and, 155, 157*t*, 158
Medication programs, 31*t*

Meetings, *see* Transition planning meetings
Memory aids, 141–142
Mental health agencies, *see* State developmental disabilities/
    mental health agencies
Mental illness, 82, 135, 145
Microsoft Office and transition activities, 72*t*, 102*f*
Mixed/hybrid model of postsecondary education, 132*t*
Money handling skills, 95–96
Monitoring progress, *see* Outcomes; Progress monitoring
Movie attendance competencies, 65*f*–67*f*
My Future form, 49*f*

Nail technician as career goal, 104
National Longitudinal Transition Study-2, 7, 37, 139, 142
National Transition Goals, 2
NCLB, *see* No Child Left Behind Act of 2001 (PL 107-110)
Needs assessment for inclusion, 38
    see also Significant support needs; Supports
Networking, 8, 9*t*, 37–38
No Child Left Behind (NCLB) Act of 2001 (PL 107-110),
    50–51, 52
Nursing career, 102*f*

Objectives, *see* Goals
Observation as informal assessment, 84
Office work, 149–150
One-Stop Career Centers
    case examples, 154
    customized employment at, 137–138
    funding and resources from, 153–154, 158
    overview of, 120, 121*t*
    role and function of, 30*t*, 87*t*
Outcomes
    community agency involvement and, 147
    community-based instruction and, 97
    data collection and evaluation of, 17, 108
    employment as intended, 98
    examples of postschool, 104–106
    expectations and, 142
    functional assessment and, 85*f*
    future orientation and, 101, 103
    interagency collaboration and, 30
    legislation and, 3, 95–96, 131
    progress monitoring, 16, 17, 104, 108, 112, 149–150
    self-determination and, 36, 101, 102*f*
    severe disabilities and, 129
    social competence and, 6–7, 8, 9*t*
    student led IEP and, 86
    student-directed planning and, 26–27, 28

Paid employment, 12*t*, 13
    see also Employment
Parent involvement in transition planning
    benefits of, 86
    concerns for student well-being and, 113–115
    dos and don'ts of, 114*t*
    functional assessment and, 85*f*
    importance of, 13, 15*t*
    promoting, 88–89, 90*f*
    responsibilities in, 113*t*
    see also Family involvement in transition planning

PATH, *see* Plan for Achieving Self Support
Peer tutors and social competence, 9*t*
Personal futures planning, 75–76
Personal interest inventory, 43
Personal learning styles, 41, 43, 47
Personal–social skills, *see* Social competence
Person-centered planning
    assessment and, 79, 91
    self-employment and, 138–139
    student-directed planning compared to, 26–27, 28, 28*t*
Person(s) responsible on transition IEP, 80–81
PL 75-718, *see* Fair Labor Standards Act of 1938
PL 93-112, *see* Rehabilitation Act of 1973
PL 99-643, *see* Employment Opportunity for Disabled
    Americans Act of 1986
PL 101-336, *see* Americans with Disabilities Act (ADA) of
    1990
PL 101-476, *see* Individuals with Disabilities Education Act
    (IDEA) of 1990
PL 102-569, *see* Rehabilitation Act Amendments of 1992
PL 105-17, *see* Individuals with Disabilities Education Act
    (IDEA) Amendments of 1997
PL 105-220, *see* Workforce Investment Act (WIA) of 1998
PL 107-110, *see* No Child Left Behind (NCLB) Act of 2001
PL 108-446, *see* Individuals with Disabilities Education
    Improvement Act (IDEA) of 2004
Plan for Achieving Self Support (PATH), 132, 138, 157*t*
Planning
    academic and career form, 10*f*–11*f*
    components of, 17, 19*f*, 20*f*, 21*f*
    for future, *see* Transition individualized education program
        (IEP); individual and community transition planning
    goals of, 25–26
    for inclusion, 37–38
    interagency, 112
    long-range, 117
    needed for transition, 6–9, 9*t*, 10*f*–11*f*, 12–13, 12*t*
    personal futures, 75–76
    person-centered, *see* Person-centered planning
    process in transition, 14, 16–17, 16*f*, 18*f*
    student-directed, 26–27, 28, 28*t*
    students' budget, 72*t*
    time to begin, 81–82, 92, 103, 114*t*, 124
    waiting lists and early, 143, 152, 158–159
Portfolio-based assessment of students, 24*t*
Postsecondary education
    accommodations for, 9, 10*f*–11*f*, 140–141, 140*t*
    case examples, 23, 24*t*, 57–58, 141–142
    current level of performance examples, 80*f*
    curriculum development and, 57–58, 59*f*, 60*t*
    as focus of transition, 78*t*
    forms for, *see* Postsecondary education forms
    goals of students and, 9*t*, 58, 77, 128–129
    high school compared with, 58, 60, 60*t*
    high school general education success and, 52
    models of, 131–133, 132*t*
    pathways to, 128–129
    preparation for, 139, 140, 140*t*, 143
    prevalence figures for, 97
    role and function of, 30*t*, 87*t*
    social competencies and, 61*f*–63*f*, 64
    Summary of Performance and, 5
    technology and success in, 56
    transition IEP and, 8–9, 10*f*–11*f*

Postsecondary education—*continued*
  as transition IEP team members, 87
  vocational rehabilitation counselor and, 118
Postsecondary education forms
  College Discussion Worksheet, 59*f*
  planning, 10*f*–11*f*
  Postsecondary Education Transition Worksheet, 46*f*
  Social Competencies Worksheet, 61*f*–63*f*
  what students need, 21*f*
Postsecondary Education Transition Worksheet, 46*f*
Postsecondary goals, *see* Goals
Poverty, 7, 9*t*, 12
PowerPoint presentations by students, 102*f*
Preferences of students, 11*f*, 26*t*, 43
Present level of performance, 78–79, 80*f*, 83
Priority registration at postsecondary education, 140
Problem behaviors, 36, 82, 111, 124*t*
Problem-solving skills, 6–7
Progress monitoring
  case examples, 149–150
  data collection and evaluation, 17, 108
  interagency planning team and, 112
  overview of, 16
  transition IEP and, 104
  see also Outcomes
Project SEARCH, 131

Quality outcomes, *see* Outcomes

Record keeping of parent absences at meetings, 89
Recreation skills, 6, 21*f*
Registration at postsecondary education, 140
Rehabilitation, *see* Vocational rehabilitation
Rehabilitation Act Amendments of 1992 (PL 102-569), 123–124
Rehabilitation Act Amendments of 1998, *see* Workforce Investment Act (WIA) of 1998 (PL 105-220)
Rehabilitation Act of 1973 (PL 93-112), 138, 148
Rehabilitation counselors, *see* Vocational rehabilitation counselors
Rehabilitation services, *see* Vocational rehabilitation services
Related services, 3, 11*f*, 15*t*
Research by students, 72*t*
Residential service agencies, 87*t*
  see also Independent living centers
Resource ownership, 147–148
Resources and web sites
  adult service system, 151, 152
  career research, 48
  community resource mapping, 57
  compliance checklist, 5
  core curriculum linked with transition, 72*t*–73*t*
  for funding, *see* Funding and community resources
  learning styles and career options, 47
  self-employment, 139
  Supplemental Security Income (SSI), 156, 157*t*
  universal design for learning, 56
Restaurant work, 1–2
Résumé writing, 72*t*
Rights
  age 22 and, 146

high school versus postsecondary, 141–142
  in transition IEP, 81
Role playing for transition planning meetings, 24*t*, 35, 36*t*
Rural settings and vocational rehabilitation, 107

Satisfaction with educational programs, 28
School program forms, 19*f*
  see also High school; Postsecondary education
SEARCH, Project, 131
Section 504 of the Rehabilitation Act of 1973, 60*t*, 139
Self-advocacy
  assessment of, 45*f*
  case examples, 141–142
  legislation on, 6
  parent information on, 88
  in postsecondary education, 58, 140, 140*t*
  student-led IEP and, 86
  Summary of Performance and, 5
  transition IEP and, 91
Self-Assessment Form, 100*f*
Self-determination
  building and teaching skills for, 101, 102*f*
  case examples, 35
  as focus of transition, 78*t*
  job success skills and, 17
  legislation on, 6–7
  overview of, 34–36, 36*t*
  social competencies and, 64
  student led IEP and, 35, 35*t*, 86, 91, 101, 102*f*
  vocational assessment and, 14
Self-employment, 95–96, 138–139
Self-evaluation tools for vocational assessment, 14
Service(s)
  coordination of, 146–147, 152
  forms for, 19*f*
  funding and resources for, *see* Funding and community resources
  goals of students versus goals of, 97–98
  high school compared to college, 60*t*
  in postsecondary education, 60*t*, 132
  related, 3, 11*f*, 15*t*
  roles of providers, 15*t*
  status of, 138
  transition, *see* Transition services
  transition services integration model and, 130
  vocational rehabilitation, *see* Vocational rehabilitation services
Service agencies, *see* Adult services agencies; Community agencies; *specific state agencies*
Service coordination, 146–147, 152
Service-learning, 12*t*
Services boards, *see* Community services boards
Severe disabilities
  assessment and, 84, 85*f*, 86
  employment and, 27, 132–133, 134
  Home- and Community-Based Services (HCBS) Medicaid Waiver Program and, 145, 147–148, 152–153
  social relationships and, 9*t*
  standardized testing and, 84, 85*f*, 86
  student involvement and, 89, 91
  vocational support services and, 142

work experiences and outcomes, 129
see also Significant support needs
Sheltered workshops
  lack of support and, 95–96
  overview of, 133–134
  settling for, 97–98
  status of, 138
Significant support needs
  community-based vocational education and, 129
  customized employment and, 137–138
  employment service organizations and, 120
  facilitator at transition planning meeting, 75
  funding and resources, 152–153
  high expectations and, 97, 142
  segregated versus competitive employment, 133–134, 135
  student involvement and, 89
  vocational rehabilitation counseling and, 117–118
  work experiences and, 127–128
  see also Severe disabilities
Situational assessment, vocational, 1–2, 118–119
1619(a) of Employment Opportunity for Disabled Americans Act of 1986 (PL 99-643), 157*t*, 158
1619(b) of Employment Opportunity for Disabled Americans Act of 1986 (PL 99-643), 157*t*, 158
Skills summary creation, 43, 44*f*–45*f*, 46*f*
Social competence
  community living and, 58, 60, 61*f*–63*f*, 64, 65*f*–67*f*, 68*f*–70*f*
  as focus of transition, 78*t*
  self-determination and, 36
  transition outcomes and, 8, 9*t*
Social Competencies Worksheet, 61*f*–63*f*, 65*f*–67*f*, 68*f*–70*f*
Social networking, 8, 9*t*, 37–38
Social problem-solving skills, 6–7
Social Security Administration
  funding and resources from, 148, 154–158, 156*t*, 157*t*
  role and function of, 30*t*, 87*t*
  self-employment and, 138
Social Security Disability Insurance (SSDI), 154–158, 156*t*, 157*t*
Social service agencies, 30*t*
Socioeconomic status, 7, 9*t*, 12
SOP, *see* Summary of Performance
Special education information for families, 88
Special educators
  as key resource, 111–112
  roles and responsibilities of, 15*t*, 86, 88, 113*t*, 134, 142–143
Specialists as consultants, 87*t*
Spelling and self-determination, 36
Spinal cord injury case examples, 141–142
SSDI, *see* Social Security Disability Insurance
SSI, *see* Supplemental Security Income
Stakeholders challenges, *see* Barriers; Challenges
Standardized testing, 83–84, 85*f*, 86
State developmental disabilities/mental health agencies
  case examples, 145
  funding and resources from, 151–153, 158
  overview of, 116–117
  transition services integration model and, 130
  see also Adult services agencies; Community agencies
State vocational rehabilitation services
  case examples, 147–148, 149–150

funding and resources in, 148–150, 158
  overview of, 87*t*, 117–119
  role and function of, 30*t*
  see also Community rehabilitation programs; Vocational rehabilitation
Strategies
  for funding and community resources, *see* Funding and community resources
  for interagency collaboration, 30–32
  for planning transition IEP, 82–84, 85*f*, 86
Strengths of students, 82, 102*f*
Student earned income exclusion, 157*t*
Student involvement in transition planning
  alternative assessment scores and, 51
  career goal exploration, 42–43, 44*f*–45*f*, 46*f*, 47–48, 49*f*
  case examples, 27
  dos and don'ts of, 114*t*
  expectations and empowerment, 142
  functional assessment and, 85*f*
  goal prioritization, 112–113
  importance of, 13–14, 15*t*
  leading IEP, 35, 35*t*, 86, 91, 101, 102*f*
  for postsecondary education, 140*t*
  preparation for, 24*t*, 31
  responsibilities in, 113*t*
  severe disabilities and, 89, 91
  on social competencies worksheet, 60, 64
  in transition IEP, 89, 91
  writing transition IEP and, 97–98
Student-directed planning, 26–27, 28, 28*t*
Substantially separate model of postsecondary education, 132*t*
Summary of Performance (SOP)
  creating, 43, 44*f*–45*f*, 46*f*
  legislation on, 5
  on transition IEP, 81
Summer work experiences, 129
  see also Employment and work experiences
Supplemental Security Income (SSI)
  overview of, 154–158, 156*t*, 157*t*
  wages and, 147–148, 157, 157*t*
Supported employment, 133, 134–137, 147–148
Supports
  assessment of, 9, 10*f*–11*f*, 26*t*, 45*f*
  case examples, 33–34, 145, 147–148
  circle of support, 75–76
  community transition planning and, 33–34
  employment and, 7–8, 9, 10*f*–11*f*, 12, 134
  funding and resources for, 146–148
  see also Funding and community resources
  inclusion and, 37–38
  legislation on, 3
  need for, 26–27
  in postsecondary education, 9, 10*f*–11*f*, 132
  versus programs as planning focus, 25*t*
  severe disabilities and, 142
  sheltered workshops and, 95–96
  see also Accommodations; Significant support needs

Task analysis approach to goals and objectives, 103
Teachers, *see* Educators
Teaching as career, 24*t*, 102*f*, 107

Teams, *see* Transition planning teams
Technical assistance, 31
Technology
    assistive, 56, 58
    challenges of, 31*t*
    transition activities linked to use of, 72*t*
Ten precious minutes, 49*f*, 71, 73
Testing, *see* Assessment; High-stakes testing
Title II of the Social Security Act, 154–158, 156*t*, 157*t*
Tools, *see* Forms
Transition
    case examples, 1–2
    curriculum developed for, *see* Curriculum development
    definition of, 3–4
    follow-up after, 18*f*, 31, 136
    forms on, *see* Forms; Transition forms
    information for families on, 88
    legislation on, 2–5
    outcomes of, *see* Outcomes
    overview of, 2, 17
    planning components, 17, 19*f*, 20*f*, 21*f*
    planning needed for, 6–9, 9*t*, 10*f*–11*f*, 12–13, 12*t*
    planning process in, 14, 16–17, 16*f*, 18*f*
    time to begin planning, 81–82, 92, 103, 114*t*, 124
    transition IEP for, *see* Transition individualized education program (IEP)
    transition planning team and, 13–14, 15*t*
    vocational assessment and, 14
Transition coordinators, 15*t*, 30–31
Transition forms
    Academic and Career Plan, 10*f*–11*f*
    Checklist for Supporting Transition Planning and Review, 18*f*
    Checklist of Important Questions for a Teacher to Consider, 19*f*
    Transition Planning Checklist, 20*f*
    What a Student Will Need Post-High School Checklist, 21*f*
    see also Forms
Transition Goals, National, 2
Transition individualized education program (IEP)
    basic elements addressed in, 76–81, 78*t*, 80*f*
    career and college advancement and, 8–9, 10*f*–11*f*
    case examples, 75–76
    family involvement in, 88–89, 90*f*
    focus questions for, 32–33
    forms for, 85*f*, 90*f*
    see also Forms
    future orientation of, 101, 103
    implementation of, *see* Implementation of transition individualized education program
    legislation on, 4–5
    meetings for, *see* Transition planning meetings
    need for, 6–9, 9*t*, 10*f*–11*f*, 12–13, 12*t*
    outcomes and, *see* Outcomes
    overview of, 16, 91–92
    self-determination and, 36*t*
    strategies for planning, 82–84, 85*f*, 86
    student involvement in, 89, 91
    time to begin planning, 81–82, 92, 103, 114*t*, 124
    transition team role in, 86–87, 87*t*
    see also Transition planning teams
    work experiences and, 129

writing, *see* Writing transition individualized education program
Transition Planning Checklist, 20*f*
Transition planning meetings
    case examples, 27, 75–76
    documentation of parents absent at, 89
    facilitators for, 75–76
    forms for, 18*f*
    person-centered, 27–28
    rehabilitation counselors at, 7–8
    student leadership for, 24*t*, 35, 35*t*, 36*t*, 86, 91, 101, 102*f*
Transition planning teams
    body language of members, 88–89
    community members on, 24*t*
    flexible scheduling and staffing for members, 30–31
    guidance counselors on, 51
    key players on, 86–87, 87*t*
    overview of, 13–14, 15*t*, 112–115, 113*t*, 114*t*
    policy compliance and makeup of, 7–8
    rehabilitation counselors on, 7–8
    roles and responsibilities of members of, 13–14, 15*t*, 16
    Social Security Administration representative on, 155
Transition program, 132*t*
    see also Postsecondary education
Transition services
    legislation on definition of, 3–4
    model of, 106, 130
    needs data to drive changes in, 26
    in postsecondary education, 132
    related services and, 3
    in transition IEP, 79
Transition services integration model, 106, 130
Transition supports, *see* Supports
Transportation, 31*t*, 78*t*
Traumatic brain injury, 27, 135, 141–142
Trial work period, 157*t*

UDL, *see* Universal design for learning
UDT, *see* Universal design for transition
Universal design for learning (UDL), 56
Universal design for transition (UDT), 56
Universities, *see* Postsecondary education

Values and beliefs of person-centered planning, 27–28
Vision for future
    current level of performance and, 79
    development of, 48
    outcome-oriented transition and, 96–97
Vision impairments case examples, 111, 124*t*
Visionary business practices, 130–131
Vocational assessment
    case examples, 1–2, 111, 124*t*
    counselor role in, 118–119
    for curriculum development, 47
    Self-Assessment Form, 100*f*
    transition and, 14
Vocational education program
    artificial limitations and, 97
    case examples, 25*t*, 127–128, 136–137
    designing and implementing, 121–122, 122*t*–123*t*
    models for, 129–133

overview of, 57, 129–130
vocational educators and, 15*t*, 113*t*
work experiences in, 12*t*, 26–27
Vocational educators, 15*t*, 113*t*
Vocational profiles and social networking, 8, 9*t*
Vocational rehabilitation
  agencies for, *see* Vocational rehabilitation services
  case examples, 1–2, 147–148
  counselors for, *see* Vocational rehabilitation counselors
  educational programs and, *see* Vocational education
      program
  eligibility, funding and resources for, 148–150, 149
  employment and, 117–118, 148
  in rural settings, 107
  specialists/job coaches, 95–96, 135–137, 147–148
  on transition IEP team, 87
  transition services integration model and, 106, 130
Vocational rehabilitation counselors
  goal strategies and, 107
  responsibilities of, 113*t*, 117–119, 149
  school cooperative relationship with, 124
  at transition IEP meetings, 7–8
Vocational rehabilitation services
  case examples, 147–148, 149–150
  funding and resources from, 148–150, 158
  overview of, 87*t*, 117–119
  role and function of, 30*t*
  see also Community rehabilitation programs; Vocational
      rehabilitation
Vocational rehabilitation specialists (job coaches), 95–96,
      135–137, 147–148
Vocational situational assessment, 1–2, 118–119
Vocational support service models, 133–139
Volunteer activities for work experiences, 12*t*

Wages
  Medicaid and, 155, 157*t*, 158
  Supplemental Security Income and, 147–148, 157, 157*t*

Waiting lists
  early planning and, 143, 152, 158–159
  interagency collaboration and, 116
Waiver Program, Home- and Community-Based (HCBS)
      Medicaid, 145, 147–148, 152–153
Walgreens hiring initiative, 130–131
Web Site design as career, 150
What a Student Will Need Post–High School Checklist, 21*f*
WIA, *see* Workforce Investment Act of 1998 (PL 105-220)
WIPA, *see* Work Incentives Planning and Assistance programs
Work, *see* Employment; *specific topics beginning with job(s)*
Work experiences, *see* Employment and work experiences
Work force centers, *see* One-Stop Career Centers
Work Incentives Planning and Assistance (WIPA) programs,
      30*t*, 147–148
Work sampling, 12*t*
Work study programs, 154
Workforce Investment Act (WIA) of 1998 (PL 105-220)
  on cooperative relationships, 123–124, 124*t*
  on grants for vocational rehabilitation programs, 148
  on One-Stop Career Centers, 153
  on self-employment, 138
Working interviews, 151
Worksheets, *see* Forms
Workshops, *see* Sheltered workshops
Writing of students and transition activities, 72*t*
Writing transition individualized education program (IEP)
  case examples, 95–96, 98, 101, 103, 105–106
  deciding on goals, 101, 103
  forms for, 99*f*, 100*f*
  getting started, 103–104
  if information needed, 98, 99*f*, 100*f*, 101, 102*f*
  overview of, 95–97, 108
  postschool outcome examples, 104–106
  support of community agencies and resources obtained,
      106–108
  what to include, 104
  see also Transition individualized education program (IEP)
  where to begin, 97–98